Mao Zedong

A Bibliography

Mao Zedong
A Bibliography

Alan Lawrance

BIBLIOGRAPHIES OF
WORLD LEADERS, NO. 3

GREGORY PALMER, SERIES EDITOR

GREENWOOD PRESS
New York • Westport, Connecticut • London

Library of Congress Cataloging-in-Publication Data

Lawrance, Alan.
   Mao Zedong : a bibliography / Alan Lawrance.
      p.   cm. — (Bibliographies of world leaders, ISSN 1056-5523 ;
   3)
   Includes index.
   ISBN 0-313-38222-6
   1. Mao, Tse-Tung, 1893–1976—Bibliography. I. Title.
   II. Series.
   Z8548.3.L38   1991
   [DS778.M3]
   016.95105–dc20   91-8424

British Library Cataloguing in Publication Data is available.

Library of Congress Catalog Card Number: 91-8424
ISBN: 0-313-38222-6
ISSN: 1056-5523

First published in 1991

Greenwood Press, 88 Post Road West, Westport, CT 06881
An imprint of Greenwood Publishing Group, Inc.

Printed in the United States of America

The paper used in this book complies with the
Permanent Paper Standard issued by the National
Information Standards Organization (Z39.48–1984).

10   9   8   7   6   5   4   3   2   1

Contents

Preface

This bibliography comprises material published in English plus some important works in other well-known languages. In the case of Mao's writings, reference is made where possible to the authorised Chinese translation, with cross-reference to other sources.

The Wade-Giles system of transcribing Chinese characters is being superseded by the Chinese phonetic alphabet, known as Pinyin. This has been used in all publications and documents put out in the People's Republic of China since 1 January 1979. It is now replacing Wade-Giles in the cataloging system of Western libraries.

The citation of works in this bibliography follows the form used in the original publication. A list of names converting Wade-Giles to Pinyin and vice versa is provided. In the biography and the commentaries I have used Pinyin throughout, with the exception of a few very well-known names such as Sun Yat-sen and Hong Kong which are given in their familiar form.

Mae-fun Chen of the University of Leeds and Hong-mei Lin at London University have provided valuable assistance, and I am grateful for the patient advice of David Fielden, Neil Allen and their colleagues at the library of the Hatfield Polytechnic.

For her masterly professional work in preparing the typescript, I am indebted to Nicola Murphy.

Some Thoughts of Mao Zedong

'There is one difficult thing in establishing oneself in life; it is being meticulous . . . A person who failed in a great undertaking and through neglect of details and whom we may take as a warning is Caesar.'

(From a jotting in Mao's handwriting in his college notebook.)

'The more books one reads, the more stupid one gets.'

(One of Mao's favourite remarks.)

So many deeds cry out to be done,
And always urgently;
The world rolls on,
Time presses.
Ten thousand years are too long,
Seize the day, seize the hour!
(From the poem, <u>Reply to Comrade Kuo Mo-jo</u>, 9 January 1963.)

We can clasp the moon in the Ninth Heaven
And seize turtles deep down in the Five Seas;
We'll return amid triumphant song and laughter.
Nothing is hard in this world
If you dare to scale the heights.

(From the poem, <u>Reascending Jinggangshan</u>, May 1965.)

'The higher one is boosted, the harder one will fall, and I am prepared to crash to smithereens.'

(From a letter to Jiang Qing, 8 July 1966.)

In response to a scholar who suggested that Communism was love, Mao replies:

> 'No, comrade. Communism is not love. Communism is a hammer which we use to destroy the enemy.'

Transcription: Wade-Giles to Pinyin; Pinyin to Wade-Giles

Wade-Giles	Pinyin
Chang Chun-chiao	Zhang Chunqiao
Chang Kuo-tao	Zhang Guodao
Chen Chang-feng	Chen Zhangfeng
Chen Po-ta	Chen Boda
Chen Tu-hsiu	Chen Duxiu
Chen Yu-ying	Chen Youying
Chiang Ching	Jiang Qing
Chieh-fang chun-pao	Jiefang junbao
Ching Kang	Jinggang
Chou En-lai	Zhou Enlai
Chu Teh	Zhu De
Chung-king	Chonqing
Dai Hsiao-ai	Dai Xiaoai
Hangchow	Hangzhou
Ho Tzu-chen	He Zizhen
Heilungkiang	Heilongjiang
Hsiang-chian ping-lun	Xiangqian pinglun
Hankow	Hankou
Hsin Hunan	Xin Hunan
Hsin Min	Xinmin
Hu Yao-bang	Hu Yaobang
Jen Pi-shih	Ren Bishi
Jenmin Jih-bao	Remin Ribao
Juichin	Ruijin
Kiangsi	Jiangxi
Ko Ching-shih	Ke Qingshi
Kuang-ming jih-pao	Guangming Ribao
Kuomintang (K.M.T.)	Guomindang

Li Jui	Li Rui
Li Li-san	Li Lisan
Li Te	Li De
Lin Piao	Lin Biao
Lin Yu-tang	Lin Yutang
Liu Shao-chi	Liu Shaoqi
Liu Ya-tzu	Liu Yazi
Lu Hsun	Lu Xun
Mao Tse-tung	Mao Zedong
Nanking	Nanjing
Pei Tai	Bei Dai
Peking	Beijing
Peng Te-huai	Peng Dehuai
Shansi	Shanxi
Shensi	Shaanxi
Siang siang	Xiang Xiang
Siao yu	Xiao yu
Soong Ching-long	Song Qing Ling
Sun Yat-sen	Sun Zhongshan
Szechwan	Sichuan
Ta Kung Pao	Da Gong Bao
Teng Hsiao-ping	Deng Xiaoping
Tien An Men	Tian An Men
Tientsin	Iianjin
Ting Ling	Ding Ling
Tsingtao	Qingdao
Tsung-yi	Zunyi
Tungshan	Dongshan
Wang Ching-wei	Wang Qingwei
Wang Jo-fei	Wang Ruofei
Wang Kwang-mei	Wang Guangmei
Wang Shih-wei	Wang Shiwei
Wen Hui Pao	Wen Hui Bao
Whampoa	Huangpu
Wu Hsun	Wu Xun
Yang Chang-chih	Yang Chanji

Yangtse Kinang	Yangzi Jiang
Yao Wen-yuan	Yao Wenyuan
Yeh Ching	Ye Qing
Yenan	Yanan

Pinyin

Wade-Giles

Bei Dai	Pei Tai
Beijing	Peking
Chen Boda	Chen Po-ta
Chen Duxiu	Chen Tu-hsiu
Chen Youying	Chen Yu-ying
Chen Zhangfeng	Chen Chang-feng
Chonqing	Chung-king
Da Gong Bao	Ta Kung Pao
Dai Xiaoai	Dai Hsiao-ai
Deng Xiaoping	Teng Hsiao-ping
Ding Ling	Ting Ling
Dongshan	Tunghsan
Guangming Ribao	Kuang-ming jih-pao
Guomindang	Kuomintang (K.M.T.)
Hangzhou	Hangchow
Hankou	Hankow
He Zizhen	Ho Tzu-chen
Heilongjiang	Heilungkiang
Hu Yaobang	Hu Yao-bang
Huangpu	Whampoa
Iianjin	Tientsin
Jiang Qing	Chiang Ching
Jiangxi	Kiangsi
Jiefang junbao	Chieh-fang chun-pao
Jinggang	Ching Kang
Ke Qingshi	Ko Ching-shih

Li De	Li Te
Li Lisan	Li Li-san
Li Rui	Li Jui
Lin Biao	Lin Piao
Lin Shaoqi	Liu Shao-chi
Lin Yutang	Lin Yu-tang
Lin Yazi	Liu Ya-tzu
Lu Xun	Lu Hsun
Mao Zedong	Mao Tse-tung
Nanjing	Nanking
Peng Dehuai	Peng Te-huai
Qingdao	Tsingtao
Remin Ribao	Jenmin Jih-bao
Ren Bishi	Jen Pi-shih
Ruijin	Juichin
Shaanxi	Shensi
Shanxi	Shansi
Sichuan	Szechwan
Song Qing Ling	Soong Ching-long
Sun Zhongshan	Sun Yat-sen
Tian An Men	Tien An Men
Wang Guangmei	Wang Kwang-mei
Wang Qingwei	Wang Ching-wei
Wang Ruofei	Wang Jo-fei
Wang Shiwei	Wang Shih-wei
Wen Hui Bao	Wen Hui Pao
Wu Xun	Wu Hsun
Xiang xiang	Siang siang
Xiangqian pinglun	Hsiang-chian ping-lun
Xiao yu	Siao yu
Xin Hunan	Hsin Hunan
Xinmin	Hsin Min

Yanan

Yang Chanji

Yangzi Jiang

Yao Wenyuan

Ye Qing

Zhang Chunqiao

Zhang Guodao

Zhou Enlai

Zhu De

Zunyi

Yenan

Yang Chang-chih

Yangtse Kinang

Yao Wen-yuan

Yeh Ching

Chang Chun-chiao

Chang Kuo-tao

Chou En-lai

Chu Teh

Tsung-yi

Chronology

1917		Becomes chairman of the Students' Society. Publishes his first article 'A Study of Physical Culture.'
1918	June	Mao graduates.
	September	Goes to Beijing and becomes an assistant Librarian in the Beijing National University Library.
1919		Visits Shanghai to see departure of work-study students going to France.
	May	Mao was travelling when news of Versailles settlement sparked off nationwide student protests (May 4th Movement). Takes job as Primary School teacher in Changsha.
		Mao becomes editor of *Xiangjiang Review* and, when it is suppressed, another student journal.
	October	Mao's mother dies.
1920	March	Mao's father dies.
	July	Appointed Headmaster of a Primary School. Marries Yang Kaihui.
1921	July	Mao is delegated to the first congress of the Communist Party, held in Shanghai.
	October	Becomes secretary of the Communist Party in Hunan.
1922		Mao fails to attend second Congress of the CCP.
	August	The Central Committee of the CCP agrees that Communists will join the Guomindang as individuals.

	September	Mao helps to organise a miners' strike.
	November	Mao resigns as Headmaster. Mao is elected chairman of the Association of Trade Unions of Hunan.
1923	January	Sun Yat-sen and Adolphe Joffe produce a joint manifesto for collaboration between the Communist parties of China and the Soviet Union and the Guomindang.
	June	At the Third Party Congress in Canton Mao is elected to the Central Committee.
	July	In Shanghai Mao works as liaison officer between the CCP and the Guomindang.
1924	January	Mao attends the First Congress of the Guomindang in Canton. Mao is elected an alternate member of the Central Executive Committee.
	February	Mao returns to Shanghai to work as liaison officer.
	May	Huangpu (Whampoa) Military Academy is founded with Chiang Kai-shek as President and Zhou Enlai as Political Commissor.
1925	January	At the Fourth Congress of the CCP meeting in Canton, Mao loses his position on the Central Committee.
	March	Sun Yat-sen dies.
	Spring	Mao returns to Hunan. Organises peasant support for the Nationalists.
	August	Mao works in peasant movement in Canton. Becomes secretary of the Propaganda

		Department of the Guomindang, and editor of *Political Weekly*.
1926	January	Mao publishes his first major works, *Analysis of the Different Classes of Chinese Society*.
	April–October	Mao is Head of the training school for peasant agitators.
	July	Northern Expedition sets out from Canton under leadership of Chiang Kai-shek.
	December	Mao addresses a conference of peasant delegates in Changsha. This is soon followed by land confiscation in Hunan.
1927		Mao investigates the peasant movement in Hunan.
	March	Publishes his *Report of an Investigation into the Peasant Movement in Hunan*.
	April	Chiang Kai-shek carries out anti-Communist coup in Shanghai.
	July	Chen Duxiu no longer effectively leader of the Party.
	August	Nanchang uprising begins.
	September	Autumn Harvest uprisings in Hunan.
	November	Mao takes refuge in the Jinggang Mountains.
1928	January	Zhu De leads uprisings in South Hunan.
	April	Zhu De's force joins up with Mao in Jinggang Mountains, forming first 'Red Army' and local soviet.

1929		Mao and Zhu De have some military successes in rural territories.
	February	The Central Committee under Li Lisan is critical of Mao's policies.
	April	Mao refutes Li Lisan's criticism.
1930	January	Mao writes to Lin Biao commenting on the policy of the Central Committee ('A Single Spark Can Start a Prairie Fire').
	June	The Politburo is in favour of urban insurrection and calls for attacks on large cities.
	July-September	Attacks on Changsha and Nanchang are ultimately unsuccessful. Li Lisan is discredited by Moscow. Chiang Kai-shek launches first major assault against the Communists. Mao's wife is executed in Changsha. Red Army has some successes in resisting Chiang Kai-shek's military campaigns.
	September	Japanese invade Manchuria.
1931		Mao is elected Chairman of the first All-China Soviet Government, and Zhu De is elected military commander.
1932	January	Japan attacks Shanghai.
	April	Central Soviet government declares war on Japan.
	June	Chiang Kai-shek's Fourth Encirclement Campaign begins.
	August	Mao's control of the Red Army and his strategic concepts are challenged by among others, Zhou Enlai. Mao becomes ill.

1933	May	Zhou Enlai is appointed general political commissor of the Red Army.
	May	Chiang Kai-shek signs Tan-Ku truce with Japanese.
	June	Land Investigation Drive begins with Mao as active participant.
	October	Chaing Kai-shek's Fifth Extermination Campaign began.
1934	January	Second All-China Soviet Congress meets in Ruijin. Mao is reelected as Chairman, but party leadership is taken over by 'Twenty-eight Bolsheviks.'
	September	Mao has fever.
	October	The Long March begins.
	November	The Guomindang army takes Ruijin.
1935	January	Zunyi Conference. Mao is elected effective leader of the army and the Party during the Long March.
	July	Jiangxi army reach Sichuan and meet troops under Zhang Guodao who have been driven from areas north of the Yangste River. Zhang and Mao disagree. Mao leads his forces to northern Shaanxi, arriving in the Fall, having lost approximately ninety percent of his initial force. Zhang's forces, also suffering great losses eventually join Mao in Shaanxi.
1936		Mao is interviewed by Edgar Snow in Shaanxi. Mao writes *On the Tactics of Fighting Japanese Imperialism* and

Strategic Problems in China's Revolutionary War.

	December	Xian Incident: Chiang Kai-shek is kidnapped by his own followers and is eventually forced to join a united front against the Japanese.
1937	July	Japanese forces begin all-out war in China. Agreement for Joint Nationalist-Communist Resistance. Soviet Government continues as an autonomous regional regime. Red Army becomes Eighth Route and New Fourth armies. Mao writes *On Contradictions* and *On Practice*.
1938		Japanese armies occupy main centres in North China. Mao writes on strategic problems: *On the New Stage*, *On the Protracted War* and *Strategic problems in the Anti-Japanese War*.
1939		Mao marries Jiang Qing. Clashes between Guomindang and Communist troops.
1940	January	Mao writes *On New Democracy* justifying the United Front policy.
	March	Puppet regime under Wang Qingwei is set up in Nanjing. More armed clashes between Chiang Kai-shek's troops and the New Fourth Army.
1941	April	The Rectification Campaign begins.
	December	Japanese attack on Pearl Harbour.
1942	January	General Stillwell appointed Chief-of-Staff in the China theatre. Rectification Campaign continues. Mao gains influence in

		the Party at the expense of Wang Ming and the Moscow-trained 'dogmatists.'
1943		'Liberated areas' are said, by Zhou Enlai, to exceed 100 million population and to have 800,000 party members.
1944		American Ambassador Hurley meets Mao in Yanan. First edition of Mao's *Selected Works* published.
1945		Mao's report *On Coalition Government* becomes basis of the the Communist demands. Encouraged by the Americans Mao goes to Chongqing to negotiate with Chiang Kai-shek.
1946		The Second Civil War, called by the Communists the War of Liberation, begins.
1947		Mao is forced out of Yanan by the Guomindang forces. In *The Present Situation and Our Tasks* Mao calls for a general offensive. Second edition of Mao's *Selected Works* published.
1948		Mao moves to Shanxi. Nationalist forces defeated in Manchuria.
1949	April	The Communist armies cross the Yangste.
	May	The People's Liberation Army take Shanghai and Wuhan.
	June	Mao's *On the People's Democratic Dictatorship*, includes a statement on the need to 'lean to one side,' that of the Soviet Union.

	August	Mao comments on the U.S. White Paper, which attempted to explain the Communist victory in China.
	September 30th	Mao elected Chairman of the Central People's Government.
	October 1st	Mao proclaims the founding of the People's Republic of China.
1950		Mao visits the Soviet Union and signs Treaty of Friendship, Alliance and Mutual Assistance.
	October	New revised edition of Mao's *Selected Works*. China enters Korean War.
1951		Mao instigates a 'thought reform' movement for intellectuals.
1952		Mao's *Selected Works* are published in three volumes. Launching of 'Five-Anti' campaign against economic corruption.
1953	Janaury	First Five-Year-Plan inaugurated.
	March	Death of Stalin.
	July	End of Korean War.
	December	Resolution on formation of Agricultural Cooperatives.
1954	April-July	Geneva Conference.
	June	Nehru and Zhou Enlai issue Five Principles of Co-existence.
1955	April	Bandung Conference of twenty-nine Afro-Asian nations.
	October	Drive for collectivisation begins.

1956		Khrushchev denounces Stalin at Twentieth Party Congress. Mao invites intellectuals to criticise the Party in the 'Hundred Flowers' movement. Mao publishes *On the Historical Experience of the Dictatorship of the Proletariat* which recognises the continuing contradictions in socialist societies.
1957	May-June	'Hundred Flowers' movement at height. Mao publishes *On the Correct Handling of Contradictions Among the People*.
	October	Sputnik launched. Sino-Soviet nuclear testing agreement signed.
	November	Mao visits Moscow for 1957 Conference of Communist Parties. Speech on 'the prevailing East wind.'
1958	February	'Great Leap Forward' announced.
	July	First communes formed.
1959		Mao replaced as Chairman of Republic by Lui Xiaoqi.
	July-August	Mao criticised at Lushan Conference.
	September	Lin Biao appointed Minister of Defence.
1960	Summer	Soviet technicians withdrawn from China.
	November	At Conference of Communist Parties in Moscow, China openly identifies Khrushchev as 'revisionist.'
1961		Soviet Party boycotts celebration of fourtieth anniversary of founding of CCP.

1962		Mao launches Socialist Education Movement in the countryside. Cuba crisis: when Khrushchev withdraws missiles from Cuba he is criticised by the Chinese for 'adventurism.' Border dispute leads to short Sino-Indian war.
1963		China steps up efforts to take leadership of Third World revolutionary movements. Mao calls for 'people of the world' to unite against U.S. China denounces Test Ban Treaty.
	December	Zhou Enlai begins tour of Africa.
1964	March	Study of Mao's works within People's Liberation Army.
	May	First publication of *Quotations from Mao Zedong*.
	Autumn	'Four Clean-ups' campaign.
	October	Khrushchev ousted from power. China tests first atomic bomb.
1965	May	PLA uniforces simplified to combat elitism.
	November	Article criticising Wu Han, later seen as start of the Cultural Revolution.
1966	March	China refuses to attend the Twenty-third Party Congress in Moscow.
	May	Mao swims in Yangste.
	July	Cultural Revolution in the universities.
	August	Red Guards formed. Mao writes his own 'big character poster.'

1967		Red Guards intensify attacks on Liu Xiaoqi and Deng Xiaoping as 'capitalist roaders.' China tests its first hydrogen bomb.
1968		'Three-in-one' revolutionary committees established throughout China. Red Guards disbanded.
	October	Mao stresses importance of manual labour for cadres.
1969	March	Chinese and Soviet forces clash on the Ussuri River.
	April	Ninth National Congress of CCP names Lin Biao as Mao's successor.
1970	August-September	At the Second Plenary Session of the Ninth Central Committee of the CCP, Lin Biao and Chen Boda are criticised.
	November	At United Nations overall majority role for admitting People's Republic of China.
1971	April	U.S. table tennis team invited to visit China.
	June	China rejects Soviet proposal for Five Power Conference on nuclear disarmament.
	July	Dr. Kissinger visits Beijing.
	October	CPR replaces Taiwan regime in U.N.
1972	February	President Nixon visits Beijing and meets Mao.
	September	Sino-Japanese agreement to reestablish relations.

1973	February	China and U.S. agree to set up reciprocal liaison offices in Washington and Beijing.
	August	Tenth Party Congress affirms that the political and organisational lines of the Ninth Congress were correct.
1974	July	At a meeting of the Politburo Mao warns against the creation of a 'Gang of Four.'
1975		Revised Constitution of the CPR is adopted at the Fourth National People's Congress. Zhou Enlai and Deng Xiaoping become Premier and First Vice-Premier of the State Council.
1976	January	Death of Zhou Enlai.
	April	Demonstrations in Tien An Men square put down by force. Deng Xiaoping removed from office.
	9 September	Mao dies.
	6 October	The 'Gang of Four' arrested.
	7 October	Hua Guofeng appointed Chairman of the CCP.

Mao Zedong's Wives and Children, 1893-1976

Wives	Children		
Yang Kaiwei 1901-1930	Son	Mao Anying	Retrieved in Shanghai; joined Mao in Yanan; went to Soviet Union; fought on Eastern Front in Tank Unit; killed in Korean War.
	Son	Mao Anqing	Retrieved in Shanghai; joined Mao in Yanan; studied engineering in Soviet Union--behaved oddly. Mao later said he had gone mad.
	Daughter	Yang Zhan	
	Son	Mao Anlang	Disappeared.
He Zizhen 1910-1984	Daughter		Placed with peasants, lost.
	Son	Mao Yong Fo	Born in Ruijin; left behind at start of Long March; later placed with peasant family in Fujian; never found.
	Son		Born prematurely and died.

	Daughter		Born on Long March.
	Daughter	Li Min	Born in Yanan, married Gong Linghua.
	Son		Born in Moscow, went to nursery school, died of pneumonia.
Jiang Qing 1914-1991	Daughter	Li Na	

I. The Life of Mao Zedong

Mao's Achievements

Many a biographer of Mao Zedong has begun by suggesting that he is probably the greatest political leader of the twentieth century. Both friends and foes have spoken of him in the superlative. His public stature has been recognised by those who have written of him as an Emperor (*The People's Emperor*[1]) and as a Messiah (*The Messiah and the Man*[2]).

To millions of Chinese, especially during the Cultural Revolution, he was 'The Great Helmsman.' To many foreigners he appeared, for a time, as the last hope for a new world. Thousands of students around the world with little real knowledge of Mao and his China called themselves 'Maoists.'

It is recounted that Mao, chatting in his cups at a restaurant after a session of the First Party Congress in 1921, asked a fellow delegate, 'who, in Chinese history, had risen to greatness through their own efforts.' His companion could suggest only the first Han Emperor and Sun Yat-sen. 'Right!' exclaimed Mao, 'I will be the third.'[3] Had Mao sought simply for power and glory there must have been easier options open to him than that of revolutionary outlaw which he was to follow for the next twenty-eight years. On several occasions he was lucky to escape with his life.

How far his career depended on good luck is not easy to judge. Mao was not a man to leave anything to chance. His friend Xiao Yu described him as 'a person who takes great pains to plan very carefully whatever he undertakes and that he is a great schemer and organizer.'[4] It has been suggested that Mao depended for much of his success on the timely support of Zhu De the military commander, and on Zhou Enlai for political advice and diplomacy. But neither of these men supported him unconditionally. He commanded their respect and their allegiance during long periods of fruitful alliance.

Mao lived long enough to compound his great achievements with great failures. In his own lifetime he was ranked with the immortals, deified in the Cultural Revolution, and subsequently, vilified for the social and economic breakdown associated with the movement.

The term 'Maoism,' originating with Harvard scholars,[5] has been in wide use since the 1960's. Before the Cultural Revolution Chinese writers held back from designating Mao's theories as Maoism. Instead, they called them Mao Zedong su-xiang (Mao's thoughts). They implied that the suffix -*ism* (zhu-yi) should be kept for such systematic doctrines as Marxism and Leninism. Nevertheless, whatever reservations one may have about the originality of Mao's thought, it now constitutes a vast body of literature.

Mao was more than just another Marxist theoretician. Like Lenin, he adapted Marx to produce a theory of revolution appropriate to his society. In Mao's case the peasantry were to be the main force. But Mao the patriot, who was also a romantic, was far from rejecting outright the heritage of his own country. He enjoyed using literary allusions to China's past, even as he condemned feudalism. He never mastered a foreign language and went abroad only twice in his life, to Moscow. Thanks to his personal style the Chinese revolution bore the stamp 'Made in China.'

Early Years: School Boy, Student and School Teacher

Mao was born on 26 September 1893 in Shaoshan in the province of Hunan in Central China. His parents were peasants, who, thanks to thrift and hard work, became relatively well off. According to many accounts, Mao's father was a harsh demanding man whom Mao came to hate, while his mother was a gentle kindly person with faith in the Gods. It has been pointed out that such stereotypes were normal in the Chinese family system. Jerome Chen believes Western biographers have overplayed the contrast between Mao's parents in their attempt to psychoanalyse Mao.

Certainly Mao's father was a determined man. To escape the burden of debts left by his own father he left home and joined the army. When he returned he managed to save enough money by petty trading to buy two and a half acres of land. Gradually the family prospered. Mao, the first born, was joined in time by two brothers and an adopted sister (his cousin). His father sent him to the local school at the age of eight anticipating that he would gain enough education to be entrusted with the family accounts.

The basic education was in the Chinese classics. Mao had a preference for old novels with stories of romance and rebellion such as *Water Margin* and *Romance of the Three Kingdoms*. Mao had to reconcile his keenness for reading with work in the fields. Often he would read late at night, his window covered by a blanket so that his father would not see the light of the lamp.

Once threatened with a beating by the school master, Mao ran off, and wandered for three days before being found. The ten-year-old boy was surprised to be welcomed back so warmly, and thereafter, he noted, both the teacher and his father treated him more considerately. 'The result of my act of protest impressed me very much. It was a successful "strike."' This story of the tribulations of the young Mao comes from his own personal account given to Edgar Snow in *Red Star Over China*.

In looking back he could not resist drawing political analogies. His father was the ruling party; in opposition was his mother, his brother and sometimes even the hired labourers. But as with other 'united fronts' there were differences within the opposition; Mao's mother sought to avoid confrontation.

Mao's differences with his father came to a climax when he was thirteen. When his father denounced him before guests as good for nothing, Mao stormed out of the house.

He was persuaded to return and apologise. Recalling the event for Edgar Snow, Mao noted: 'That when I defended my rights by open rebellion my father relented, but when I remained weak and submissive he only cursed and beat me the more . . . I learned to hate him.' This startlingly unfilial comment was removed from early Chinese language editions of Snow's book.[6]

At thirteen Mao was married, against his wishes, to a girl of nineteen. There were practical considerations for such a marriage within the social tradition, but Mao was not prepared to cooperate. 'I did not consider her my wife and gave little thought to her.' They parted and it is believed that she married again.

By the time he was fifteen Mao was determined to pursue his education. He wished to go to a new primary school thirteen miles away which taught some of the new 'Western' learning. Friends and relatives lent him some money and he was able to persuade the headmaster of the school to admit him in spite of his age and his size.

Thus, Mao came to spend a year at Dongshan where he got on well with most of the teachers. His classmates, mostly well-dressed sons of landlords, made fun of the large, uncouth newcomer.

On the recommendation of the school, he gained a place at the Xiangxiang Middle School in Changsha, the capital of Hunan province. He travelled forty miles on foot and by boat, and arrived highly excited at his first sight of a big city and at the prospect of joining such a 'great school.' But before long he was caught up in the political enthusiasm when Sun Yat-sen's revolutionary forces attempted to seize the city in October 1911. He enrolled in the republican army and served for six months as an orderly to the officers mess. As an intellectual he felt it was beneath his dignity to carry water and used a substantial part of his meagre salary to pay a water-carrier. The rest of his money went on newspapers--in one of which he read his first article on socialism.

Leaving the army after six months Mao scanned advertisements for courses of study. He enrolled successively at a police school, a soap-making school, a law school and a commercial school. His father was at this time reconciled to supporting his son while he studied and sent money for his school career. In fact, Mao had decided he could better teach himself, reading avidly all day in the Hunan Provincial Library. A recently opened Teacher Training College was offering free tuition for potential primary school teachers. Mao did well in the entrance examination (in fact he wrote papers for two friends who were also admitted) and at the age of nineteen entered Hunan Normal School in Spring 1913. It was an enlightened school. Mao stayed for five years.

One of the teachers who was particularly respected by Mao was Yang Changji (Yang Chang-chih) a professor of ethics who had studied in Japan, England and Germany. He was a man of high ideals who believed in the virtue of strengthening his will by taking a cold bath every morning. Mao learnt from this man to respect Western learning but not to be subservient to Westerners. Imbued with the precept of a healthy mind in a healthy body Mao wrote his first published work 'A Study of Physical Culture' for the magazine *New Youth*.

One summer Mao went on a walking tour with his friend Xiao Yu. With a change of clothes, a sketch pad and an umbrella they tramped from village to village staying in the homes of the peasants. Another summer, with two other friends, he lived in a hut high on a mountain. And most of the time they talked, as young men will, of how they would put the world, and China in particular, to rights. In his later years at the College Mao became a leading figure, active in student affairs, and corresponding with students at other colleges on matters of political concern. He helped to found the New People's Study Society in April 1918. Its aims were 'to reform China and the world.' There were several such societies inspired by the periodical *New Youth* (Zhou Enlai helped to start the Awareness Society in Tianjin).

In May 1918, Mao received his degree. In the summer he went on another walking tour of Hunan province, taking note of the customs of the villagers and the relative status of landlords, tenants and the very poor landless peasants. He then joined a group which was committed to sending progressive students to study abroad. He went to Beijing to help organise the work-study programme for France. Apparently he did not pursue the possibility of going abroad himself. He met up with his old teacher, Yang, who had recently moved to Beijing, and took a job as assistant librarian in the University Library. The chief librarian was Li Dazhou, a leading Marxist who had welcomed the Bolshevik Revolution in Russian, but neither he nor the Dean of Literature and editor of *New Youth*, Chen Duxiu, took much, if any, notice of Mao, who often found himself snubbed by some of the well-known users of the library when he tried to engage them in conversation. Nevertheless, it was his first serious contact with Marxist ideas.

Early in 1919, Mao went to Shanghai to see off a group of students who were going to France, and from there returned to Changsha. He was travelling when the news of the Versailles settlement sparked off the May 4th demonstrations in Beijing. Back in Changsha he taught for a short time as a primary teacher, a job which he found tedious and wearing. 'All day long we eat chalk dust,' he complained. Meanwhile his mother was taken ill and died in October 1919 of acute tonsillitis.

In 1919, Mao became editor of a new magazine the *Xiangjiang Review*. The second issue contained the first instalment of a major article by Mao 'The Great Union of the Popular Masses' calling for the setting up of a revolutionary united front of peasants and workers. When the Changsha government banned the journal Mao started another which in turn was banned. In November he found a *cause celebre* when a young woman, forced into an arranged marriage, cut her throat as she was being put into the bridal chair. Mao wrote nine passionate articles decrying the injustice which had led to Miss Chao's suicide.

At the beginning of 1920, Mao had occasion to go back to Beijing as a leading participant in protests against the local warlord of Hunan. Almost immediately he was caught up in personal affairs. In January, his revered Professor Yang died. In March, his father died of typhoid. On his way home to arrange the family affairs, Mao stopped at Shanghai for a time. He worked as a laundryman and saw more of Chen Duxiu, with whom he had long discussions on Marxism. Back in Changsha Mao was appointed Headmaster in a Primary School attached to the Teachers College. With his first respectable salary Mao was in a position to set up house. He took as his wife, Kaihui, the daughter of Professor Yang, a pretty and intelligent girl whom he had long admired. The date of their marriage is unknown. It may be that they simply agreed to live together. Their first son, Anying, was born soon afterwards.

As a Marxist in the United Front

By now a convinced Marxist, Mao organised a Changsha Communist party and began to recruit students for a Socialist Youth Corps. When the Comintern sent a Dutch agent, Maring, to organise the six separate Communist groups in China into a national party, each group sent two delegates to a meeting at Shanghai. Mao was one of the delegates to this first Party Congress, which, in order to avoid the police, conducted most of its business in a boat on a lake.

For the next two years he led the movement to unionise the urban workers of Hunan. This episode in his career has been rather overshadowed by his later preoccupation with rural reorganisation.

Mao did not attend the Second Party Congress in Shanghai, because as he said he 'forgot the name of the place where it was to be held and as I could not find any of my comrades I missed it.' He was present at the Third Congress held in Guangzhou (Canton) in May 1923 when the decision was taken to join with Sun Yat-sen's Nationalist Party, the Guomingdang. Mao himself opposed the proposal for the united front, which was being pressed by the Russians, but he was nevertheless elected to the Central Committee of the Communist Party.

In 1924, Mao combined his work in the Central Committee of the Party with membership in the Central Executive Committee of the Guomindang in Shanghai. The summer of 1924 saw the setting up of the Hunan (Whampoa) Military Academy and the KMT-CCP entente seemed to be flourishing. Mao's coordinating activities were successful enough for him to be attacked for 'rightism.' Mao returned 'for a rest' to his native village in Hunan.

Meanwhile, in March 1925, Sun Yat-sen died, and on the advice of the Comintern agents Borodin and Galen, Chiang Kai-shek became the new Commander-In-Chief. Popular uprisings in Shanghai and Canton (May 30th Incident) had repercussions across the country. According to Mao the Hunanese peasantry became very militant and Mao began to organise peasant unions. The landlords demanded his arrest and he fled to Canton where he was put in charge of the Peasant Movement Training Institute. He wrote his first major analytical article 'Analyses of the Different Classes of Chinese Society' in the winter of 1925-6, but Chen Duxiu objected in particular to Mao's proposals for the vigorous organisation of the peasants.

At this time he was also editing the *Political Weekly* for the KMT. Preparations were in hand for a march North. Mao urged the peasants to support this 'Northern Expedition' when it set out from Canton in 1926 and moved into Hunan province. Chiang Kai-shek followed the troops in his headquarters train. Mao, as chief of the KMT Propaganda Department, was on the same train. He was smarting from the criticism of fellow communists like Li Lisan and Chen Duxiu who believed that the party's role was to win over the cities and to leave the 'petty-bourgeois' peasants to the KMT. In fact, the vanguard of the expedition under Zhu De found that the peasants were more than ready to revolt. The scenes of anarchy and rebellion as peasants turned on the landlords, forcing them to flee for their lives, shocked KMT troops. The Communist Party Central Committee was impressed. Mao was to make a tour of inspection. He produced his classic 'Report on an Investigation into the Peasant Movement in Hunan,' published in March 1927. By late summer 1926 the nationalist army had reached the Yangtze at Hankou and within a month the three-city urban complex now called Wuhan, had fallen. The revolutionary government moved into Wuhan.

Mao went to Wuhan to defend his policies at a conference in April 1927. It was interrupted by news that Chiang Kai-shek had instigated an appalling massacre of his left-wing supporters in Shanghai. In the ensuing political confusion and recriminations Chen Duxiu was to be deposed as CCP Secretary.

As a Revolutionary Leader in the Countryside

Mao went back to Hunan. The earlier peasant movements had been suppressed. Meanwhile, an attempt to seize the city of Nanchang, the 'Nanchang uprising,' led by Zhou Enlai, Zhu De and others, failed and some of the dispersed communists, including Mao, took to the mountains at Jinggang on the borders of Hunan and Jiangxi. From this remote base Mao set about organising what was to be known as the Autumn Harvest Rising. He interpreted his instructions radically and proposed to confiscate the land of small as well as large landlords and to set up soviets--although, at that time such a policy was opposed by the Comintern.

The Autumn Harvest Uprising began on 9 September with four 'regiments' comprising coal miners, peasants and soldiers who had defected from the Guomindang. Mao himself was captured by the Guomindang and taken to their headquarters to be shot. He offered a bribe which the officer refused, and then broke away and hid in some rough grass. Miraculously, a thorough search failed to uncover him. At nightfall he made his way back to the safety of the mountains. The uprising began with some successes, but then dissension led to fighting between the various regiments. The citizens of Changsha wisely refused to throw their lot in with the rebels. The operation was called off and Mao retreated to the Jinggang Mountains. The Politburo put the blame on Mao. He was dismissed from his position as Alternate Member. Meanwhile Mao made a working alliance with the bandit leaders of secret societies who were already installed in the relatively remote mountains on the border of Hunan and Jiangxi. He later claimed: 'While I remained on Jinggangshan they were faithful Communists and carried out the orders of the Party. Later on . . . they returned to their bandit habits. Subsequently they were killed by the peasants, by then organized and sovietized and able to defend themselves.'[7]

Mao's wife, Yang Kaihui, had been left behind in Changsha where she was later captured and killed. During 1928 he began to live with He Zizhen, 'a small delicate woman with a pretty face and a shy modest manner.'[8] She was 18, Mao was 35.

In May 1928, Zhu De and his force came into Hunan and joined up with Mao.[9] This was one of the most important events in Mao's career. 'It is legitimate to suppose,' writes Dick Wilson, 'that if this union had not come off, Mao would have remained at best a discredited provincial leader.'[10] At a conference on 20 May 1928 at Maoping, the leaders drew up the main lines of their practical policy in the field. This included the well-known lines:

> The enemy advances, we retreat
> The enemy halts and encamps, we harass
> The enemy seeks to avoid battle, we attack
> The enemy retreats, we pursue.

Meanwhile, such orders as came through from the Politburo, were often unrealistic and sometimes contradictory. It is suggested that Mao more than Zhu was prepared to ignore such instructions. Politically, Mao seems to have imposed his leadership winning over some of Zhu's senior men such as his political Commissar Chen Yi, and Lin Biao, at that time a battalion commander.

In October Mao summed-up the position in the base area in his article 'Why is it that Red Political Power can Exist in China?' In this he claimed that the long-term survival of encircled small areas was 'a phenomenon which has never occurred anywhere else in the world.' But the economic difficulties were almost intolerable. In November, Mao's report to the Central Committee entitled *The Struggle in the Jinggang Mountains* included a plea for help: 'Send a few doctors with Western training and some iodine.'

Mao claimed that the army could triumph over its hardships because of the practice of democracy. 'The newly captured soldiers in particular feel that our army and the Guomindang army are worlds apart. They feel spiritually liberated, even though material conditions . . . are not equal to those in the White Army.'[11]

But the masses were slow to respond at first keeping aloof from the Red Army's propaganda. Mao wrote: 'We have an acute sense of our isolation which we keep hoping will end.'

Meanwhile, another military force joined Mao-Zhu.[12] This was led by Peng Dehuai who was to be one of the stalwarts of the Communist military leadership.

 In 1929, Li Lisan, the new leader of the Communist Party Central Committee, ordered Mao to disband the Red Army and to move to Shanghai to help implement proletarian revolution. Mao refused, reaffirming his commitment to the peasant revolution.

In the summer of 1930, Li Lisan ordered the capture of several major cities in Central China, including Wuhan and Changsha. The failure of one such attack led to the torture and public execution of Mao's wife, Yang Kaihui.

Mao gave up his hopes of easy victory. In the summer of 1931, leading figures of the Central Committee moved from their hiding places in Shanghai

to Jiangxi where a Chinese Soviet Republic was proclaimed on 7 November
1931, with Mao as Chairman. For several years Mao appeared to have been
severely constrained by the Central Committee. However, if at times he
appeared to be little more than a figure head, he was now in direct
communication with the national leaders of the party. The Central Committee, dominated by the Returned Student group trained in Moscow, favoured
conventional military operations in which the Red Army would meet the
enemy head on. Mao's strategy of 'luring the enemy' into hostile country
was in line with his conviction that 'The Red Army fights not merely for the
sake of fighting, but exclusively to agitate among the masses, to organize
them, to arm them, and to help them establish political power.'

By this time Chiang Kai-shek was able to mount such pressure, in a
series of encirclement campaigns led by German officers, as to ensure the
destruction of the Jiangxi Soviet. The Long March began in October 1934
as a desperate attempt to break out with only a vague idea of joining up with
other dispersed Soviets. As Mao later told Edgar Snow 'if you mean did we
have any exact plans the answer is we had none.' Many of the women and
children were left behind. Mao left two children with peasants but took his
second wife He Zizhen with him. She was pregnant, suffered injuries in a
dive bombing attack and gave birth. Mao himself was far from fit, he was
convalescing from malaria when the march began. He had political battles
to fight. At Zunyi in January 1935 Mao called for an 'enlarged' meeting of
the Politburo. He persuaded his old opponents to accept his strategic
concepts and his leadership. Mao was elected Chairman of the Politburo; for
the first time the Party had chosen its leader without the blessing of
Moscow. Zhou Enlai who had been associated with Mao's opponents did a
neat switch to Mao's side.

By the end of October 1935 some eight thousand of the original ninety-
thousand troops arrived at the Red base in Shaanxi, the end of a six-
thousand-mile journey. Mao was forty-three years old; he was described as
a thin, stooping, 'gaunt, rather Lincolnesque figure' by Edgar Snow, who
arrived at the Red Headquarters in 1936 and wrote his classic *Red Star Over
China*, presenting Mao to the world.

The Second United Front: Mao at Yanan

Even before the Long March in January 1933, Mao had stated his wil-
lingness to cooperate with any anti-Japanese forces. The Zunyi conference
had endorsed such a proposal, and later on 1 August 1935, the Communists
issued an *Address to the People of China* calling for combined efforts against
the Japanese.

In the process of history, the Japanese aggression was to benefit the Communists. Mao later said as much to visiting Japanese delegations. In December 1936 Chiang Kai-shek was kidnapped by his own troops who forced him to agree to a united front with the Communists. In July 1937, the Japanese opened their major offensive to conquer China. They forced Chiang onto the defensive; he retreated westwards to Chongqing. The cities and the railroads were held by the conventional forces of the Japanese. In the countryside, the Communist armies roamed widely and won adherents, moving among the people 'as a fish in water.' By 1945 Red China had ninety million people led by one million party members and defended by nearly one million soldiers.

At the headquarters in Yanan, life was hard but it was relatively peaceful. After the Japanese chose to extend themselves in a world war against the United States, Mao and his comrades found time to study and debate. Late into the night the Chairman prepared his speeches defining the Marxist struggle in its Chinese context, doing ideological battle with those who opposed him, especially the Moscow trained.

The senior 'Bolshevik,' Wang Ming, had arrived with orders from Moscow that the Party should be subordinate to the Guomindang and the army should be integrated with the nationalist troops under Chiang Kai-shek's command. Mao was able to resist such pressures and waged an ideological campaign which isolated Wang Ming and confirmed his own position. 'On Practice' and 'On Contradiction' were two of Mao's lectures, later polished up and reissued, which gave a practical and Chinese emphasis to Marxist studies. While Zhu De was responsible for the military campaigns and for organising the highly successful Eighth Route Army behind the Japanese lines, and while Zhou Enlai was developing his role as the suave diplomat, Mao set himself up as the ideologue, and as a moulder of men's minds. For two years, 1942-44, the rectification campaigns stressed the importance of 'struggle' in the development of 'correct' thinking. Above all, Mao developed the 'mass line' in which 'from the people, to the people' really did mean consultations at the rice roots.

One feature of the rectification campaign was the Yanan forum on Art and Literature which opened in May 1942 emphasising that writers and artists should serve society. By this time Mao had a new wife, Jiang Qing, who attended the conferences as his secretary and was thereafter to assume a particular interest in 'cultural' reform. Jiang Qing, a vivacious actress from Shanghai, had earlier supplanted He Zizhen. Although the Yanan style was not particularly puritanical, the comrades had been shocked. They were also anxious that the newcomer should not have too much political influence. Eventually they had allowed Mao to have a divorce and He Zizhen had been sent to Moscow for medical treatment.

Mao's teaching was highlighting the practice of Marxism in the context of a Chinese revolution: 'Our comrades must understand that we do not study Marxism-Leninism because it is pleasing to the eye or because it has some mystical value . . . Marxism-Leninism has no beauty, nor has it any mystical value. It is only extremely useful.' As for those who opposed him, he was content that they should acknowledge their errors and repent.

'Our aim in exposing errors and criticising shortcomings, like that of a doctor curing a sickness, is solely to save the patient and not to doctor him to death . . . In treating an ideological or a political malady one must never be rough and rash but must adopt the approach of curing the sickness to save the patient.'

By 1944 Mao was dominant in Yanan. His ideas were preeminent. Wang Ming was to claim that Mao spoke of the fundamental need for a new *Maoist* faith. Mao said 'we must take our example from Mahomet who turned people to a new faith by force with the sword in one hand and the Koran in the other.'

Liu Shaoqi and Lin Biao were among those who helped to glorify Mao at this time. In 1943 Liu had published an article showing that Mao's policies over the past twenty years had been in line with Bolshevik precedents--his opponents had been the Chinese Mensheviks. Thus did Liu legitimize Mao's leadership for Comintern historiography.

The Civil War

With the end of the World War in sight the Americans tried to bring Communists and Guomindang together. They sent General Hurley, unannounced, to Yanan in November 1944. He leapt from his plane with an Indian war-cry, believing it to be a suitable greeting in bandit country! He and Mao appeared to get on well enough. Mao was so encouraged that he put out, via General Wedemeyer, a feeler for an invitation to visit Roosevelt in Washington. This failed, as it was almost bound to anyway, because it was not supported by Hurley.

The cause of reconciling the Communists and the Guomindang proved hopeless, although Mao spent over six weeks in Chongqing in talks with Chiang Kai-shek in the fall of 1945. Intermittent negotiations continued into 1946. A cease-fire agreement broke down and both sides prepared to fight to the finish.

The story of the Civil War, while revealing the fundamental flaws on the part of the Nationalists, was not a story of continuous success for the Communists. In March 1947 their headquarters at Yanan became untenable due to air attacks. In a hasty withdrawal Mao survived an air attack on his jeep which left bullet holes in the roof. Moreover, in their haste, Mao and

Jiang Qing had left the children behind. Mao-mao was never heard of again; the daughter Li Na was found in a peasant's house and sent to Zhou Enlai's wife for safe-keeping.

Meanwhile, the Communists began to take the offensive. As the Red armies gained increasing success Mao began to concentrate on extending the domestic policies, which had been tested in base areas, into newly liberated regions. Eventually with the collapse of Chiang Kai-shek's forces the Communists swept into power. Corruption, mismanagement and rampant inflation in the Guomindang region brought Mao to Tian An Men quicker than he had dared hope. In September 1949 he proclaimed: 'Our nation will never be insulted again. We have stood up.'

Leaning to One Side: The Early Years of the People's *Republic*

On 30 June 1949, Mao had made a speech in which he argued that China had no alternative but to 'lean to one side,' the Soviet side of the Cold War. We now know that the situation at the time was not as clear cut as a simple reading of the speech would indicate. Documents released in Washington and London after thirty years have revealed that in the summer of 1949 Zhou Enlai, probably with Mao's knowledge, attempted to sound out the United States and Great Britain on the possibility of economic aid. This 'Chou Demarche' came to nothing, but its significance must be that the Chinese leaders in 1949 were not wholeheartedly committed to a state of economic dependence on the Soviet Union.

Their doubts were to be vindicated during the following winter when Mao led a Chinese mission to the Soviet Union. He was later joined by Zhou Enlai, the Premier and Foreign Minister, and it has been suggested that this was a sign of failure on Mao's part since he had made so little progress in his negotiations with Stalin that Zhou Enlai's support was felt to be necessary. Stalin drove a tough bargain. In the Sino-Soviet Treaty which was signed on 17 February 1950, the provisions for joint-stock companies smacked of the old imperialist relations while the credits, £300 million for five years, were minimal. However, it was a lot better than nothing and Soviet advisers moved in. Their influence was manifested in many ways over the next few years, perhaps most conspicuously in 'wedding cake' style architecture.

The eruption of the Korean War in June 1950 has yet to be fully explained. According to Khruschchev, Stalin had asked Mao what he thought of Kim Il Sung's plan to attack the South and Mao dismissed the question as a local matter which would not bring in the United States. In the event, the Korean War was to cost China an estimated 900,000 lives; one of those who died was Mao's oldest son. Moreover, the war ensured for many years to come that the People's Republic would be anathema at the United Nations, and encouraged Chiang Kai-shek, in his refuge on Taiwan to harass the mainland and dream of reconquest.

It was against this background that the party had to implement its reforms: campaigns such as the Three Anti's (against corruption, waste and bureaucracy), together with land reform. Inevitably perhaps, there was bloodshed. Although Mao had urged that only a percentage of the worst offenders should be killed, this undoubtedly encompassed a large number, some say two million.

An early challenge to Mao's leadership of the people's Republic came from the northeast provinces (formerly Manchuria) where Gao Gang was in charge. Gao was undoubtedly an efficient administrator and it has never been proved that he conspired with Stalin to promote Russian interests in the Northeast. A series of articles, none of them actually naming Gao, began to whittle away his reputation. It was a slow but effective process culminating in Gao's suicide. Some of his followers were purged. Mao was rid of a rival.

Much influenced by the Russians, 1953 saw the inauguration of the first five-year plan for industrial development. It also saw the completion of the first stage of land reform, 700 million mou (1/3 acre) had been redistributed to 300 million peasants. Thus the peasants gained their land; one mou in the south, two mou in central China and three mou in the north. But almost immediately with the Resolution on the Formation of Agricultural Cooperatives, December 1953, they were being driven towards coopera- tivization. Mao himself was anxious to set the pace in moving from mutual aid teams to semi-socialist cooperatives. He listened avidly to the members of his own personal guard who he chose to send back to their own villages to assess the prospects for reform. He travelled fairly extensively, 'more than Confucius' he said, and in 1955 presided over the publication of a compen- dia of optimistic reports entitled *The Socialist Upsurge in China's Countryside*.

Meanwhile, it had been decided that the time had come to nationalise China's independent capitalist businessmen. Henceforth, they had to exist on fixed interest and salaries.

In February 1956, Khrushchev made his famous attack on Stalin at the Soviet Party's Twentieth Congress. Mao had mixed feelings but pre- dominantly he feared the implications of Khrushchev's speech. He began to voice his doubts about the whole Sino-Soviet relationship. On 25 April 1956 he delivered an address to the Politburo 'On the Ten Major Relationships.' Socialism should be accelerated, there should be some decentralization of industry, bureaucrats in party and government should be pruned by as many as two-thirds. Counter-revolutionaries must be eliminated, but they should be reformed rather than killed.

At this time there was growing opposition within the Politburo to Mao's policies. This was reflected in the Eighth Party Congress in which Liu Shaoqi and others reminded Mao of his own professed regard for collective leadership. The Secretariat of the Party was reorganised so that it could operate effectively without Mao and with Deng Xiaoping as the new Party Secretary.

The 'Hundred Flowers' and the 'Great Leap'

Mao's appeal to the intellectuals, 'to let a hundred flowers bloom, a hundred schools of thought contend,' is open to various interpretations. It may have been a genuine recognition of the value of freedom of expression if China was to develop economic and social strategies independent of the Soviet advisers. Whatever his motive, he soon changed his mind and many who spoke out found that they had been trapped into identifying themselves as enemies. By the summer of 1957 the 'blooming' was over and those who were now seen to be 'poisonous weeds' were in dire trouble; some managed to emigrate. 'On the Correct Handling of Contradictions Among the People' was published to define the limits of criticism in relation to the Party.

In foreign affairs Mao disapproved of Khrushchev's attempts to improve relations with the United States. Visiting Moscow in November 1957 Mao addressed the meeting of Communist and Workers parties. He declared that the 'East Wind was prevailing over the West Wind' and implied that the Soviet Union should use its recently demonstrated capability in sputniks and rocketry to embark on a more active confrontation with the United States.

Meanwhile, economic difficulties in China, for example, the disastrous harvest of 1956, highlighted the inadequacies of Soviet aid and the inappropriateness of the Soviet development model. It was such considerations which impelled Mao formally to inaugurate the 'Great Leap Forward' on 1 February 1958. Using her own resources with the maximum mobilization of human effort China would, in fifteen years, surpass Great Britain in industrial development. For Mao the 'Great Leap' was an answer to the critics and the doubters, a response to the disappointing achievements of the Five Year Plan. The achievement of 'socialism' was to be speeded up; rural China was to be organised into self-reliant Commune units. Living and working together the peasants would be forged into a truly revolutionary corps, while at the same time industry would be diversified. Within a year it was becoming clear that the Communes would not work. Both as economic and social units they were too large. As bases for rural industry they suffered from over ambitious leaders, lacking expertise and technical resources.

When the Central Committee met at Wuchang in December, Mao found himself defending the Great Leap Forward. Meanwhile, the more radical aspects of the Commune movement, for example, single-sex barracks, were halted and the possession of small private plots guaranteed. Among those who opposed Mao were Zhou Enlai, Zhu De and Peng Dehuai, Minister of Defence. Already it had been agreed that Lui Xiaoqi would succeed him as Chairman of the Republic and this was implemented by the National People's Congress meeting at the end of April.

In June, Mao went home for the first time in thirty-two years to visit his birthplace. He wrote a poem, 'Shaoshan revisited,' and wept as he reminisced with those who had known his wife Yang Kaihui. By July he was at Lushan, facing an outspokenly hostile central committee meeting. The lead was taken by Peng Dehuai.

There were long bitter recriminations replete with coarse language. Mao admitted many of his mistakes. 'I understand nothing about industrial planning . . . Comrades in 1958 and 1959 the responsibility was mine and you should take me to task.' They did. The transcripts of the Lushan meeting show Mao suffering from a verbal battering which at times left him gibbering almost incoherently to the point where his replies are almost impossible to translate into English.

Chou Enlai made some attempt to defend Mao now that he was down, while Liu Xiaoqi turned on him. As for Peng he had apparently gone too far. His fate was to be dismissed to run a Sino-Soviet state farm in Heilongjiang. Lin Biao replaced him as Minister of Defence.

From the Sino-Soviet Rift to the Cultural Revolution

The opening of the new decade saw the widening of the Sino-Soviet Rift. Mao disapproved of the Soviet initiative for summit talks in the U.S. When Khruschev dropped in on his way home from the U.S. in 1959 and, at a banquet in his honour, attacked those who wanted to 'test by force the stability of the capitalist system,' Mao was unimpressed and continued to stress the need for vigilance in dealing with the imperialists.

Already in June 1959 the Soviet Union had abrogated its agreement to share nuclear weapon technology with China. The following year, in July, Moscow recalled all its advisers and at the Moscow conference in November 1960 the Chinese openly identified Khruschev as revisionist. Differences over the Sino-Indian War and the Cuban crisis compounded Mao's scorn for the Soviets. Different political objectives separated the two Communist powers and were not lessened by the negative personal chemistry of the two ex-peasant leaders.

The fall of Khrushchev in 1964 was followed by a temporary lull in the dispute, but within months Chinese official polemics were denouncing Khrushchev's successors. The escalation of the American War in Vietnam did not bring the supporters of North Vietnam any closer together. Mao was more firmly opposed to cooperation than Liu Shaoqi. The Chinese refused to attend a meeting of Communist parties in March 1965 which produced a statement on Vietnam calling for 'united action.' In rejecting this appeal the Chinese argued that the policies of the new Soviet leaders were as revisionist as those of Khrushchev and that Soviet revisionism was the ally of U.S. imperialism.

Mao's antagonism to American imperialism went further than that of his rivals in the Politburo. To would-be revolutionaries throughout the world Maoism appeared to offer an alternative route to socialism. In the first half of the 1960's, before the chaos of the Cultural Revolution turned China inwards and the excesses of the Red Guards alarmed friends and foes alike, it was not inappropriate for China, estranged from the Soviet revisionists, to appear as the leader of the Third World. Mao's concept of the 'Intermediate Zone' was a challenge to both of the super-powers.

From 1960 Mao was increasingly dependent for support on the People's Liberation Army which Lin Biao was turning into 'a great school of Mao Zedong thought.' Seeing 'new bourgeois elements arising in the Party and the educated elite, Mao pressed for a Socialist Education Movement in 1962. This blossomed in 1964 with the 'Four Clean-Ups,' a campaign intended to inculcate enthusiasm for a classless society and to encourage maximum economic growth.

The movement started in the countryside and was then extended to the cities. A number of intellectuals and artists were disgraced for un-revolutionary and revisionist work.

In November 1965, a Shanghai newspaper published an article, instigated by Mao himself, which criticised the playwright Wu Han, the Deputy Mayor of Beijing, on the grounds that his play 'Hai Rui Dismissed from Office' was a covert attack on Mao. This article was later hailed as the first bugle call of the Cultural Revolution.

In the first months of 1966 Mao was mobilising support against his perceived enemies. When in May a lecturer at Beijing University put up a poster which denounced some of the university authorities as well as the First Secretary of the Communist Party, Mao saw that it was published in the *People's Daily*. A mood of rebellion spread through colleges and schools across China. Mao offered his own slogan 'To rebel against reactionaries is justified.' Meanwhile, to confute those who had suggested that he was not in good health, he went for a swim in the Yangste. With 5000 young swimmers in attendance, he covered 9 miles in 65 minutes, going downstream.

Beginning in August, a ferment of public denunciations, big character posters and Red Guard rallies began to characterise the Chinese scene. On 18 August, Mao and his close comrade-in-arms, Lin Biao, welcomed a mass rally of a million young people. A '16 point decision' adopted on 8 August was intended to provide guidelines and keep the revolution under control. However, the violence, chaos and bloodshed of the ensuing months led eventually to the restoration of order by the PLA.

By the beginning of 1967 Mao was urging caution on the more extreme radical leaders. He told the Shanghai leftists, Zhang Chunqiao and Yao Wenyuan that it was wrong to demand the abolition of 'heads.' He opposed the idea of calling the People's Republic 'The Chinese Peoples Commune': 'Where would we place the Party? Where would we place the Party Committee? There must be a nucleus no matter what we call it.'

But Mao was content to watch his opponents in the Party being destroyed. In October 1968 the Central Committee confirmed the removal of Liu Shaoqi from all his posts and named Lin Biao as 'the close comrade-in-arms and successor of Comrade Mao Zedong.'

From time to time Mao expressed doubts about the cult personality. 'I was quite uneasy at some of his (Lin Biao's) thinking' he had written to Jiang Qing in 1966. 'I have never believed that the several booklets I wrote would have so much supernatural power. Now after he exaggerated them the whole nation has exaggerated them.'[13] Lin had published over 350 million copies of that breviary of Mao's thoughts, the *Little Red Book*, by January 1965. It became indispensible not only as a guide to the correct political line but as a panacea, a literal life saver. Doctors reported that patients who studied it recovered from burns ninety-five percent more often than those who did not and that those who read it during surgery needed no anesthetic. A locomotive driver reported that, thanks to Mao's Thought, he was able to make his train, 'a rotten old piece of goods sold us by the Soviet Union,' go much faster. This deification of Mao lampooned in the *Miracles of Chairman Mao* (see no. 571), was to last until his death.

The exuberant phase of the Cultural Revolution was over by 1969. The Maoist line--putting politics in command and emphasising faith before works, the virtue of Redness over expertise--was to last. The cry of 'Mao Zhuxi Wan Sui' (Long Life to Chairman Mao) was to follow him through his declining years in the 1970's.

Rapprochement with the U.S.: The Unwinding of the Cultural Revolution

Remarking wryly to Edgar Snow in 1970 that he was soon going to see his maker, Mao was nevertheless about to seize a remarkable opportunity. The U.S. President Nixon, realising that America's anti-China policy was counter-productive and seeking a way out of the Indo-Chinese *impasse*, had let it be known that he would like to do a deal.

The hint was taken. Edgar Snow was one of the channels through which Mao indicated that a Nixon visit would be welcome. 'I'm only a lone monk with a leaky umbrella,' said Mao, as he saw Snow to the door. This apparently endearing remark was deceptive. In Chinese it is a pun. 'I recognize no law: nothing is sacred.' The old man was saying that he had no principles which would preclude him from doing a deal with the leader of the capitalist world.

Meanwhile, one irksome factor for Mao was removed by the death of his heir, Lin Biao. Ever since Lin had been confirmed as Mao's successor at the Ninth Party Congress in March 1969, Mao had been barely able to conceal his doubts about this arrangement. In desperation, a Lin faction, led by his son, conspired to kill the Chairman. This turned out to be a fiasco which led to the attempted escape of Lin by air to Moscow. The plane crashed in Outer Mongolia. At least that is the official story, but there is an alternative version that Lin was not on the plane but met his death, after a last supper with Mao and Zhou Enlai, who had arranged to have his car blown up as it went off down the drive.

The death of Lin in September 1971 was welcome anyway; Lin had been among those who objected to the Nixon visit scheduled for February 1972. The visit was a triumphal turning point, an indicator of the standing of Mao's China in world affairs. China had indeed come a long way since the Communists 'entered the cities.'

China's leaders were the same old men. Zhou Enlai, three years younger than Mao, went into hospital in April 1974. Mao's wife Jiang Qing who had become more conspicuous since the Cultural Revolution as a radical-propagandist through the arts, became associated with other 'leftists' anxious to ensure a radical succession. Mao seemed to have taken a middle ground. He proposed the reinstatement of Deng Xiaoping to take charge of the work of the Central Committee during Zhou's illness. He criticised the radicals at a Politburo meeting on 3 May 1975: 'Don't function as a gang of four . . . Why don't you unite with the more than two hundred members of the Central Committee of the Party? A few banding together is no good, never any good.'

The death of Zhou in 1976 increased the hopes of the radicals. But Mao appointed Hua Guofeng. He also seemed to have some confidence in Deng Xiaoping. Old adversary that he was, he had been relatively open in his criticism of Mao. Mao once pointed him out to Khruschev: 'See that little man there? He's highly intelligent and has a great future ahead of him.' But this was not apparent in April 1976. Deng was blamed for the circumstances of the riots in Tien An Men Square when an occasion for mourning the late Zhou Enlai became a demonstration in favour of his policies. Hua was confirmed as Premier and made Senior Vice-Chairman of the Party, according to Hua's story, 'upon the personal proposal of Chairman Mao.'

In June 1976, Mao had what was to be the last meeting with his colleagues. His wife was not invited. He told them that he was not going to leave a will. He had no faith in such a formality. He commented 'I have predicted that full-scale capitalist restoration may appear in China. I think it will be bad then . . . It is my idea that there shall be no presidency for the country. The best solution is for the Politburo to produce a tripartite leadership of old, middle-aged and young cadres. It is up to the Politburo to decide if Jiang Qing will be included . . . After I die send my remains to Xiangtan, Hunan. I don't believe in ghosts . . . You too should be brave. Get rid of that scholarly air. In this world revolution is still the main stream. Will it do without struggle?'

In July there came a devasting earthquake. It was the portent for the end of a dynasty. On 9 September 1976, Mao died.

Notes

1. Dick Wilson, *Mao. The People's Emperor.* (London: Hutchinson, 1979), and e.g. George Paloczi-Horvath. *Mao Tse-tung. Emperor of the Blue Ants.* (London: Secker and Warburg, 1962).
2. Dennis Bloodworth, *The Messiah and the Mandarins.* (London: Weidenfeld, 1982).
3. Wilson, *Mao. The People's Emperor*, pp. 95-96.
4. Ibid., p. 95.
5. Jerome Chen, *Mao and the Chinese Revolution.* (London: O.U.P., 1965). p. 3.
6. Wilson, *Mao. The People's Emperor*, p. 26.
7. Edgar Snow, *Red Star Over China.* (London: Gollancz, 1968), p. 167.
8. Wilson, *Mao. The People's Emperor*, p. 129.
9. Seven years older than Mao, Zhu came from a well to do Sichuanese peasant family. Two of his brothers were killed in action and his wife and son were murdered. At one time an opium addict, he was cured and went to Europe where he studied at Gottingen. He was nicknamed 'The Cook.' The story was that once, when captured, he had saved himself by shouting: 'Don't shoot, I'm only the cook.'
10. Wilson, *Mao. The People's Emperor*, p. 131.
11. Ibid., p. 136.
12. The two men were so closely linked that the peasants referred to them as one person.
13. Wilson, *Mao. The People's Emperor*, p. 396.

II. The Sources

China has not been an easy country for the researcher in modern history. As a totalitarian state in which, to paraphrase Mao, 'Politics is put in command,' freedom of speech and information has been trimmed. The study of Mao Zedong himself, always a controversial figure, and not less so at the height of his power and influence, has been constrained by the dearth of reliable information.

This does not mean that there is a lack of data. On the contrary, the Communists have always set great store by their printing machines--they humped one along with them on the Long March--and Mao himself has been nothing if not prolific with pen and tongue. The main problem is that the literature published by the Party and Government has always been 'official,' that is, dedicated to the prevailing political line, and there is very little ancillary and circumstantial evidence against which it can be tested.

What we have learnt in the West about Mao has come out occasionally and in great spurts. For example, Mao, the almost unknown 'bandit,' was discovered by Edgar Snow, and one or two other intrepid travellers such as Agnes Smedley who went to Yanan in 1936-37. Snow's *Red Star over China* is a classic with its account of Mao's life to that date in his own words. Then after Liberation, the Foreign Languages Press prepared an apparently comprehensive anthology of selected works in four volumes. A fifth volume of selected works was published in April 1977 in Chinese, and in August 1977 in English translation.

Meanwhile, a veritable floodgate was opened in the 1960's with the so-called 'Red Guard publications' which found their way out via Hong Kong. Much recent scholarly work on Mao has depended on the insights which were let loose, often inadvertently, in the mass of Cultural Revolution literature and documentation.

These materials include *Mao Zedong ssu-hsiang wan sui!* (Long Live Mao Tse-tung's thought!), translated in full in *Current Background* 891, and *Mao Tse-tung ssu-hsiang wan sui*, 1967 and 1969, which became available in 1973 in photo-offset editions produced by the Institute of International Relations, Taipei, Taiwan. They had apparently been originally produced in the People's Republic for limited distribution.

The 1967 volume covers the period 1959-61, and the 1969 volume covers the mid-50's to late 60's. Consisting of speeches and articles not previously available, they are translated in *Current Background* 892.

Mao's death in 1976 has, of course, shifted the bounds of critical research in China, but is unlikely to have liberated it completely. For example, some books and pamphlets as well as certain issues of periodicals and newspapers have not been allowed to circulate among non-Chinese, and have been taken out of the country. They have been designated *neibu* because they contain material which the authorities consider to be too sensitive for foreign scrutiny. Such works may not even be listed in the Cumulative National Bibliography.

In order to compensate, a prodigious source of information has been provided over the years by the China Watchers. Based in Hong Kong and financed by the United States, these agencies have provided a continuous source of information conveniently published in English. The two major agencies have been the United States Consulate General and the Union Research Institute.

The Consulate General's press and translation unit has produced a steady stream of materials since it was set up in 1950 until the 1970's. Its main publications were as follows:

Current Background, published from June 1950 to August 1978, usually weekly. Each issue focuses on a single aspect and is compiled from newspapers and periodicals. From time to time a chronology of principal developments is published.

Survey of China Mainland Press, published from November 1950 until 1973. The survey carries main press releases of the New China News Agency and translations of key articles from the *People's Daily*.

Extracts from China Mainland Magazines, published irregularly from August 1955 until August 1978. In 1962 its name changed to *Selections from China Mainland Magazines*. It gives translations in full of key periodical articles.

Current Background, *Survey of China Mainland Press* and *Extracts from China Mainland Magazines* have been regularly indexed since 1956. All three publications are available from Clearinghouse, U.S. Department of Commerce, Springfield, Virginia.

Current Scene, published monthly from 1962 until January 1979, is a series of documented monographs on various aspects of economic, political and educational change in China.

The Union Research Institute, set up in Nanjing in 1949, was reestablished in Hong Kong in January 1951. It scanned and produced extracts from over 300 Chinese newspapers and periodicals from the People's Republic, from Taiwan and other parts of Asia. Its main publications are:

China News Analysis published weekly from August 1953 until November 1976.

Communist China Problem Research Series has produced issues on specific topics, such as education.

The Union Research Service series, a twice weekly translation service of materials from Chinese mainland regional newspapers not generally available. The U.R.I. sources are particularly valuable for the 1950's and 1960's. Since then the service has gradually atrophied. Its original archive files have been acquired by the Hong Kong Baptist College.

In the Republic of China (Taiwan) the government established in 1961 an Institute of International Relations to collect and disseminate materials on the People's Republic. It has published a monthly journal, *Issues and Studies* (since October, 1964) as well as books and articles on a variety of topics pertaining to communist China.

In the United States of America the Joint Publications Research Service, part of the Clearinghouse for Federal Scientific and Technical Information of the Department of Commerce, was set up in March 1957 to provide government agencies with translations of foreign documents, divided into Social Science and Scientific-Technical Sections. The Social Science Section includes materials from important Chinese journals such as *Hongqi* (Red Flag), *Zhenfa Yenjui* (Political and Legal Research), *Jingji Yenjui* (Economics Research), *Renmin Jiaoyu* (People's Education).

The Joint Publications Research Service published *Communist China Digest*--a summary of information on various aspects of life in China. When the U.S. press monitoring unit in Hong Kong was closed down in 1979, the JPRS series was entitled *China Report* and was reorganised into six subseries: agriculture; economic affairs; political, sociological and military affairs; plant and installation data; science and technology, and *Red Flag*.

In the United Kingdom the British Broadcasting Corporation has published (since before Liberation) a daily *Summary of World Broadcasts (Far East)*. This is also on microfilm and can be obtained in many libraries.

Universities and Libraries in the United States

Universities

Universities in the United States which have centres for Chinese Studies include the following: California (Berkeley), Columbia, Harvard (currently engaged in Mao studies), Cornell, the University of Michigan and the University of Washington. The University of California publishes 'Studies in Chinese Government Terminology' from 1956 and 'China Research Monographs' beginning in 1967. Stanford University has *The Hoover Institution on War, Revolution and Peace*, a research centre and library. It began collecting materials on Chinese communism in 1945.

Libraries

Libraries in the United States which have centres for Chinese Studies include the following:

- The Library of Congress, Washington.
- The Far Eastern Library of the University of Chicago.
- The Harvard-Yenching Library of Harvard University, Cambridge.
- The East Asian Library of Columbia University, New York.
- The Center for Chinese Studies Library of the University of California, Berkeley.
- The Asian Library of the University of Michigan, Ann Arbor.
- The Bentley Historical Library at the University of Michigan has established an archive to collect trip reports, including private diaries by Americans who visited China in the 1970's.
- The Far Eastern Library of the University of Washington, Seattle.

Journals Published in the United States

Asian Survey, Berkeley, California. First issue March 1 1961 when it succeeded the *Far Eastern Survey* (1932-1961), Monthly.

Chinese Law and Government, New York. A journal of translations.

Communist Affairs, Los Angeles.

Foreign Broadcasting Information Service, Washington D.C. provides transcriptions of Chinese Communist radio broadcasts and also publishes special issues on selected topics.

The Journal of Asian Studies, Ann Arbor, Michigan. First issue November 1 1941, Quarterly.

Pacific Affairs, Honolulu and Vancouver.

Problems of Communism, Washington, D.C.

Major Libraries in China

- The Peking Library
- Shanghai Municipal Library
- The Social Science Library of the Chinese Academy of Sciences

Chinese Publications

Compendia

The People's University (Renmin Daxiu) compiles and publishes annually a file of articles on a wide range of topics. This series is known as *Fuyin Baokan Ziliao* (Duplication of Press Materials). Publication began in 1978, was opened to foreigners in 1980-81, declared *neibu* in 1982-3 and reopened to foreigners in 1984.

New China Monthly (Xinhua Yuebao) has appeared since 1949 (from 1956-1961 it was on a semi-monthly basis). Consists of collected New China News Agency items. It contains the major directives, speeches, editorials, commentaries and news dispatches plus a chronology of the events of the month. The pre-Cultural Revolution chronology section of the periodical has been collected, photographed and republished by the Center for Chinese Research Materials Association of Research Libraries, Washington D.C. under the title *New China Monthly Chronology of National and International Events of Significance* (1972) in three volumes.

Newspapers

The Chinese Communist Party Central Committee began to publish *Renmin Ribao* (People's Daily) soon after Liberation and since 1958 has published *Hongqi* (Red Flag) as its leading theoretical journal.

In Shanghai *Wenhui Bao* is the leading paper.

The English language paper published in Beijing since 1981 is *China Daily*.

Pre-Liberation English language newspapers published in China. Useful foreign coverage of events in China particularly in the interwar years can be found in contemporary periodicals such as *North China Herald* (weekly edition of the *British Work China Daily News* and the American *China Weekly Review* both published in Shanghai; *South China Morning Post*, Hong Kong.

Publications in English from the People's Republic of China

- *China Pictorial* (Monthly)
- *China Reconstructs* (Monthly)
- *Chinese Literature* (Monthly)
- *Hsinhua (Xinhua) News Agency Release*
- *Hsinhua Weekly Issue*
- *People's China*, published semi-monthly from 1950-1957 and then succeeded by the weekly *Peking Review*
- *Peking Review* (until 1978)
- *Beijing Review* (from 1979)

The Chinese press has become somewhat less constrained in recent years. For example, *Outlook* (Liaowang), a periodical published by the New China (Xinhua) News Agency since 1981, has reported on activities within the government. Published reminiscences of high level cadres have given insights into the political and personality conflicts within the Party from the 1920's to Mao's death. The speeches and writings of high-level figures other than Mao have become available, for example, the selected works of Zhu De (Chu Te), Chen Yun (Ch'en Yun), Zhou Enlai (Chou En-lai), Liu Shao-qi (Liu Shao-chi), Dong Biwu (Tung Pi-wu) and Deng Xiaoping (Teng Hsiao-ping).

Other Research Centres and Libraries

The United Kingdom

The School of Oriental and African Studies, University of London, which has an excellent library, and which publishes *The China Quarterly*, first issue January 1960.

The Department of Chinese Studies, University of Leeds.

East Asia Centre, University of Newcastle on Tyne.

The University of Durham.

Cambridge University.

The University of Essex.

The British Library.

Australia

The Australian National University and the Australian National Library.

West Germany

The *Institut fur Asienkunde*, Hamburg.

France

The Centre de Recherche et de documentation sur la China Contemporaine de l'Ecole des Hautes Etudes en Sciences Sociales, 54 Boulevard Raspail, Paris, has an extensive collection of books, periodicals and microfilms in Chinese, Russian and Western languages on modern China.

Japan

The National Diet Library, the Institute for Developing Economics and the Toyo Bunko, which publishes *Kindai Chugoku Kenkyu*.

Hong Kong

The Universities Service Centre, the Chinese University, and the Hong Kong University.

India

Asian Recorder, A Weekly Digest of Asian Events has been published in New Delhi since 1955. It includes extracts from the world's press and gives considerable space to China.

III. Published Works of Mao Zedong

A. Collections of Mao's Works Published in English in China
(Arranged alphabetically by title.)

1. Mao Tse-tung. 'Comrade Mao Tse-tung on Educational Work.' Parts 1-5. *Chinese Education* 2, nos. 1-2 (Spring-Summer 1969): 35-67; 2, no. 3 (Fall 1969): 37-57; 2, no. 4 (Winter 1969-70): 63-72; 3, no. 1 (Spring 1970): 20-41; 3, no. 4 (Winter 1970-71): 265-82. All five parts originally published as book by People's Educational Publishing House in Beijing, 1958.

2. _____ *Four Essays in Philosophy*. Peking: Foreign Languages Press, 1966. This booklet includes three of Mao's important theoretical essays: 'On Practice' (July 1937), 'On Contradiction' (August 1937) and 'On the Correct Handling of Contradictions Among the Peoples' (February 1957). (For further details see nos. 64, 65 and 103). The fourth 'essay' is a brief extract from the 'Draft Decisions of the Central Committee of the CCP on Certain Problems in Our Present Rural Work.' This extract entitled 'Where Do Correct Ideas Come From?' was written by Mao personally in May 1963.

3. _____ *Mao Tse-tung on Art and Literature*. Peking: Foreign Languages Press, 1960. Translated from the Chinese text published by the People's Literature Publishing House, December 1958. The writings are arranged chronologically. Most of them are also printed in the *Selected Works of Mao Tse-tung* but some later items have been included in this selection.

4. _____ 'Mao's Letters on Literature.' Published, *Beijing Review*, vol. 25, no. 22 (31 May 1982): 5-6. Fifteen of Mao's private letters to writers and artists, written between 1939 and 1949, were published on 23 May 1982 in *Renmin Ribao* to mark the 40th anniversary of Mao's *Talks at the Yanan Forum on Literature and Art*. The letters were follow-ups to Mao's *Talks* and reflect the close friendship between Mao and the recipients.

5. _____ *Selected Military Writings*. Peking: Foreign Languages Press, 1963. 408. 1st edition. This important selection covers Mao's works on

guerilla warfare from the period 1936 to 1938 (including 'On Protracted War') as well as writings from 1928 'Why is it that Red Political Power Can Exist in China?' and 'The Struggle in the Chingkang Mountains.' It also includes two well-known statements from 1929-30: 'On Correcting Mistaken Ideas in the Party' and 'A Single Spark Can Start a Prairie Fire.' The final section of the book comprises numerous brief statements, directives, telegrams and commentaries by Mao covering the period 1941-49. It includes the reissued Rules of Discipline for the Army and excerpts from the well known 'On Coalition Government' and 'The Present Situation and our Tasks' report to the Central Committee of the CCP in December 1947.

6. _____ *Selected Readings from the Writings of Mao Tse-tung*. Peking: Foreign Languages Press, 1966. Translation of Chinese edition published in 1966.

7. _____ *Selected Works*. 5 vols. London: Lawrence and Wishart Ltd., 1954-1957. Also published by International Publishers, New York. Translation of first Chinese edition of Mao's selected works published in Beijing 1951-53. This edition has been repudiated by the Chinese, who regard the Selected Works published in English by the Foreign Languages Press in Beijing as the correct version. (See no. 8). 'Chinese Communist Party Central Committee issues explanatory remarks on the "Selected Works" of Mao Tse-tung.' *Survey of the China Mainland Press*, 194, 19 (13 October 1951).

8. _____ *Selected Works of Mao Tse-tung*. Peking: Foreign Languages Press, 1965. Vol. 1, 347. Vol. 2, 468. Vol. 3, 290. Vol. 4, 459. English translation of second Chinese edition of *Selected Works of Mao Tse-tung* published in 1960. Vol. 1 prints writings from 'The First Revolutionary Civil War Period' March 1926 to August 1937. Vol. 2 covers the 'War of Resistance against Japan' to May 1941. Vol. 3 covers the 'War of Resistance against Japan' up to August 1945. Vol. 4 selects key documents from the 'Third Revolutionary Civil War Period' up to September 1949. The 5th volume was published in 1977, see no. 9.

9. _____ *Selected Works of Mao Tse-tung*. Peking: Foreign Languages Press, 1977. 518. Vol. 5. This volume includes key works by Mao between 21 September 1945 and 18 November 1957. Almost half the material had not been previously available. This volume is a very important contribution to documentation of Mao's thinking, particularly for the period July 1956 to December 1957. Selectivity has produced some significant omissions; for example, Mao's laudatory comments on Stalin, 16 December 1949 and 8

March 1953, are omitted together with other items on the theme of Soviet friendship. None of Mao's messages of support to Ho Chi Minh are included.

10. _____ *A Selection of Letters by Mao Zedong with Reproductions of the Original Calligraphy.* Beijing: 1983. *The Selected Letters of Mao Zedong* published in Chinese comprised 372 of Mao Zedong's letters from 1920 to 1965, most of them published for the first time. This is an English language edition of some of these letters. An introductory article to this Selection was published in *Beijing Review.* See: 'A revolutionary's outlook,' *Beijing Review*, 26, 52 (26 December 1983): 18-19.

11. _____ *Serve the People. In Memory of Norman Bethume. The Foolish Old Man Who Removed the Mountains.* Peking: Foreign Languages Press, 1967. 11. This pamphlet which reproduced three of Mao's articles, originally written in 1944, 1939 and 1945 respectively, was widely used in schools and colleges during the Cultural Revolution. The articles were known then as 'the three constantly read articles.'

12. _____ 'Six letters from Mao Zedong.' *Beijing Review*, vol. 26, no. 52 (26 December 1983): 14-18. A translation of several letters from a new publication in Chinese *The Selected Letters of Mao Zedong*, compiled by the Central Committee's Research Centre of Party Literature, to mark Mao's 90th birthday. Includes letters to Song Qing Ling (18 September 1936); to Qin Bangxian, director of *Jiefang Ribao* (Liberation Daily), (31 August 1944); to Liu Shaoqi, Zhou Enlai and others (19 February 1956); to Huang Yanpei, then Chairman of the China Democratic National Construction Association, (4 December 1956) enclosing two poems Mao has recently written, *Beidaihe* (1954) and *The Changjiang River* (1956) later published as *Swimming*; to Zang Kejia, a celebrated poet, (26 December 1981) and to Lu Dingyi and others (18 July 1964). These letters include comments on the importance of freedom of expression, e.g. writing to Lu Dingyi Mao defends the practice of drawing from nude models. 'It would be wrong to be influenced by feudal ideas and forbid the practice. Even if some bad things happen, it doesn't matter. We should be willing to make some small sacrifices for the sake of art.'

13. _____ *The Socialist Upsurge in China's Countryside.* Peking: Foreign Languages Press, 1957. Condensed version of articles published with preface and introductory notes in 3 vols. in Chinese in 1955. The preface and introductory notes were written by Mao, 27 December 1953, and published separately in *Peking Review*, 7, 52 (25 December 1964): 19.

14. _____ *Quotations from Chairman Mao Tse-tung.* 2nd edition. Peking: Foreign Languages Press, 1967. 312. Known as 'The Little Red Book,' famous during the Cultural Revolution. Consists of short extracts from Mao's *Selected Works* and other writings up to 1964. Of the 426 quotations, 163 are taken from 9 articles. The extracts tend to reflect the period when Mao's influence was at its height. For example, 36 extracts come from 'On the Correct Handling of Contradictions Among the People' published in 1957. This second edition, translated into English, has a foreword by Lin Biao, dated 16 December 1966, stressing the importance of Mao's thought for the masses as 'an inexhaustible source of strength and a spiritual atom bomb of infinite power.'

The book was originally designed especially for the People's Liberation Army and the early editions had a limited circulation among zealots in the Party and Government. It became widely available in late 1966, when the first English edition was also published, and became universally known after it was held aloft by Red Guards at mass rallies beginning on 18 August 1966. The second English edition has only one textual change: two sentences in which Mao quoted Liu Shaoqi were removed. Also available as Schram, ed. *Quotations from Chairman Mao Tse-tung,* no. 30 and *Mao Tse-tung's Quotations* introduced by Fraser, no. 20.

B. Edited Collections of Mao's Works Published Outside China
(Arranged alphabetically by surname of editor.)

15. Altaisky, M. I., ed. *Maoism as it Really Is.* Moscow: Progress Publishers, 1981. 283. Translated by Cynthia Carlisle. Subtitled: Pronouncements of Mao Zedong, some already known to the public and others hitherto not published in the Chinese press. The aim of this Soviet collection is to 'lift the veil' on . . . 'the acute political and ideological struggle within the Communist Party of China over the basic issues of the Chinese Revolution, China's relations with the Soviet Union . . . and the world communist movement. It is an exposure of the reactionary anti-Marxist nature of Maoist ideology and policy.'

16. Brandt, Conrad, Benjamin Schwartz and John Fairbank. *A Documentary History of Chinese Communism.* New York: Atheneum, 1971. 552. A collection of documents covering development of Chinese Communist movement up to 1949 with commentaries introducing documents. Includes extracts from a number of Mao's best known speeches and articles between 1927 and 1949: 'Report on an investigation of the peasant movement in Hunan,' February 1927, (pp. 77-88); 'Report to the Second All-China Soviet Conference' (pp. 226-39); 'On the New Democracy,' January 19, 1940 (pp.

260-75); 'On Coalition Government,' 24 April 1945 (pp. 295-318); 'Correcting unorthodox tendencies in learning, the Party, and literature and art,' 1 February 1942 (pp. 372-92); 'Opposing Party formalism,' 8 February 1942 (pp. 392-407); 'Speech made at the forum on literature and art at Yenan,' 2 May and 23 May 1942 (pp. 408-419); 'On the People's Democratic Dictatorship,' 1 July 1949 (pp. 445-61).

17. Chen, Jerome. *Mao Papers: Anthology and Bibliography*. London and New York: Oxford University Press, 1970. 221. This volume consists of three parts: (1) There is an introductory essay on Mao's literary style, showing, for example, the influence of Lu Xun's writings (pp. xviii-xx) and some detailed commentary on the editing of Mao's *Selected Works* since 1942 (pp. xxviii-xxxi). (2) The collection has examples of hitherto untranslated works, including letters, speeches and instructions from 1917 to 1969 and is particularly pertinent to the period of the Cultural Revolution (1966-69). (3) A chronological bibliography of Mao's writings in English and Chinese including those not translated into English.

18. Compton, Boyd. *Mao's China: Party Reform Documents 1942-1944*. Seattle: University of Washington Press, 1952. 278. Covers a critical period in the ideological history of the party. Includes several documents by Mao translated here for the first time. The editor provides a useful introduction on Mao's thought.

19. Fan, K. T. *Mao Tse-tung and Lin Piao: Post-Revolutionary Writings*. New York: Doubleday, Anchor Books, 1972. 536. Claims to contain all the major public writings and statements of Mao and Lin from 1949 to 1970. A useful paperback original allowing the student to compare the works of Mao and his heir-designate in a single volume.

20. Fraser, S. E. *Mao Tse-tung's Quotations: The Red Guard's Handbook*. Introduction by Stewart E. Fraser. Nashville, Tenn: Peabody International Center, George Peabody College for Teachers, 1967. 312. This is a reproduction of the Beijing 1966 English language edition (see no. 14) plus an introduction on the background to the quotations and their role in the Cultural Revolution.

21. Fremantle, Anne. *Mao Tse-tung. An Anthology of his Writings*. New York: New American Library, 1962. 300. This Mentor edition presents a basic selection of Mao's political, philosophical and military writings, which have been previously published in English by the Foreign Languages Press, Beijing. Included is Mao's speech 'On the Correct Handling of Contradic-

tions Among the People,' 27 February 1957, with certain additions. The editor's introduction presents a sympathetic overview of Mao's career to 1960.

22. Gelder, G. S. *The Chinese Communists*. London: Gollancz, 1946. 290. Prints a selection of Mao's writings translated by the Russian Research Centre, Harvard University. Includes: 'On Coalition Government,' 'On the Disbandment of the Communist International 1943,' 'Report of Comrade Mao Tse-tung on the occasion of the 22nd anniversary of the Chinese Communist Party,' 1 July 1942.

23. Kau, Michael Y. M. and John Leung. *The Writings of Mao Zedong, 1949-1976*. Vol. 1, September 1949-December 1955. London: M.E. Sharpe, 1987. 800. The first of a projected five volume series intended to be the most complete collection of Mao's post-1949 works.

24. Levy, Richard. *A Critique of Soviet Economics* by Mao Tse-tung, translated by M. Roberts. New York: Monthly Review Press, 1977. 157. This book is a translation of Mao's notes on a textbook issued by the Soviet Academy of Sciences in 1957 and his notes, written in 1959, on Stalin's *Economic Problems of Socialism in the USSR* (1952).

25. MacFarquhar, Roderick, Timothy Cheek and Eugene Wu. *The Secret Speeches of Chairman Mao. From the Hundred Flowers to the Great Leap Forward*. Cambridge, Massachusetts: Harvard University Press, 1989. 561. This volume, No. 6, in the Harvard Contemporary China Series, contains translations of speeches by Mao from the period 1957-1958. They are published here, in their original form, for the first time and are full of revelations which were cut out of the official versions. Thus, they provide valuable new insight into the 'Hundred Flowers' movement and the 'Great Leap Forward.' The editor comments 'We all found these Mao texts difficult because none appear to have been formal prepared speeches; rather, they were rambling monologues. The Chairman was allusive, tangential, colloquial, earthy.'

26. Martin, Helmut. *Mao Zedong Texte 1949-1976*. Munich, GFR: Carl Hanser-Verlag, 1979-1982. 7 vols. (approx 600 pages each). A comprehensive collection of Mao's post-1949 writings. All the items are printed in Chinese (or in the case of texts which appeared only abroad in English or the original language of publication). The more important, about 70 percent of the pages, are translated into German as well. The introduction in volume 1

has been published separately in an English translation as *Cult and Canon. The Origins and Development of State Maoism*. (See no. 953).

27. Rejai, Mostafa. *Mao Tse-tung On Revolution and War*. Garden City, New York: Doubleday, 1969. 355. Offers an analytical treatment of the principal elements of Mao Tse-tung's thought. Designed as a general introduction for student and layman alike. A selection of readings in 6 chapters, each preceded by an introductory note: (I) Imperialism, Revolution and War; (II) Stages of Revolutionary Development; (III) Dynamics of Revolution: United Front; (IV) Dynamics of Revolution: The Army; (V) Dynamics of Revolution: The Communist Party; (VI) The Global Strategy.

28. Schram, Stuart R. *Mao Tse-tung Unrehearsed: Talks and Letters 1956-71*. Harmondsworth: Penguin, 1974. 352. Also available as *Chairman Mao Talks to the People: Talks and Letters 1956-71*. New York: Pantheon, 1974. Contains twenty-six statements and speeches from material divulged by Red Guard publications during the Cultural Revolution. They are valuable for the expression of Mao's thinking on political, economic and philosophical matters, as historical documents shedding light on events in the period 1956-71 and as samples of Mao's entertaining literary style.

29. _____ *The Political Thought of Mao Tse-tung*. New York: Praeger, 1969. 479. First published in 1963, this important study has been updated and expanded. It incorporates thirty new extracts by Mao including some little known but increasingly relevant older writings and major new materials from the post-1963 period. In the extensive introduction Schram reexamines the development of Mao's thought, assesses its originality and traces the direction of China under Mao.

30. _____ *Quotations from Chairman Mao Tse-tung*. New York: Frederick A. Praeger, 1968. 182. This is a translation of the Beijing edition of the *Quotations* which became a symbol of the Cultural Revolution (see no. 14). The editor provides a very useful introductory essay which explains the origins of the *Little Red Book* and comments on its contemporary significance.

31. Selden, Mark. *The People's Republic of China. A Documentary History of Revolutionary Change*. New York: Monthly Review Press, 1979. 718. These documents have been chosen to illustrate the theme of China's socialist development, and 'to clarify the dynamic linking the masses of Chinese people with the Communist Party and its leader, Mao Tse-tung.' The selections from Mao's writings include major items from the *Selected Works*

as well as a variety of writings, speeches and informal remarks collected and published by Red Guards during the Cultural Revolution. Some of the documents are translated here for the first time.

32. Shaw, Bruno, ed. *Selected Works of Mao Tse-tung.* New York: Harper and Row, 1970. 423. (Harper Colophon Books). This is an abridged version of Volumes 1-4 of the *Selected Works* printed in English in Beijing in 1965. There is a very brief introduction. Shaw's aim is to present a readable but complete abstract of the 4 volumes of the *Selected Works,* by retaining the substance but omitting redundancies, repetitions and 'many of the minute details of battles the Communist troops fought during the Civil War,' which take up pages of the original work.

33. Snow, B. *Mao Tse-tung: Selected Works.* Abridged edition. New York: Harper Colophon Books, 1970. A shorter version of the 4 volumes of Mao's *Selected Works* published in Beijing in 1965.

34. Steiner, Arthur H. *Maoism a Sourcebook: Selections from the Writings of Mao Tse-tung.* Los Angeles: University of California Press, 1952. 142. Mimeographed collection of Mao's writings between 1934 and 1951, described by Steiner as 'representative samplings.' The criteria for selecting the 19 items were: 1) the fidelity with which they represented Mao's views at the time; 2) the intrismic interest of the issues covered; 3) the importance attached to the text in official Communist circles; and 4) to whom the work was directed--primacy being given to Mao's directives to party and government officials. The selection begins with the *People's Daily* commentary on the first volume of Mao's *Selected Works* (published in 1951) covering Mao's writings from 1926-1937. Includes some of the best known writings from this period, available in *Selected Works* and other sources.

35. *What Peking Keeps Silent About.* Moscow: Novosti Press Agency Publishing House, 1972. 48. Pamphlet with numerous brief quotes from Mao in different periods chosen to demonstrate how far Mao has gone in abandoning his former positions since he repudiated cooperation with the Soviet Union. The Introduction (which is unsigned) denounces Mao for repudiating Marxism-Leninism and characterises Maoism as an eclectic mixture of 'feudal Chinese philosophy . . . petty-bourgeois socialism, petty-bourgeois and peasant views, bourgeois-nationalist views, great-power chauvinism, Trotskyite and anarchistic ideas.'

C. Mao's Works Published During the Cultural Revolution
and Reproduced Outside China (Arranged by title.)

36. Mao Tse-tung. 'Chairman Mao on Revolution in Education.' *Current Background*, no. 888 (22 August 1969): 1-20. Originally published in Chinese in Peking, 1967. Collection of statements by Mao from period 1927-1967 in chronological order.

37. _____ 'Chairman Mao's Activity in Revolutionary practice.' *Current Background*, no. 900 (30 January, 1970): 1-47. Originally published as booklet entitled 'Material for Study.' Translated by U.S. Consulate Hong Kong. Reviews Mao's life up to 1966 and includes some previously untranslated statements by Mao on education.

38. _____ 'Comments on Educational Reform.' *Issues and Studies* (Taiwan) 6 (January 1970): 79-86. Includes ten excerpts from statements attributed to Mao before, and during, the Cultural Revolution.

39. _____ *Long Live Mao Tse-tung's Thought!* Translated in *Current Background*, 1969, no. 891 and 892. Valuable collections of materials emanating from Red Guard and other sources during the Cultural Revolution.

40. _____ 'Mao Tse-tung's Instructions Concerning the "Great Proletarian Cultural Revolution". *Current Background* no. 885 (31 July 1969): 1-48. Translations of excerpts from Mao's instructions published in Chinese newspapers between May 1966 and June 1968.

41. _____ *Miscellany of Mao Tse-tung Thought (1949-1968)*. Washington, DC: Joint Publication Research Service, U.S. Department of Commerce 1974, no. 61269. Slightly shorter version of *Long Live Mao Tse-tung's Thought*, 2 vols., publisher unknown, 1967, 280 and 1969, 720. Published in China during Cultural Revolution and reprinted in Taiwan (in Chinese). Extensive commentaries on these new writings were published in *China Quarterly*, nos. 57, 60, 61 and 62 (1974-75), each article focussing on particular aspects of Mao's thought.

42. _____ 'Supreme Instructions.' *Current Background*, no. 897 (10 December 1969): 1-60. Collection of Mao's statements up to March 1969 published as booklet and circulated during Cultural Revolution in China.

D. Individual Works in Chronological Order

To 1921 (First Party Congress)

43. Mao Tse-tung. *Une etude de l'education physique*. Translated by Stuart R. Schram. Paris: Mouton, 1962. This is a full translation of Mao's first significant published article 'A study of physical education,' New Youth, 1 April 1917, vol. III, no. 2. Mao recommends a system of physical exercises for strengthening body and character. He states 'The principal aim of physical education is military heroism.' Extract in English in Schram, *Political Thought of Mao Tse-tung* (see no. 29): 152-60.

44. _____ 'The Fundamental Question of the Problem of Reconstructing Hunan--the Republic of Hunan.' *China Quarterly*, no. 68 (December 1976): 751-77. Originally published 16 September 1920. Introduction and translation by A.W. McDonald Jr.: 'Mao Tse-tung and the Hunan self-government movement, 1920: an introduction and five translations.'

45. _____ The Great Union of the Popular Masses.' Translated by Stuart R. Schram. *China Quarterly*, no. 49 (January/March 1972): 76-87. This is a translation of an article that first appeared in three instalments in nos. 2, 3 and 4 of *The Hsiang River Review* on 21 and 28 July and 4 August 1919. No copy of this periodical is available outside China translation made from collection of historical materials on the party history of the Chinese Communist Party compiled by the Higher Party School in Beijing. Schram describes this as Mao's most important writing of the May Fourth period.

46. _____ 'Historical and Comtemporary Evidence of the Burden China has put on Hunan.' *China Quarterly*, no. 68 (December 1976): 751-77. Originally published on 17 September 1920. Introduction and translation by A.W. McDonald Jr.

47. _____ 'The Hunan Self-Government Movement Should Arise.' *China Quarterly*, no. 68 (December 1976): 751-77. Originally published 26 September 1920. Introduction and translation by A.W. McDonald Jr.

48. _____ 'Miss Chao's Suicide.' *Survey of the China Mainland Press*, no. 2011 (12 May 1959). Extracted from several articles published in the Changsha *Da Gung Bao*, beginning 16 November 1919. See also Roxane Witke, 'Mao Tse-tung, Women and Suicide in the May Fourth era,' *China Quarterly*, no. 31, 1967, pp. 128-47. (See no. 303). Mao comments on a young woman who committed suicide rather than go through with an

arranged marriage. He treats this as an example of the evils of tight social constraints on individual freedom.

49. _____ 'More on the "Promotion Movement".' *China Quarterly*, no. 68 (December 1976): 751-77. Originally published 28 September 1920. Introduction and translation by A.W. McDonald Jr.

50. _____ 'Proposal for "The Revolutionary Government of Hunan . . . ".' Drafted by Mao Tse-tung, Lung Chien-Kung and Peng Huang. *China Quarterly*, no. 68 (December 1976): 751- 77. Originally published 9 October 1920. Introduction and translation by A.W. McDonald Jr.

1921 (First Party Congress) to 1935 (End of Long March)

51. Mao Tse-tung. *Analysis of the Classes in Chinese Society*. Peking: Foreign Languages Press, 1956. 17. 1st edition. Also available as C. Benton, ed. *Mao Tse-tung: Analysis of the Classes in Chinese Society*. America Asia Studies, 1985. Written in March 1926. Also printed in *Selected Works,* vol. 1, 13-22 (see no. 8).

52. _____ *Report of an Investigation into the Peasant Movement in Hunan*. 1st edition. Peking: Foreign Languages Press, 1953. Written in March 1927. Based on first-hand investigations during a 32 day visit to Hunan province, Jan-Feb 1927. A defence of the role of the peasant in making revolution. Mao gives a lively description of the practices of the peasant associations and assesses their potential for spearheading the process of reform in the countryside. Also in *Selected Works*, vol. 1, 23-62 (see no. 8).

53. _____ 'Why is it that Red Political Power can exist in China' from a Resolution drafted for the Second Party Congress of the Jiangxi-Hunan border region, 5 October 1928. In *Selected Works of Mao Tse-tung*, Peking: Foreign Languages Press, 1965. Vol. 1, 63-72.

54. _____ 'The Struggle in the Chingkang Mountains.' Report submitted to the Central Committee, Chinese Communist Party, 25 November 1928. In *Selected Works of Mao Tse-tung*. Peking: Foreign Languages Press, 1965. Vol. 1, 73-104. Account of the conflict in the mountains on the Jiangxi-Hunan border.

55. _____ *On the Rectification of Incorrect Ideas in the Party*. 1st edition. Peking: Foreign Languages Press, 1953. Written December 1929 as a resolution for the Ninth Party Congress of the Fourth Army. This was a key

directive in consolidating an ideological basis for the Red Army. Also published as 'On Correcting Mistaken Ideas in the Party' in *Selected Works*, vol. 1, 105-116. (See no. 8). There are considerable differences between the original and the later versions of this text, see Schram, *The Political Thought of Mao Tse-tung*, 272-75 (see no. 29).

56. _____ *A Single Spark can Start a Prairie Fire*. 1st edition. Peking: Foreign Languages Press, 1953. 22. Written January 1930, in criticism of the pessimistic views of certain leading comrades. Also in *Selected Works*, vol. 1, 117-28 (see no. 8).

57. _____ *Red China: President Mao Tse-tung Reports on the Progress of the Chinese Soviet Republic*. London: Martin Lawrence, 1934. 36. This pamphlet prints Mao's report to the Second National Soviet Congress at Ruijin, Jiangxi, 22 January 1934. The brief Introduction claims that it is the first official report on progress in the Chinese Soviet Republic to be published in English. The main subjects of the report were the development of the Revolution in China, the growth of the Red Army and extension of Chinese Soviet territory, the intensification of Agrarian Revolution, the conditions of the working class, emancipation of women and raising the cultural level.

1935 (End of Long March) to 1949 (Liberation)

58. Mao Zedong. *On the Tactics of Fighting Japanese Imperialism*. Peking: Foreign Languages Press, 1953. Report by Mao to Conference of Party activists in December 1935 after Politburo meeting which decided the bourgeoisie could ally with the workers and peasants in resisting Japanese imperialism. Also in *Selected Works*, vol. 1, 153- 78 (see no. 8).

59. _____ 'Appeal of the Central Soviet Government to the Ko-lao-hui,' 15 July 1936. Translated as appendix to Schram's 'Mao Tse-tung and the Secret Societies,' *China Quarterly*, no. 27 (July-September 1966): 11-13 (see no. 865). Mao appeals to the members of this society throughout China to cooperate in resisting the Japanese. He points out that the 'Ko-lao-hui' and the Soviets have much in common. 'You support striking the rich and helping the poor; we support striking at the local bullies and dividing up the land. You despise wealth and defend justice and you gather together all the heroes and brave fellows in the world; we do not spare ourselves to save China and the world.'

60. _____ *Strategic Problems of China's Revolutionary War*. Peking: Foreign Languages Press, 1954-65. Written in December 1936 and first published in Chinese in 1941. Also printed as 'Problems of Strategy in China's Revolutionary War,' *Selected Works*, vol. 1, 179-254 and available as 'Strategic Problems of China's Revolutinary War: How the Chinese People's Army Won?' *China Digest 6*, no. 3-5 (7-12, May-September 1949).

61. _____ 'Problems of War and Strategy.' Originally published in Chinese 6 November 1936. In *Selected Works of Mao Tse-tung*. Peking: Foreign Languages Press, 1965. Vol. 2, 219-235.

62. _____ 'More Mao Zedong's writings published.' *Beijing Review*, vol. 24, no. 29 (20 July 1981): 5. Refers to a letter written by Mao in 1937 in Yanan (and published on 11 July 1981 in *Renmin Ribao*). Mao is emphasising that the death sentence on Huang Kegong, a Party member, for murdering a woman student who refused to marry him must be carried out for the sake of Party discipline. *Jiefangjun Bao* (Liberation Army Daily) published this letter, together with a commentary on its significance 40 years later. Reference is also made to the recent publication in *Renmin Ribao* of five previously unpublished telegrams and four news reports. These were concerned with guerilla warfare in north China.

63. _____ *The tasks of the Chinese Communist Party in the Period for Resistance to Japan*. 1st edition. Peking: Foreign Languages Press, 1956. 44. This is a report delivered at the National Conference of the CCP in Yanan, May 1937. Mao discusses problems inherent in the 'United Front' policy and the need to resolve certain internal contradictions. Also in *Selected Works*, vol. 1, 263-84 (see no. 8).

64. _____ *On Practice*. Peking: Foreign Languages Press, 1951. Article originally written in July 1937. One of Mao's most important articles interpreting Marxist theory on the relation between knowledge and practice. Also in *Selected Works*, vol. 1, 295-309 (see no. 8).

65. _____ *On Contradiction*. Peking: Foreign Languages Press, 1952. 61. Written August 1937. Much cited article giving Maoist version of Marxist dialectic in social theory. Also in *Selected Works*, vol. 1, 311-47 and available as: *On Contradiction*. New York: International Publisher, 1953. 61. See *China Quarterly*, no. 19 (July-September 1964): 38-46 for article which suggests *On Contradiction* was not written in the summer of 1937 and *China Quarterly*, no. 29, pp. 155-165 for review article by Schram which suggests evidence supports earlier publication.

66. _____ *Mao Zedong's 'On Contradiction.' An Annoted Translation of the Pre-Liberation Text.* Nick Knight (ed). Nathan, Queensland: Griffith University, Griffith Asian Papers Series no. 3, 1981. 53. Indicates all the textual variations in the published versions of this famous article between 1937 and 1952.

67. _____ *Mao Tse-tung on Guerrilla Warfare.* Translated by Samuel B. Griffith. New York: Praeger, 1961. Translation of Mao's 'On Guerrilla Warfare' written in 1937. It is not certain that the whole work was written by Mao, but he apparently checked the whole volume and it reflects his theory of guerrilla warfare. The chapter 'Strategic Problems in the Anti-Japanese Guerrilla War' is attributed directly to Mao and is also printed in *Selected Works*, vol. 2, 79-112 (see no. 8). Griffith has also written a valuable summary analysis of Mao's guerrilla strategy. (See no. 898).

68. _____ *Basic Tactics.* Translated by Stuart R. Schram. London: Pall Mall Press, 1967. 149. Introduction by Schram explaining historical context and Mao's evolution from politician to guerilla, and his policies and political style in 1938. *Basic Tactics* was originally a course of lectures to students at the Anti-Japanese Military Political University in early 1938. This book has a foreword by General Samuel B. Griffith.

69. _____ *On Protracted War.* Peking: Foreign Languages Press, 1954. 140. Delivered as lectures 26 May to 3 June 1938 at the Yanan Association for the Study of the War of Resistance against Japan. Also in *Selected Works*, vol. 2, 113-94 (see no. 8).

70. _____ 'Dialectical Materialism.' Translated by Dennis J. Doolan and Peter J. Golas. *China Quarterly*, no 19 (July-September 1964): 38-46. Originally published in June 1938. Republished in Shanghai in March 1940. One of Mao's first essays in Marxist theory. Commentary by translators.

71. _____ *The Role of the Chinese Communist Party in the National War.* 1st edition. Peking: Foreign Languages Press, 1956. 33. Report to the Sixth Plenary Session of the Sixth Central Committee delivered in October 1938. Considers the problems of securing the interests of the revolutionary movement in the context of the 'United Front.' Also in *Selected Works*, vol. 2, 195-212 (see no. 8). A section of the original Report, praising the Guomindang, has been omitted. See Schram, *The Political Thought of Mao Tse-tung*, (see no. 29), 228-29.

72. _____ 'New Situation in China; abridged report to the Sixth enlarged Plenum of the Communist Party of China, 1938.' *Labour Monthly*, 21 (July 1939): 437-44; (September-October 1939): 553-60 and 629-36.

73. _____ 'Outline of the second imperialist war.' *Labour Monthly*, 22 (April 1940): 240-8. An Addendum to the Staff Conference at Yanan, 14 September 1939. Says war began with invasion of North Eastern provinces (Manchuria) in 1931. Gives his analysis that while the USSR has become impregnable, the 'capitalists are like mad dogs . . . They are forced to fly at the throats of their imperialist rivals throughout the world.' Says outbreak of the 'second imperialist war follows directly from Chamberlain's and not only Hitler's desire to fight for the effective prevention of war demanded the participation of the Soviet Union.' Concludes that China, the Soviet Union and all the peoples' movements for freedom and independence must together build a strong and unshakeable united front.

74. _____ *The Chinese Revolution and the Chinese Communist Party.* Published in Chinese, November 1939, translated into English 22 March 1949, by Huang Li. Shanghai, 1949. 19. This is a text-book written in the winter of 1939-40 jointly by Mao and other comrades in Yanan. Discusses *inter alia* the bourgeois democratic character of the revolution at that stage and the need for Communist leadership. Also in *Selected Works*, vol. 2, 305-34. Also available as *The Chinese Revolution and the Chinese Communist Party.* Peking: Foreign Languages Press, 1954 or in *Current Background*, no. 135.

75. _____ *On New Democracy.* Peking: Foreign Languages Press, 1954. 84. This was issued in January 1940 and in it Mao indicates the kind of system he foresaw for China when the Communists came to power. The 'new democracy' would be a people's republic led by the revolutionary classes and would be a transition stage before the introduction of socialism. Also in *Selected Works*, vol. 2, 339-84.

76. _____ *Mao Tse-tung's 'Democracy,' a Digest of the Bible of Chinese Communism.* Commentary by Lin Yutang with expurgated passages restored. New York: Chinese News Service, 1947. 23. (See no. 75).

77. _____ *China's 'New Democracy.'* With an introduction by Earl Browder. New York, New Century Publications, 1945. 72. (See no. 75).

78. _____ 'On Conducting Rural Surveys,' 13 September 1941. *Beijing Review*, 22, 1 (5 January 1979): 12-15. This talk was delivered to a women's

life investigation group. Earlier in the year Mao had called for the elimination of the 'subjectivism, sectarianism and stereotyped Party writing' spread by Wang Ming. Shortly after Wang Ming was removed from his posts as President of the Chinese Women's College and secretary of the Women's Work committee of the Party Central committee. Mao gave this talk.

79. _____ *Mao Tse-tung Talks at the Yenan Forum on Art and Literature.* 1st edition. Peking: Foreign Languages Press, 1956. 51. Speeches made in May 1942. Mao discusses the need for art and literature to serve the masses and how to achieve this aim. Justifies ideological struggle against petty-bourgeois intellectionalism. Also in *Selected Works*, vol. 3, 69-98 (see no. 8).

80. _____ *Mao Zedong and the Political Economy of the Border Region: a Translation of Mao's Economic and Financial Writings.* Translation by A. Watson. Cambridge: Cambridge University Press, 1980. 271. Also published in part as 'Economic and Financial Problems in the Anti-Japanese War' December 1942, and in *Selected Works*, vol. 3, 111-16 (see no. 8). Mao's report was delivered to a Senior Secretaries conference in Yanan in 1942. This was the most comprehensive statement on economic problems made by Mao during the Yanan period. It was not reproduced in full after 1949. Part I, in the 1953 edition of the *Selected Works* contains an important addition 'This self-supporting economy, which has been developed by the troops and the various organisations and schools is a special product of the special conditions of today. It would be unreasonable and incomprehensible in other historical conditions, but it is perfectly reasonable and necessary at present.'

81. _____ *Our Study and the Current Situation.* Appendix: Resolution on some questions in the history of our Party. 1st edition. Peking: Foreign Languages Press, 1955. 116. Speech of 12 April 1944 summing-up previous discussions on the theme of ideological unity. Also in *Selected Works*, vol. 3, 163-226 (see no. 8). The speech was made during discussion held by senior cadres in Yanan on the history of the CCP. The discussion was designed to promote the 'correct' understanding of the Party's history and in particular to provide the correct line on the 1931-34 period, when a 'leftist' faction was in control of the Party. This edition includes as an appendix the CCP Central Committee Resolution of 20 April 1945: 'Resolution on Some Questions in the History of our Party.' (21-116).

82. _____ *On Coalition Government.* 1st edition. Peking: Foreign Languages Press, 1953. 118. In this report to the Seventh Congress

(April-June 1945) Mao reviews the role of the Communist and the Guomindang in the anti-Japanese struggle. He points to the danger of civil war and outlines the principles of 'New Democracy' to be established after the thorough defeat of the Japanese. This would be a united-front democratic alliance which would unite the majority of the people. Schram (*Political Thought of Mao Tse-tung*, no. 29) points out that in his original speech Mao made concessions to the Guomindang which were eliminated from later published versions. Also in *Selected Works*, vol. 3, 205-270 (see no. 8). Available also as: *The Fight for a New China.* New York: New Century Publishers, 1945. 80.

83. _____ 'Address before the Seventh National Congress of the Chinese Communist Party: summary.' *Amerasia*, 9 (18 May 1945): 150-58. The Congress was held in April 1945.

84. _____ *People's Democratic Dictatorship.* Peking: Foreign Languages Press, 1950. 24. Report delivered June 1949 in commemoration of the 28th anniversary of the Communist Party of China. With the defeat of the Guomindang assured, Mao's speech dealt with current problems and the policy options open to the new regime. He appeared to stress the need for China to 'lean to one side,' that of the Soviet Union. 'Sitting on the fence will not do, nor is there a third road.' Also in *Selected Works*, vol. 4, 411-24.

1949 (Liberation) to 1959

85. Mao Tse-tung. *China Wins Economic Battles--'Fight for a fundamental turn for the better in the financial and economic situation.'* Peking: Foreign Languages Press, 1950. 58. Report to the Third Plenary Session of the Seventh Central Committee, 6 June 1950. Now that the Chinese mainland has been liberated, except for Tibet, Mao anticipates the partial demobilisation of the PLA before the end of the year. He notes the growing strength of the Soviet bloc, and warns that a third world war is not impossible. In domestic policy he stresses agrarian reform, stablisation of prices, reform of intellectuals and Party organisations. See also *Peking Review II*, 43 (25 October 1968): 5, and *Selected Works*, vol. 5, 26-31 (see no. 9).

86. _____ *Closing Speech* at the Second Session of the First National Committee of the Chinese People's Political Consultative Conference, on 23 June 1950. *Survey of the Chinese Mainland Press* 4000 (14 August 1967): 12. Mao anticipates the transition from 'New Democracy' to socialism. He stresses that those who constantly serve the peeople need not fear that, in the

future, they will be rejected and denied the opportunity to live and work. Mao says China must unite firmly with the Soviet Union and other socialist countries. Also in Fan, *Mao Tse-tung and Lin Piao: Post-Revolutionary Writings*. 93-95 (see no. 19).

87. _____ 'Statement at the Eighth Session of the Central Peoples' Government Council, on 28 June 1950.' *Peking Review*, 37 (11 November 1958): 10.

88. _____ 'Give Serious Attention to the Discussion of the Film "The Life of Wu Xun".' 20 May 1951. *Peking Review*, 10, 23 (2 June 1967): 5. Written for the *People's Daily* as an editorial which opened the campaign to criticize the film. The Wu Xun legend, the film and the campaign are described in R. Witke, *Comrade Chiang Ching* (see no. 257), pp. 238-244. Also in *Survey of the Chinese Mainland Press* 4000 (14 August 1967): 11; and in *Selected Works*, vol. 5, 37-58 (see no. 9).

89. _____ *Comments* on the Work of Suppressing and Liquidating Counter-Revolutionaries, on 27 September and 19 December 1950, and 17 and 24 January, 28 February, 30 March, 15 June, 18 September and 1 October 1951. Joint Publications Research Service, U.S. Department of Commerce, no. 61269-1. (20 February 1974): 6-8.

90. _____ 'Opening Address at the Third Session of the First National Committee of the Chinese People's Political Consultative Conference,' on 23 October 1951. *Peking Review*, 6, 47 (22 November 1963): 11. Also in *Survey of the Chinese Mainland Press* 4000 (14 August 1967): 11; and in *Selected Works*, vol. 5, 59-63 (see no. 9).

91. _____ 'Speech at the Fourth Session of the First National Committee of the Chinese People's Political Consultative Conference,' on 7 February 1953. *People's China*, 5 (1 March 1953): 3. Also in *Current Digest of the Soviet Press*, 5, 6 (21 March 1953). Mao blames United States intransigence for the failure of the armistice negotiations in Korea. He stresses the need to study 'the advanced scientific techniques of the Soviet Union.' He stresses the need for leading cadres to 'get right down among the rank and file to check up on the work.' Also in Fan, *Mao Tse-tung and Lin Piao: Post-Revolutionary Writings*, 101-2 (see no. 19).

92. _____ 'The greatest friendship' a tribute written on the occasion of Stalin's death, on 8 March 1953. *Current Digest of the Soviet Press*, 5, 7 (28 March 1953). This article has been omitted from *Selected Works of Mao*

Tse-tung, vol. 5, together with the items on the theme of friendship and solidarity with the Soviet Union. (See no. 9).

93. _____ 'Introductory note to the "Second Instalment of Material on the Hu Feng Counter-Revolutionary Clique"'on 24 May 1955. *Peking Review*, 10, 31 (28 July 1967): 6. 11, 37 (13 September 1968): 21. 12, 37 (7 September 1969): 15. 12,39 (26 September 1969): 6. Republished during the Cultural Revolution. Excerpts in *Selected Works*, vol. 5, 176-83 (see no. 9).

94. _____ 'Introductory note to the "Third Instalment of Material on the Hu Feng Counter-Revolutionary Clique"' on 10 June 1955. *Peking Review*, 12, 37 (7 September 1969): 15. Republished during the Cultural Revolution.

95. _____ *On the Question of Agricultural Cooperation*. Beijing: Foreign Languages Press, 1966. Report to Communist Party Conference of Party Secretaries of provincial, municipal and autonomous region Committees on 31 July 1955. First published in translation by Foreign Languages Press in 1955. Also in *Selected Works*, vol. 5, 184-207 (see no. 9). In urging on the process of cooperativisation in the countryside Mao anticipates that by Spring 1958 half the rural population will be in semi-socialist cooperatives and some collectives will have been established throughout the country. By 1960 the semi-socialist transformation will be complete and yet more collectives would be set up. In the event, this program was to be speeded up in the Great Leap Forward.

96. _____ Speech at the Sixth Planary (Enlarged) Session of the Seventh Central Committee of the CCP, on 11 October 1955. Joint Publications Research Service, U.S. Department of Commerce, no. 61269-1 (20 February 1974): 14-26. A broad overview of progress in agricultural reform and its relevance to the role of the national bourgeoisie and the position of the better-off peasants. Also in *Survey of the Mainland China Press* 4000 (4 August 1967): 16. Included under title 'The Debate on the Co-operative Transformation of Agriculture and the Current Class Struggle.' In *Selected Works*, vol. 5, 211-33 (see no. 9).

97. _____ Speech at the Supreme State Conference, on 25 January 1956. *Peking Review*, 14, 37 (10 September 1971): 7. Also in Joint Publications Research Service, U.S. Department of Commerce, no. 61269-1 (20 February 1974): 45.

98. _____ 'On the Ten Major Relationships.' *China Quarterly*, 69 (March 1977): 221-38. Speech at an enlarged conference of the Politburo on 25

April 1956. Mao proposes inter alia 'that the Party and Government organs should be streamlined and that two-thirds of their numbers should be axed.' Mao is concerned to mobilize all positive factors to serve socialism. He notes weaknesses in Soviet development strategy and defines a self-reliant Chinese road to development. Also *Selected Works*, vol. 5, 284-307 (see no. 9) and in *Mao Tse-tung Unrehearsed* (Penguin edition), 61-83. Also in *Peking Review*, 1 (1 January 1977): 10-25.

99. _____ Opening Address at the Eighth National Congress of the CCP, 15 September 1956. In *Eighth National Congress Documents*. Peking: Foreign Languages Press, 1956. 7-11. And in *Peking Review*, 6, 51 (20 December 1963): 9. Overview of China's domestic situation in 1956, in which Mao suggests need to examine Soviet experience in creating a socialist society. He also considers China's foreign policy and need to support third world national liberation movements. Extract in Fan, *Mao Tse-tung and Lin Piao: Post-Revolutionary Writings*. 143-47. (See no. 19).

100. _____ 'In Commemoration of Dr. Sun Yat-sen,' written on 12 November 1956. *Peking Review*, 12, 9 (28 February 1969): 6. Article on the occasion of the ninetieth birthday of Dr. Sun Zhongshan (Sun Yat-sen). Mao says that China has completed the democratic revolution left unfinished by Sun and is now in the process of a socialist revolution. Also in *Selected Works*, vol. 5, 330-31 (see no. 9). See also *Beijing Review*, 24 (19 October 1981): 13.

101. _____ *On the Historical Experience of the Dictatorship of the Proletariat*. Peking: Foreign Languages Press, 1957. 20. Pamphlet reproducing editorials in the People's Daily of 5 April 1956 and of 29 December 1956. The 5 April editorial article although unsigned has been attributed to Mao, deals with (1) the inevitable continuation of contradiction in society and (2) considers Stalin's place in history in the light of the criticism of Stalin unleashed in February at the Twentieth Congress of the CPSU. For December editorial see also *Current Digest of the Soviet Press*, 81, 52 (6 February 1957): 14-17.

102. _____ 'Comments at a Conference of Provincial and Municipal Party Committee Secretaries' January 1957. Joint Publications Research Services, U.S. Department of Commerce, no. 61269-1 (20 February 1974): 46-53. Published as 'Talks at a Conference of Provincial, Municipal and Autonomous Region Party Committees.' The first talk of 18 January criticises ideological wavering and deviation on the progress of agricultural

cooperation. The second on 27 January covers foreign policy. Also in *Selected Works*, vol. 5, 350-83.

103. _____ *On Correct Handling of Contradictions Among the People.* Peking: Foreign Languages Press, 1957. 26. Also available as: *On the Problem of the Correct Handling of Contradictions Among the People.* New York: New Century Publishers 1957. Mao's February 1957 speech, publicly released June 1957, signified the 'anti-rightest' campaign to end criticism of the regime. Commentators outside China speculated on possible changes to the text. See also *Selected Works*, vol. 5, 384-419 (see no. 9). The full text plus editorial and bibliographical comment can be found in: *Communist China 1955-1959, Peking Documents and Analysis, 273-94.* Cambridge, Mass: Harvard University Press, 1962.

104. _____ Speech at the CCP National Conference on Propaganda Work. Peking: Foreign Languages Press, 1957. Pamphlet reproducing Mao's speech on 12 March 1957. This speech pointed out that the majority of intellectuals did not really understand Marxism. Mao proposed that intellectuals should work in factories and in the countryside in order to remould their own thinking and attitudes. Version also available in *Selected Works*, vol. 5, 422-35 (see no. 9).

105. _____ Editorial: 'The Bourgeois orientation of Wen Hui Pao over a period of time,' 14 June 1957. *Peking Review*, 11, 37 (13 September 1968): 25. cf. 'Wen Hui Pao's Bourgeois Orientation should be criticized' in *Selected Works*, vol. 5, 451-56 (see no. 9). The paper is reprimanded for the inadequacy of its self-criticism.

106. _____ 'Comment on Class Education in a talk with Leaders from Shanghai Motive Power Institute.' Printed in *Revolutionary Education in China*, ed. Peter J. Seybolt. White Plains, New York: International Arts and Sciences Press, 1973. 26. Speech delivered 9 July 1957. Mao appears to anticipate continuing revolution by arguing that 'it is necessary to "set a fire going" at regular intervals' and in supporting the use of the big-character posters in political struggle. Also published as 'Beat Back the Attacks of the Bourgeois Rightists' in *Selected Works*, vol. 5, 457-72. (See no. 9).

107. _____ Talk with the Secretaries of the Provincial and Municipal Party Committees at Tsingtao: 'The Situation in the Summer of 1957,' July 1957. *Peking Review*, 11, 43 (25 October 1968): 5. Also published as 'The Situation in the Summer of 1957' in *Selected Works*, vol. 5, 473-82.

108. _____ Speech at the meeting of the Supreme Soviet of the USSR celebrating the 40th anniversary of the October Revolution, 6 November 1957. *Peking Review*, 1, 37 (11 November 1958): 10. Mao's speech is diplomatic about the achievements of the Russian Revolution and the Twentieth CPSU Congress, but indicates scepticism about peaceful coexistence with U.S. imperialism. 'If the imperialist warriors are determined to start a third world war, they will bring about no other result than the end of the world capitalist system.' See Fan, *Mao Tse-tung and Lin Piao: Post-Revolutionary Writings*, 211-19 (see no. 19).

109. _____ Talk at a Meeting with Chinese Students and Trainees in Moscow, on 17 November 1957. *Peking Review*, 1, 37 (11 November 1958): 9. Speech in which Mao claims that in the struggle between socialism and capitalism 'the East wind prevails over the West wind.'

110. _____ Speech at the Moscow Meeting of Representatives of the Communist and Workers' Parties, 18 November 1957. *Peking Review*, 6, 36 (6 September 1963) and 1, 37 (11 November 1958): 9. Speech in which Mao reiterates that 'Today the East wind prevails over the West wind' to signify Communist ascendancy over capitalist forces. Two brief extracts from the speech are printed in *The Selected Works of Mao Tse-tung*, vol. 5, 514-18 (see no. 9) under titles 'A Dialectical Approach to Inner-Party Unity' and 'All Reactionaries are Paper Tigers.'

111. _____ 'Sixty work methods,' 31 January 1958. *Peking Review*, 16, 32 (10 August 1973): 11. Also in *Chinese Law and Government*, 5, 1 (Spring 1972): 93- 117; and in *Current Background*, 892 (21 October 1969): 1-14.

112. _____ 'Uninterrupted Revolution,' January 1958. *Beijing Review*, 22, 1 (5 January 1979): 11. One of *The Sixty Points of Methods of Work* (see no. 111). Inaugurating the 'Great Leap Forward' Mao states 'What we need now is a technological revolution so that we can catch up or surpass Britain in 15 years or a little longer.'

113. _____ Article for inaugural issue of *Hongqi*: 'Introducing a Cooperative,' 15 April 1958. *Peking Review*, 1, 15 (10 June 1958): 6 and 12, 39 (26 September 1969): 8.

114. _____ Four Speeches to Second Session of the Eighth National Party Congress on 8, 17, 20 and 23 May 1958. Joint Publications Research Service, U.S. Department of Commerce, no. 61269-1 (20 February 1974):

91-118. Also includes speech at Conference of heads of delegations to the Second Session of the Eighth National Party Congress on 18 May 1958.

115. _____ Remarks during an inspection tour of Anhui, Hubei and Jiangxi Provinces in September 1958. *Peking Review*, 1, 32 (7 October 1958): 4 and 1, 33 (14 October 1958): 4f. Reprinted in *Peking Review*, 12, 48 (28 November 1969): 8 and 14, 52 (31 December 1971): 7. Includes statement following provincial tour.

116. _____ Directives issued during inspections of Nankai and Tianjin Universities 13 August 1958 and Wuhan University 12 September 1958. *Chinese Education*, 2, 3 (Fall 1969): 45f. Also in *Chinese Sociology and Anthropology*, 2, 1-2 (Fall-Winter 1969-1970): 44.

117. _____ 'On the Question of Whether Imperialism and All Reactionaires Are Real Tigers.' *Peking Review*, 20, 37- 38 (13 September 1977): 7-8. Commentary on 1 December 1958 in which Mao states: 'The answer is that they are at once real tigers and paper-tigers.'

118. _____ 'On dialectics,' 1959. Joint Publications Research Service, U.S. Department of Commerce, no. 61269-1 (20 February 1974): 201-25.

119. _____ Critique of Stalin's 'Economic Problems of Socialism in the Soviet Union.' Joint Publications Research Service, U.S. Department of Commerce, no. 61269-1 (20 February, 1974): 191-199. Originally written early in 1959. Published in Red Guard publication of 1967. See also 'A Critique of Soviet Economics' translated by Moss Roberts, Monthly Review Press, 1977.

120. _____ Speech at the Conference of the Politburo of the Central Committee at Zhengzhan, 27 February 1959. *Chinese Law and Government*, 1, 4 (Winter 1968-69): 23f; also in Joint Publication Research Service, U.S. Department of Commerce, no. 52029 (21 December 1970): 33.

121. _____ Letter to Production Team Leaders 29 April 1959. Joint Publications Research Service, U.S. Department of Commerce, no. 61269-1 (20 February 1974): 170.

122. _____ Speeches at and after the Lushan Conference 23 July 1959 and 6 August 1959. *Chinese Law and Government* 1, 4 (Winter 1968-69): 27-43, 45f.

123. _____ Foreword to 'Empiricism or Marxism-Leninism?,' 15 August 1959. *Chinese Law and Government*, 1, 4 (Winter 1968-69): 72.

124. _____ Speech at an enlarged meeting of the Military Affairs Committee of the Central Committee of the CCP and the Foreign Affairs Conference, 11 September 1959. *Chinese Law and Government*, 1, 4 (Winter 1968-69): 79-84.

1960 to 1969

125. Mao Tse-tung. *Long Live Leninism: In Commemoration of the 90th Anniversary of the Birth of Lenin*. Peking: Foreign Languages Press, 1960. 56. Pamphlet reproducing editorial in the *People's Daily* of 20 April 1960. Mao's authorship uncertain.

126. _____ Talks with guests from Asia, Africa and Latin America in May 1960. *Peking Review*, 3, 20 (17 May 1960): 5f.

127. _____ *Chairman Mao Tse-tung's Important Talks with Guests from Asia, Africa and Latin America*. Peking: Foreign Languages Press, 1960. 10. Pamphlet summarizing content of talks held by Mao with delegations from Latin America and Africa on 3 May 1960, a delegation from Latin America on 8 May, delegations from Iraq, Iran and Cyprus on 9 May, delegations from Japan, Cuba, Brazil and Argentina on 14 May, and with a Japanese writers' delegation on 21 June. The general emphasis of the report on Mao's remarks is to attack U.S. imperialism and assert Chinese support for movements against Western imperialism and colonialism.

128. _____ Reading notes on the Soviet Union's 'Political Economics' written in 1961, date not known exactly. Joint Publications Research Service, U.S. Department of Commerce, no. 61269-2 (20 February 1974): 247-313. Excerpts were published as: 'Mao on Soviet Economics and other subjects: Excerpts from Reading Notes to the Soviet Political Economy.' *Monthly Review Press*, 29 (March 1977): 1-20.

129. _____ Speech before a Central Committee Conference in Peking, 12 June 1961. Joint Publications Research Service, U.S. Department of Commerce, no. 50792 (23 June 1970): 44f.

130. _____ Letter to Jiangxi Communist Labour University on 31 July 1961. *Current Background*, 891 (8 October 1969): 36. Also in *Mao Papers*

(see no. 17) 9-10. Mao applauds the system of part-time work, part-time study at school and university level, as a model for other provinces to adopt.

131. _____ 'A Talk on the Question of Democratic Centralism.' Speech at an enlarged session of the Central Work Conference (also known as the 7000-strong meeting), on 30 January 1962. *Peking Review*, 11, 21 (24 May 1968): 10f. Also in Joint Publications Research Service, U.S. Department of Commerce, no. 50792 (23 June 1972): 39-58; and an abbreviated version is in *Mao Papers*, 36-39 (dated 1966). Also in *Mao Tse-tung Unrehearsed* (see no. 28) 158-187. This speech was made to an audience of 7000 cadres who had been called to Beijung to discuss policy issues. Mao appears genuinely concerned with the democratic aspect of 'democratic centralism.' For example, he says 'Now there are some comrades who are afraid of the masses initiating discussion and putting forward ideas which differ from those of the leaders and leading organisations . . . This attitude is extremely evil.' He concludes 'In short, let other people speak out. The heavens will not fall and you will not be thrown out. If you do not let others speak, then the day will surely come when you are thrown out.'

132. _____ Speech at the Tenth Planary Session of the Eighth Central Committee of the CCP, on 24 September 1962. *Chinese Law and Government*, 1, 4 (Winter 1968-69): 85-93, and *Peking Review*, 10, 23 (2 June 1967): 17. Also in *Mao Tse-tung Unrehearsed* (see no. 28) 188-96. A wide-ranging speech on problems at home and abroad including comments on the current nature of the class struggle.

133. _____ Speech at the Hangchow Conference, May-June 1963. Joint Publications Research Service, U.S. Department of Commerce, no. 61269-2 (20 February 1974): 318-24.

134. _____ Draft Resolution of the Central Committee of the CCP on some problems in Current Rural Work. ('The first ten points.') 20 May 1963. *Current Background*, 885 (31 July 1969) (which dates resolution 11 September 1960). *Peking Review*, 10, 11 (10 March 1967) attributes Resolution to Mao. Also in *Mao Tse-tung and Lin Piao: Post-Revolutionary Writings* (see no. 19) 267-269. This resolution includes 'Where do correct ideas come from?' Mao contends that ideas come from social practice, such as the struggle for production, the class struggle and scientific experiment.

135. _____ A Proposal Concerning the General Line of the International Communist Movement, (letter of the Central Committee of the CCP, 14 June 1963). Peking: Foreign Languages Press, 1963. Pamphlet. Also in *Peking*

Review., 6, 25 (21 June 1963): 6-22. Also see *China Quarterly*, 15 (July-September 1963): 192-96, for a condensed version. Mao's authorship uncertain. The letter blames Khruschev for ruining communism in Russia and its prospects throughout the world.

136. _____ Statement Supporting the American Negroes in their Just Struggle Against Racial Discrimination by U.S. Imperialism. Written on 8 August 1963. *Peking Review*, 6, 32. Also in *Political Thought of Mao Tse-tung* (see no. 29) 409-12. This statement was made at the request of an American negro leader, Robert Williams, at that time in Cuba. It refers to recent examples of prejudice and injustice in the United States and accuses the Kennedy Administration of 'cunning two-faced tactics.'

137. _____ 'Origin and Development of the Differences between the Leadership of the CPSU and ourselves.' (Comment 1 on the Open Letter of the Central Committee of the CPSU of 14 July 1963). Written 6 September 1963. *Peking Review*, 6, 37 (13 September 1963: 6-20. This and the following eight Comments (see nos. 138, 139, 140, 141, 142, 143, 144, 145 below) show the Chinese Communist Party's line at this stage of Sino-Soviet discord. See also CCP letters to the CPSU (nos. 147, 149, 151). Whoever was the author of these documents, Mao as Party Chairman must have endorsed their contents.

138. _____ 'On the Question of Stalin.' (Comment 2 on the Open Letter of the Central Committee of the CPSU of 14 July 1963). Written 13 September 1963. *Peking Review*, 6, 38 (20 September 1963): 8-15.

139. _____ 'Is Yugoslavia a Socialist Country?' (Comment 3 on the Open Letter of the Central Committee of the CPSU of 14 July 1963). Written 26 September 1963. *Peking Review*, 6, 39 (27 September 1963): 14-27.

140. _____ 'Apologist of Neo-Colonialism.' (Comment 4 on the Open Letter of the Central Committee of the CPSU of 14 July 1963). Written 22 October 1963. *Peking Review*, 6, 43 (25 October 1963): 6-14.

141. _____ 'Two Different Lines on the Question of War and Peace.' (Comment 5 on the Open Letter of the Central Committee of the CPSU of 14 July 1963). Written 19 November 1963. *Peking Review*, 6, 47 (22 November 1963): 6-16.

142. _____ 'Peaceful Coexistence. Two diametrically opposed policies.' (Comment 6 on the Open Letter of the Central Committee of the CPSU of

14 July 1963.) Written 12 December 1963. *Peking Review*, 6, 51 (20 December 1963): 6-18.

143. _____ Comment on Comrade Ko Ching-shih's report 12 December 1963. *Peking Review*, 10, 23 (2 June 1967): 8. Also in Joint Publications Research Service, U.S. Department of Commerce, no. 49826 (12 February 1970) 26 (dated as December 1965) and in *Mao Papers* (see no. 17) 86. Mao refers to the lack of progress in socialist transformation of the arts. 'Isn't it absurd that many communists are enthusiastic about promoting feudal and capitalist art, but not socialist art?'

144. _____ 'The Leaders of the CPSU are the greatest splitters of our times.' (Comment 7 on the Open Letter of the Central Committee of the CPSU). Written 4 February 1964. *Peking Review*, 7, 6 (7 February 1964): 5-21.

145. _____ Instructions given at the Spring Festival concerning Education Work on 13 February 1964. Joint Publications Research Services, U.S. Department of Commerce, no. 61269-2 (20 February 1974): 326-36. Also in *Mao Papers*, (see no. 17) 93-97; and in *Mao Tse-tung Unrehearsed* (see no. 28) as 'Remarks at the Spring Festival' 197-211. Includes Mao's comments on the present examination system '. . . it is like an ambush . . . My suggestion is to publish the questions first, let the students study them and answer them with the help of their books.' Mao's comments on the stultifying effect of abstract learning include the following: 'Students should be permitted to doze off when a lecturer is teaching. Instead of listening to nonsense, they do much better taking a nap to freshen themselves up. Why listen to gibberish anyway?' 'Let us drive opera singers, poets, playwrights and men of letters out of the cities, and drive all of them to the countryside.' 'One must not read too much. Books by Marx should be read, but not too many of them. A few dozen volumes will do. Too much reading will lead you to the opposite of what you expect to be, a bookworm, a dogmatist, a revisionist.'

146. _____ Talk on the Problems of Philosophy. Joint Publications Research Service, U.S. Department of Commerce, no. 61269-2 (20 February 1974): 397-402. Also in *Mao Tse-tung Unrehearsed* (see no. 28) 212-30 under title 'Talk on Questions of Philosophy.' The talk was given on 18 August 1964. Mao argues that comrades who study philosophy should go down to the countryside.

147. _____ Letter of the Central Committee of the CCP to the Central Committee of the CPSU 20, 27 and 29 February 1964. *Peking Review*, 7, 19 (8 May 1964): 10-18.

148. _____ 'The Proletarian Revolution and Khreshchev's Revisionism.' (Comment 8 on the Open Letter of the Central Committee of the CPSU of 14 July 1963). Written 31 March 1964. *Peking Review*, 7, 14 (3 April 1964): 5-22.

149. _____ Letter to the Central Committee of the CCP to the Central Committee of the CPSU. Written 7 May 1964. *Peking Review*, 7, 19 (8 May 1964): 7-10. Also in *Current Digest of the Soviet Press*, 30, 16 (19 August 1964): 3f.

150. _____ 'On Khrushchev's Phoney Communism and Its Historical Lessons for the World.' (Comment 9 on the Open Letter of the Central Committee of the CPSU of 14 July 1963. Written 14 July 1964. *Peking Review*, 7, 29 (17 July 1964): 7-28.

151. _____ Letter of the Central Committee of the CCP in reply to the letter of the Central Committee of the CPSU dated 15 June 1964 . Written 28 July 1964. *Peking Review*, 7, 31 (31 July 1964): 5-11.

152. _____ Talk with the Nepalese Education Delegation, 29 August 1964. Joint Publications Research Service, U.S. Department of Commerce, no. 41884 (18 July 1967): 1. Also in *Mao Papers* (see no. 17) 21-23. Mao attacks Chinese education system for being too academic and abstract and stresses the need for students to learn from both 'books and work' and to make contact with peasants and workers.

153. _____ Talk on the four clean-ups movement. Joint Publications Research Service, U.S. Department of Commerce, no. 61269-2 (20 February 1974): 437-44. Talk given 3 January 1965.

154. _____ Some Problems currently arising in the course of the rural Socialist Education Movement. ('The twenty-three articles') 14 January 1965. *Chinese Education*, 1, 3 (Fall 1968): 38-53. Note *Peking Review*, 10, 11 (10 March 1967): 15 attributes this statement to Mao, so authorship (presumably) uncertain.

155. _____ Talk at the Hangchow Conference, 21 December 1965. *Peking Review*, 10, 23 (2 June 1967): 22. Also in *Mao Tse-tung Unrehearsed* (see

no. 28) as 'Speech at Hangchow' 234-41. Mao attacks bookish philosophy, puts forward proposals for reforming university education, stresses the need for practical work and experience in the countryside.

156. _____ Talk at an enlarged meeting of the Politburo, 20 March 1966. Joint Publications Research Service, U.S. Department of Commerce, no. 61269-2 (20 February 1974): 375-80.

157. _____ Letter to Comrade Lin Biao commenting on the 'Report for Making Greater Success of Farming by Armed Force Units' from the General Logistics Department of the Military Commission. 7th May 1966. *Peking Review*, 9, 32 (5 August 1966): 8. Also in *Mao Papers* (see no. 17) 103-105. Mao suggests that the army should 'serve as big school' for politics, military affairs and culture. It should engage in agricultural production and set up workshops to produce foods for its own use.

158. _____ Speech at a 'certain conference' 21 July 1966. Joint Publications Research Services, U.S. Department of Commerce, no. 49826 (12 February 1970): 31f. Also in *Mao Papers* (see no. 17) 129 (dated 2 September 1966) and in *Mao Tse-tung Unrehearsed* (see no. 28) as 'Talk to Leaders of the Centre' 253-55. Mao warns against repressing the students and commends their 'big-character posters.'

159. _____ Address to Regional Secretaries and Members of the Cultural Revolution Group under the Central Committee on 22 July 1966. Joint Publications Research Services, U.S. Department of Commerce, no. 49826 (12 February 1970): 32ff (dated 2 July 1966). Also in *Mao Tse-tung Unrehearsed* (see no. 28) 256-59. Mao criticizes the work teams for obstructing the Cultural Revolution in the schools.

160. _____ Decision of the Central Committee of the CCP concerning the Great Proletarian Cultural Revolution. ('The Sixteen Point Decision.') 8 August 1966. *Peking Review*, 9, 33 (12 August 1966): 6-11. Also in *Mao Papers* (see no. 17) 117-27. This important document lays down guidelines for the unfolding of the Cultural Revolution.

161. _____ Speech at the Eleventh Plenary Session of the Eighth Central Committee on 12 August 1966. Joint Publications Research Services, U.S. Department of Commerce, no. 41884 (18 April 1967): 4f, and no. 42349 (25 August 1967): 34 and no. 49826 (12 February 1970): 7f. Also in *Mao Tse-tung Unrehearsed* (see no. 28) 262-63.

162. _____ Comments during a Review of the Red Guards, 18 August 1966. *Peking Review*, 10, 20 (12 May 1967): 5. Also in *Mao Papers* (see no. 17) 127 (dated 19 August 1966) and 132 (dated 12 November 1966). Brief comments on the importance of the mass line and the role of the Red Guards.

163. _____ 'Twenty Manifestations of Bureaucracy.' January 1967. Joint Publications Research Service, U.S. Department of Commerce, no. 49826 (12 February 1970): 40-43.

164. _____ Speech at an enlarged meeting of the Military Affairs Commission, 21 January 1967. *Peking Review*, 11, 3 (19 January 1968): 11. Joint Publications Research Services, U.S. Department of Commerce, no. 49826 (12 February 1970): 40. Also in *Mao Papers* (see no. 17) 47, 140 (dated 27 January 1967 and 1 June 1967).

165. _____ Conversations with Chang Chun-chiao and Yao Wen-yuan, 12 February 1967. *Peking Review*, 10, 10 (3 March 1967): 10. Also in *Mao Papers* (see no. 17) 136 (dated 23 February 1967) and in *Mao Tse-tung Unrehearsed* (see no. 28) 277-79. Zhang and Yao were the two principal leaders of the 'Shanghai Commune' formed on 5 February 1967. At this point Mao is repudiating the ultra-leftists. He warns against anarchism and states "if instead of calling someone the 'head' of something, we call him 'orderly' or 'assistant,' this would really only be a formal change. In reality these will still always be 'heads.'

166. _____ Directive concerning the 'Great Strategic Plan' for the Great Proletarian Cultural Revolution. 7 March 1967. *Peking Review*, 11 (15 March 1968): 5. Also in *Mao Papers* (see no. 17) 136. Includes instruction for the work of the PLA in schools and universities, as part of the 'three in one combination.'

167. _____ Instructions during an Inspection Tour in the Central and Southern parts of China, September 1967. *Peking Review*, 10, 48 (24 November 1967) and in Joint Publications Research Services, U.S. Department of Commerce, no. 61269-2 (20 February 1974): 463-67 (dated July-September 1967). Also in *Mao Papers* (see no. 17) 146-50 (dated October and November 1967).

168. _____ Conversation with responsible persons of the Beijing Red Guard Congress, 28 July 1968. Joint Publications Research Service, U.S. Department of Commerce, no. 61269-2 (20 February 1974): 469-97.

1970 to 1976

169. Mao Tse-tung. Editorial: 'Leninism or Social Imperialism?,' 22 April 1970 in People's Daily. *Peking Review* 13, 17 (24 April 1970): 5-15. Mao's authorship uncertain.

170. _____ Statement: 'People of the World Unite and defeat the U.S. Aggressors and their Running Dogs,' on 20 May 1970. *Peking Review*, Special Issue (23 May 1970): 8f.

171. _____ Talks with responsible local comrades during a tour of inspection (August-September 1971). *Chinese Law and Government*, 5, 3-4 (Fall-Winter 1972-73): 31-42.

172. _____ Talk with Maurice Couve de Murville in November 1971. *China Quarterly*, 55 (July-September 1973): 43.

173. _____ Talks with Madame Sirimavo Bandavanaike of Sri Lanka and Foreign Minister Maurice Schumann of France in June-July 1972. *China Quarterly*, 55 (July-September 1973): 44f.

174. _____ Conversations with Madame Nguyen Thi Binh, Foreign Minister of the Provincial Revolutionary Government of the Republic of Vietnam on 29 December 1972. *Peking Review*, 16, 1 (5 January 1973): 5 and 17, 24 (14 June 1974): 3.

175. _____ Comments at a meeting with Henry Kissinger, on 17 February 1973. *Peking Review*, 16, 8 (23 February 1973): 3.

176. _____ Comments at a meeting with French President Georges Pompidou on 12 September 1973. *Peking Review*, 16, 37 (14 September 1973): 3f.

177. _____ Comments at a meeting with Japanese Foreign Minister Masayoshi Ohira on 5 January 1974. *Peking Review*, 17, 2 (11 January 1974): 3.

178. _____ 'Directives on the Dictatorship of the Proletariat' on 22 February 1975. *Peking Review*, 18, 9 (28 February 1975): 5.

IV. General Biographies and Other Works Covering Mao's Life

Books

179. Archer, Jules. *Chou En-lai*. New York: Hawthorn Books, 1973. 188. This biography includes some account of Zhou's (Chou's) relationship with Mao Zedong over many years.

180. _____ *Mao Tse-tung*. New York: Hawthorne, 1972. 211. Popular introductory biography covering whole of Mao's life up to the visit by President Nixon in 1972. The first ten chapters cover period up to liberation. A fairly brief survey of Mao in power and a short concluding chapter on Mao's thought.

181. Bergere, Marie-Claire. *La Republique Populaire de Chine de 1949 a nos jours*. Paris: Armand Colin, 1987. 282. Presents the main 'traits' of the political, economic and social evolution of China since 1949. The third part covers 'La Victoire du Pragmatisme 1976-1986.'

182. Bloodworth, Dennis. *The Messiah and the Mandarins. The Paradox of Mao's China*. London: Weidenfeld and Nicolson, 1982. 331. Claims to be 'a study in irony' . . . 'matching the magnitude of Mao's achievement against the enormity of his errors.' The author believes that the 'key to Mao lies in his Chineseness.' He traces 'the ancient mental reflexes and modern social pressures, the influences of blood and environment that formed this outstanding, unorthodox, and flexible revolutionary-thinker, teacher, poet, soldier and political leader, and then contrived his inexorable conversion with the passage of years into an old man withered by the dogmatism he had so despised when young.'

183. Bodard, Lucien. *Mao*. Paris: Gallimard, 1970. 253.

184. Bogdanov, Nikolai. *Erzahlungen uber Mao Tse-tung*. Berlin: Verlag Kulter und Fortschrift, 1952. 134. Translated by Veronica Erselen.

185. Boorman, Howard L. *Mao Tse-tung, the lacquered image*. Bombay: Manaktalas, 1965. 75. Essay first published in *China Quarterly*, October-December 1963. Book has an epilogue by C.R.M. Rao bringing it up to 1965. This is a brief biography attempting to place Mao at seventy in the context of twentieth-century Chinese history.

186. Brugger, Bill. *Contemporary China--An Introductory History*. London: Croom Helm, 1977. Based on Brugger's lecture course for undergraduates, this book provides a detailed, generally sympathetic history of Mao's China from the 1940's to the mid-1970's.

187. Carter, Peter. *Mao*. London: Oxford University Press, 1976. 161. A popular introductory biography which gives greater attention to the period before Liberation. It sets Mao's personal life in the context of political affairs, both inside and outside China.

188. _____ *One of the great epics of our century--the rise to power of Mao Tse-tung and the land he led into the 20th century*. New York: New American Library, 1980. 197. A clear chronological account of Mao's career.

189. Chang, Kuo-sin. *Mao Tse-tung and his China*. Hong Kong: Heinemann Educational Books Ltd., 1978. 228.

190. Chen, Jerome. *Great Lives Observed: Mao*. Englewood Cliffs, New Jersey: Prentice-Hall, 1969. 176.

191. _____ *Mao and the Chinese Revolution*. London: Oxford University Press, 1965. 419. A pioneering work based on primary sources. It covers the period from Mao's childhood to Liberation. Part 2 has thirty-seven poems by Mao translated by Jerome Chen and Michael Bullock.

192. Ching, Ping and Dennis Bloodworth. *Heirs Apparent*. London: Secker and Warburg, 1973. 236. This book highlights the personalties and political characteristics of the Chinese Communist leaders and their relationships with Mao Zedong. It covers the period from the 1920's to 1972. The authors have tried (successfully) to present a readable story. They use nick-names and reveal such personal foibles as eating and drinking habits. Among many interesting insights is the description (p. 93) of the 'Mao Tse-tung Mass' as celebrated in the reform-through-labour camp established at Yanan for members of religious sects.

193. Chou Eric. *Mao Tse-tung. The Man and the Myth*. London: Cassell, 1982, 289.

194. Craig, Dietrich. *People's China--A Brief History*. New York: Oxford University Press, 1986. 327. Intended as an undergraduate textbook based on English language versions of primary sources such as Mao's *Selected Works*.

195. Domenach, Jean-Luc and Philippe Richer. *La Chine 1949-1985*. Paris: Imprimerie Nationale, 1987. 532. Covers political, social, economic changes and foreign policy, in three sections. The second section 'Maoism in the State' is especially well written. The authors divide the Cultural Revolution into an 'insurrectional' phase (1965-67) and a period of 'militarization' (1967-71). They point out that the Cultural Revolution failed both because of 'Mao's excessive zeal as an innovator' and because of his reluctance to let the movement run its full course.

196. Domes, Jurgen. *The Internal Politics of China, 1949-1972*. London: Hurst, 1973. 274. 'A scholarly summary of major policies, events and personalities in the national politics of the People's Republic of China' (*China Quarterly*).

197. Ebon, Martin. *Lin Biao. The Life and Writings of China's New Ruler*. New York: Stein and Day, 1970. 378. Written at the time when Lin was expected to succeed Mao. Includes a number of Lin's works extolling the virtues of Chairman Mao.

198. Elegant Robert S. *China's Red Leaders*. London: The Bodley Head, 1952. 264. Chapter 10 on Mao Tse-tung, describes his arrival in Beijing in March 1949. Summarises the formative influences on Mao and raises the question of 'whether Maoism represents a substantive as well as a formal heresy of orthodox Lenin-Stalinism.'

199. _____ *The Centre of the World. Communism and the Mind of China*. London: Metheun and Co. Ltd, 1963. 379. A wide ranging survey of Chinese history from 1600 to the present, of the growth of the Communist Party and its role once in power, and of problems facing the Party. The author comments on the attitudes of individuals responding to the demands of Maoism. Chapter 9 specifically discusses 'The Vision of Mao Tse-tung' looking at his childhood, his personality and sources of his ideas.

200. Fairbank, John King. *China Watch*. Cambridge, Mass.: Harvard University Press, 1987. 219. Professor Fairbank has arranged into five parts

25 of his reviews on books about China. He points out political and social continuities in Chinese history. *Inter alia* he explains the primacy of 'redness' over 'expertness' and the attitudes and behaviour of Mao Zedong after he became 'The One Man.'

201. Fitzgerald, C P. *Mao Tse-tung and China*. London: Hodder and Stoughton, 1976. 166. Biography of Mao covering his entire life by a well-known scholar of Chinese history, but written as a popular, not a scholarly, account of Mao's life and achievements.

202. Fonseca, Gondin da. *Afonso de Albuquerque e Mao Tse-tung*. Sao Paulo: Editora Fulgor, 1963. 78.

203. Franz, Uli. *Deng Xiaoping, China's Erneverer: eine Biographie*. Stuttgart: Deutsche Verlags-Austalt, 1987. 350. A detailed account of Deng's life from his youth in Sichuan, to France, Moscow and back in China in the Communist Party guerilla movement. Shows Deng as a 'pragmatist' in the politics of the People's Republic but does not really explain how he came to take this role.

204. Fromentin, Pierre. *Mao Tse-tung: Le Dragon Rouge*. Paris: Editions Medicis, 1949. 212. A popular, rather romantic account of Mao's life from boyhood to leader of the Chinese Communist Party and the Red Army, explaining the political context in which Mao's politics evolved. Final chapters discuss probable nature of Chinese Communism and relations with Stalin, the implications of a Communist China for the U.S. and for Indo-China.

205. Garder, Michel. *Mao Tse-toung*. Paris: La Table Ronde, 1960. 126. (Collection 'Meneurs d'hommes,' 9).

206. Gittings, John. *China Changes Face. The Road from the Revolution, 1949-1989*. Oxford: Oxford University Press, 290. A lively, well-written analysis of changes in China since Liberation. Offers interesting insights into Mao's objectives and policies.

207. Gray, Jack. *Mao Tse-tung*. Guildford: Lutterworth Press, 1973. 88. (Makers of Modern Thought Series) An overview of Mao's early career followed by some assessment of the success of economic reforms. Part 3 discusses the relevance of Maoism in China, in developing countries and in advanced countries.

208. Gray, Jack, ed. *Modern China's Search for a Political Form*. New York: Oxford University Press, 1969. 379. This symposium originated in the 1965-66 programme of the Working Group on China and the World organised by Chatham House. It comprises ten essays contributed by experts from various disciplines on the theme of revolutionary political development in modern China. It begins with the historical antecedents of the Communist revolution and concludes with some analysis of the Cultural Revolution.

209. Guillermaz, Jacques. *The Chinese Communist Party in Power, 1949-1976*. Folkestone, Kent: Dawson, 1976. 614. Translated by Anne Destenay. First published as *Le parti Communiste Chinois au pouvoir*. Paris: Payot, 1972. English edition revised and updated. This is the second volume of Guillermaz's history of Communist Party. Author says 'I have tried as far as possible to find a viewpoint situated within the Chinese system, not in order to justify it . . . but to share the ideas and reasoning of its leaders and to understand the feelings and behaviour of the masses.' Primary emphasis on institutions and policies, not personalities, but frequent references to Mao.

210. Hamilton, John Maxwell. *Edgar Snow: A biography*. Bloomington: Indiana University Press, 1988. 343. A useful biography of the man who discovered Mao in Yanan, and who subsequently visited Mao on several occasions.

211. Han Suyin. *The Morning Deluge: Mao Tse-tung and the Chinese Revolution, 1893-1953*. London: Jonathan Cape, 1972. 615. This first volume takes Mao from his schooldays through the stages of his career as a revolutionary leader to Liberation and the early years of The People's Republic. There is little analysis of Mao's thought. This biography is very favourable to Mao and uses polemical texts from the period of the Cultural Revolution.

212. _____ *Wind in the Tower: Mao Tse-tung and the Chinese Revolution 1949-1975*. London: Cape, 1976. 404. This is the second volume of her biography of Mao. Part 1 covers 'The Building of New China' up to 1962 and Part 2 looks at 'The Cultural Revolution and After.' The account is focussed on Mao's ideas, writings and speeches but fills in the political context as necessary. A strongly pro-Mao account and interpretation. Shows Mao as 'a complex thinker, a modest man--and moreover, a man merciful to his enemies--uncorrupted by power, realising the dangers and temptations presented to those who govern, and putting his trust in the revolt of the common man as the safeguard against all tyranny.'

213. Harris, Nigel. *The Mandate of Heaven. Marx and Mao in Modern China*. London: Quartet Books, 1978. 307. Covers Mao's policies throughout his period in power and begins with brief survey of the road to power. A political analysis, not a biographical work, but Mao naturally emerges as the central figure in the historical sections, Part 1 and Part 2. Later parts examine the party's relation to workers and peasants, the degree of equality and democracy achieved in China, the significance of China's foreign policy and the role of Maoists abroad.

214. Harrison, James Pinckney. *The Long March to Power: A History of the Chinese Communist Party, 1921-72*. New York: Praeger, 1972. 647. Gives weight to role of other Communist leaders as well as Mao, and notes Mao often cautious and pragmatic in his policies, not always a romantic revolutionary. Antidote to presentations of Mao influenced by Cultural Revolution.

215. Ho Kan-chih. *A History of the Modern Chinese Revolution*. Peking: Foreign Language Press, 1959. 627. A chronological history of the communist movement in China from 1919 to 1956. Includes details of the military campaigns. Photographs.

216. Hollingworth, Clare. *Mao*. London: Triad Paladin, 1987. 366. Originally published by Jonathan Cape, 1985. 372. Draws on a great deal of new information which has come to light since Mao's death. Centers on Mao's political struggles, particularly in the Cultural Revolution. Part III, 'The Years of Decline' takes the story of Maoism through to the trial of the Gang of Four. Part IV, 'In Perspective,' includes notes on ten men who opposed Mao.

217. Howard, Roger. *Mao Tse-tung and the Chinese People*. London: George Allen & Unwin, 1977. 412. New York: Monthly Review Press, 1977. 384. This book covers Mao's life from his early years to his death in 1976. An uncritical biography which draws heavily on quotations from Mao himself and accepts Mao's position even over controversial issues like the Cultural Revolution.

218. Huang, Yu-chuan. *Mao Tse-tung: a Chronology of His Life*. Hong Kong: Union Research Institute, 1970. 544. Not strictly a chronology, rather a collection of raw materials relating to Mao's life, including extensive extracts taken from the official Beijing edition of Mao's *Selected Works*. Includes extracts from wide range of secondary sources, some familiar in the West, others drawn from Hong Kong books and periodicals. The extracts

often contain contradictory accounts. The compiler does not guide the reader through this rather random and confusing collection, but includes materials of interest to serious Western students of Mao.

219. Hughes, Richard. *Foreign Devil. Thirty Years of Reporting in the Far East*. London: Century Publishing, 1984. 320. Includes some anecdotal material on Mao Zedong; for example, chapter 17, 'The Unpublished Thoughts of Chairman Mao.'

220. Karlsson, Per Olof. *Mao Tse-tung*. Stockholm: Seelig, 1966. 159.

221. Kolpas, Norman. *Mao*. Harlow, Essex: Longman, 1981. 69. Very basic introductory biography, extensively illustrated in the Longman Great Lives series. Includes a map and a chronology.

222. Krieg, Ernst. *Mao Tse-Toung, l'empereur rouge de Pekin*. Paris: Editions de Saint-Clair, 1966. 255.

223. Ladany, Laszlo. *The Communist Party of China and Marxism, 1921-1985*. London: C. Hurst & Company, 1988. 588. Subtitled 'A Self Portrait' this book relies entirely on what the Communist Party has revealed about itself. For the period 1921-49 it relies mainly on revelations that appeared in the Communist press in the early 1980's when Chinese historians of the party were relatively free to write. For the period after 1949 it summarizes what was reported in the weekly *China News Analysis* which was written by the author during the years 1953-1982. The foreward by Robert Elegant states 'Ladany offers a portrait of the Chairman (Mao) that differs significantly from previous portraits. Yet, every alteration in the familiar physiognomy is substantiated by Mao's contemporaries and colleagues.'

224. Lee, Ching Hua. *Deng Xiaoping: The Marxist road to the forbidden city*. Princeton, New Jersey: The Kingston Press, 1985. 254. A useful biography of the political survivor, purged and rehabilitated three times, who has done so much to reverse Mao's programmes. The author shows that Deng is economically liberal but politically conservative. Deng is not a great theoretician but that it is hardly surprising in view of his pragmatic reputation. 'It doesn't matter whether the cat is black or white, so long as it catches mice,' was his saying. A readable account of the man who Mao predicted would 'shake the world' and who was described by Jiang Qing as 'that Fascist dwarf.'

225. Levy, Roger. *Mao Tse-toung*. Paris: Seghers, 1965. 175.

226. MacGregor-Hastie, Roy. *The Red Barbarians. The Life and Times of Mao Tse-tung*. London: Boardman and Co Ltd, 1961. 224. This is an optimistic socialist view of Mao up to 1960. The author appears not to recognise errors in the Great Leap Forward.

227. Migot, Andre. *Mao Tse-toung*. Paris: Editions Planete, 1965. 312.

228. Moise, Edwin E. *Modern China. A History*. London: Longman, 1986. 256. A clear introductory account.

229. Paloczi-Horvath, George. *Mao Tse-tung: Emperor of the Blue Ants*. London: Secker and Warburg, 1962. 424. A political biography of Mao up to 1962. Emphasis on relations with the USSR.

230. Payne, Robert. *Mao Tse-tung*. New York: Weybright and Talley, 1969. 303. Originally published as: *Mao Tse-tung, Ruler of Red China*. New York: Schuman, 1950. 'A study of the mind of Mao Tse-tung from his birth in a small village in Hunan to his arrival in Peking as the Conqueror of China in 1949.' Concentrates on 'the influences which went to form his mind.'

231. Payne, Robert. *Portrait of a Revolutionary: Mao Tse-tung*. New York: Abelard-Schuman, 1961. 311. Revised edition of 1950 book with an additional chapter.

232. Poole, Frederick King. *Mao*. London: Franklin Watts, 1984. 96. (New York: Franklin Watts, 1982). Brief biography of Mao covering his whole life. Journalistic account which seeks to cover political context and political relevance of Mao's actions. One in a series of candid biographies of people who have had major influence in the twentieth century.

233. Purcell, Hugh. Mao Tse-tung. New York, Wayland/St. Martin's Press, 1977. 96. (Wayland History Makers). A concise introductory biography.

234. Pye, Lucian W. *Mao Tse-tung. The Man in the Leader*. New York: Basil Books Inc., 1976. 346. Seeks to examine Mao's personal qualities as revealed in his upbringing and personal relations and to explain his charismatic appeal and his 'extraordinary ability to manage the emotions of others while remaining aloof himself.'

235. Radio Free Europe. *Mao Tse-tung: his rise and his role.* New York: National Committee for a Free Europe, 1953. 21.

236. Rice, Edward E. *Mao's Way.* Berkeley: University of California Press, 1972. 596. The author's duties as American Consul General at Hong Kong during the Cultural Revolution included supervising the 'China watchers' a large unit engaged in monitoring and translating the China Mainland Press. This book written after his return to the U.S. sets out to show that the Cultural Revolution has its roots in earlier movements such as the Great Leap and the Hundred Flowers campaign. The author aims to draw out Mao's personality and character, in its historical context, from his childhood to 1970. Half the book deals with the period 1965-1970. A final chapter 'Going Mao's Way' gives a rather simplistic picture of the social impact of the Cultural Revolution based on reports by foreign visitors. In pp. 499-519 is a useful Who's Who to the leading persons mentioned in the text.

237. Roberts, Elizabeth Mauchline. *Mao Tse-tung and the Chinese Communist revolution.* London: Methuen, 1970. 96.

238. Robottom, John. *Mao Tse-tung.* (Making of the Modern World series). London: Longmans, 1974. 32. A clear, introductory textbook.

239. Roy, Claude. *Premieres clefs pour la Chine: une vie de Mao Tse-Toung.* Paris: Editeurs francais reunis, 1950. 84.

240. Scharping, Thomas. *Mao Chronik.* Munich: Carl Hansen-Verlag, 1976. 235. A chronicle of Mao's life citing all the major events and using brief quotations from his political writings. Draws on extensive Chinese and Western sources.

241. Schram, Stuart. *Mao Tse-tung.* Harmondsworth, Middlesex: Penguin Books, 1966. 351. A Pelican original in the series 'Political Leaders of the Twentieth Century,' by an acknowledged scholar. A detailed sympathetic account to about 1960.

242. Schram, Stuart R. and Helene Carrere d'Encausse (eds). *Marxism and Asia.* London: Allen Lane, The Penguin Press, 1969. 404. This analyses includes some useful documents on Maoism, e.g. extracts from Mao's works 'On New Democracy' (pp. 251-58); and (pp. 259-61) Liu Xiaoqi's report to the Seventh Congress of the CCP May 1945 which stipulated that 'the thought of Mao Tse-tung constitutes the sole, correct and orthodox theory which must guide all the work of the Party.' This was a decisive stage in the

development of the Mao cult includes (pp. 253-61) extracts from Lin Biao's 'Long Live the Victory of People's War,' September 1965, exalting Mao's strategy, and stressing its relevance to the world situation.

243. Schurmann, Franz and Orville Schell. *China Readings 3: Communist China: Revolutionary Reconstruction and International Confrontation 1949 to the Present.* Harmondsworth, Middlesex: Penguin Books, 1968. 647. This book of readings includes two assessments of Mao, one by Edgar Snow, the other 'Mao Tse-tung Reassessed' by Mark Gayn was an unpublished working paper for the China Conference in Chicago, February 1966. Gayn met Mao in 1947 in Yanan, and returned to China 18 years later. Includes extracts from Mao's writings 'On Contradiction' and three of his poems.

244. Schwartz, Benjamin Isadore. *Chinese Communism and the Rise of Mao.* Cambridge, Massachusetts: Harvard University Press, 1951. 258. (Reprinted Harper Torchbooks, 1967). Reprinted, with new preface, by Harvard University Press, 1979. This is a history of the Chinese Communist Party up to 1933. The last two chapters discuss the 'triumph' of Mao in the Jiangxi Soviet and in the Party, and assess the essential features of Maoist strategy.

245. Smedley, Agnes. *The Great Road. The Life and Times of Chu Teh* (Zhu De). New York: Monthly Review Press, 1956. 460. Zhu De's life story as told to Agnes Smedley provides an account of the travails of the Chinese Communists before they reached Yanan, which can be matched with Snow's *Red Star.* 'Agnes Smedley provides both a sociological classic on rural China and a narrative of the Revolution, with few gaps from start to finish, as it appeared to its leading military figure.'

246. Snow, Edgar. *Red Star Over China.* First Revised and Enlarged Edition. London: Gollancz, 1968. 543. First published by Random House in 1938. This is a classic account in which Snow, a young American journalist, penetrated the military blockade and entered the Communist controlled area of Northwest China in 1936. He was the first Westerner to reach the Communist headquarters and he talked at length to Mao during the four months he spent there. The book includes Mao's own account of his life, the story of the Long March, an assessment of the Soviet being created in the Northwest, conversations with peasants and Snow's experiences with the Red Army. *Red Star* played an important role in making Mao and the Chinese Communist movement known in the West.

247. Spence, Jonathan, D. *The Gate of Heavenly Peace: the Chinese and their Revolution 1985-1980.* New York: Viking Press, 1981. 465. The author

follows the history of the Chinese revolution through the lives and writings of the great writers, historians and poets. He deliberately 'places the familiar careers of political leaders Mao and Chiang Kai-shek at the edge of his story.'

248. Solomon, Richard H. *Mao's Revolution and the Chinese Political Culture*. Berkeley: University of California Press, 1971. 604. The author describes his work as 'a study of one of the twentieth century's most influential political leaders in his personal struggle to adapt the weighty cultural inheritance of a quarter of mankind to the political and economic challenges of a new era.' In summing up the interplay between revolutionary leader and cultural legacy he stresses that Mao has tried 'to liberate in disciplined, politicized fashion the aggressive emotions which were denied legitimate expression in the political culture of dependency. Where the Confucian order stressed emotional restraint as the basis of personal discipline, . . Mao . . . saw resentment and hatred as the motivational basis of mass political participation.' Based on interviews as well as wide range of written sources.

249. Terrill, Ross. *Mao: A Biography*. New York: Harper, 1980. 481. This is a chronological account of Mao's career in which the author examines the sources of his social and political ideas, describes his rise to influence and power, and analyses his strengths and weaknesses. Nearly one-third of the book is devoted to Mao's last decade. Terrill's view is .pa that the Cultural Revolution, far from being 'the culmination of Maoism' was 'a charade in a hothouse.'

250. Terrill, Ross. *The White-Boned Demon: a biography of Madam Mao Zedong*. London: Heinemann, 1984. 446. The author writes 'In Jiang Qing we . . . come face to face with a living personality of universal dimensions whose spirit speaks to the heart of ambitious women--and not a few men-- everywhere . . .. This book tells Jiang's story on the basis of the eloquent "unofficial" voices of China: oral eyewitness accounts from the grass roots; testimony of those Chinese now outside China who watched, knew, hated or loved Jiang Qing; documents of the Peking elite that were directed at a small readership but have reached me in the West.' A very readable account of her life from childhood to her trial, when 'she gave off more life and spirit than all the other defendants put together.' By refusing to confess she made herself a landmark in the history of communist trials.

251. Thornton, Richard C. *China: A Political History, 1917-1982*. Boulder, Colorado: Westview Press, 1982. 518. Detailed account of leadership

conflicts in the Communist Party, written from standpoint that 'the Communist period has been a backward step in China's evolutionary experience.'

252. _____ *China: The Struggle for Power 1917-1972*. Bloomington, Indiana: Indiana University Press, 1973. 448. Examines Mao's manoeuvres to achieve and maintain power in the Party throughout his polical life and the attempts by other leading Communists to bypass Mao or to overthrow him. Also looks at relation of Chinese Party to the Soviet Party.

253. Uhalley, Stephen. *Mao Tse-tung: A Critical Biography*. New York: New Viewpoints, 1975. 233. Laudatory and uncritical biography relying on secondary sources, but useful on Yanan period and gives a clear chronological treatment of the Cultural Revolution. The author believes that Mao has influenced more people during his lifetime than anyone else in history. 'Mao wants a truly communist society peopled by a transformed "new socialist" man.'

254. Wang Fanxi. *Chinese Revolutionary Memoirs: 1919-1949*. New York: Oxford University Press, 1979. 349. The author, having joined the Chinese Communist Party in the 1920's, became a Trotskyist, was expelled, was imprisoned by the Guomindang until 1937, and was finally purged by the CCP after Liberation. These memoirs give an account from one revolutionary's view point of a rather obscure period in the history of the Chinese revolution.

255. Wilson, Dick. *Chou. The Story of Zhou Enlai 1898-1976*. London: Hutchinson and Co, 1984. 349. A useful overview of Zhou's life, but less satisfactory as an analysis of Zhou's impact on the political development of modern China. Some of the new material comes from hagiography written after his death. The author states that Zhou's relationship with Mao 'was to determine the whole shape and course of the People's Republic.'

256. _____ *Mao. The People's Emperor*. New York: Doubleday, 1980. 530. A detailed well-written biography which includes excerpts from Mao's writings, speeches and conversations. The reminiscences of Mao's wives, friends and acquaintances help to provide a revealing picture of 'the last of the great dominating figures of our century.' The 'Olympian' who retained his peasant habits to the end, and whose 'tragedy was that he could not in the end bring about all the reforms which he wanted.'

257. Witke, Roxane. *Comrade Chiang Ching*. London: Weidenfeld and Nicolson, 1977. 549. A lively account of the life and career of Madame Mao from her childhood to her trial as one of the 'Gang of Four.' Based largely on interviews with the author in the Summer of 1972. Well illustrated with photographs.

258. Yang, Zhong Mei. *Au Yao Bang: A Chinese Biography*. Armonk, New York: M.E. Sharpe, 1988. 208. This biography, written by a scholar born and raised in the People's Republic, includes important information on the people and events central to the history of the Chinese Communist Party from the late 1920's to the present.

259. Zach, Manfred. *Mao Tse-tung*. Esslingen: Bechtle, 1969. 87.

260. Zhong Wenxian. *Mao Zedong. Biography--Assessment--Reminiscences*. Beijing: Foreign Languages Press, 1986. 238. Published to commemorate the tenth anniversary of Mao's death. This selection of twenty articles begins with a biographical sketch by the editor and then reprints a chapter from Edgar Snow's *Red Star Over China* which recounts Mao's life on the basis of a number of interviews. The second part of the book comprises assessments of Mao by Zhou Enlai and Deng Xiaoping. The third section reprints personal reminiscences of Mao by various individuals who met him or worked with, and includes 'Recollections of Our Father' by Mao's son and daughter-in-law, Mao Anqing and Shao Hua.

Articles

261. Boorman, Howard L. 'Mao Tse-tung: the Lacquered Image.' *China Quarterly*, 1963 (October-December): 1-55. This biographical essay was written on the occasion of Mao's seventieth birthday.

262. _____ 'The Literary World of Mao Tse-tung.' *China Quarterly*, no. 13 (January-March 1963): 15-38. Boorman believes that the 'Juxtaposition of strategic and artistic instincts in Mao Tse-tung is so unusual in the post-Churchillian world that the case merits more than passing note.' This article surveys the evolving political influences which have shaped Chinese imaginative writing in the 40's and 50's, with particular attention to literary policies as expounded by Mao. Boorman concludes that 'Mao Tse-tung himself is the outstanding exception to the canons of proletarian and utilitarian literature which he has brought to his country and his people.'

263. _____ 'Liu Shao-chi: A Political profile.' *China Quarterly*, no. 10 (1962): 1-22. Examines the career and political prospects of the man who, at the time of writing, seemed destined to succeed Mao. The author believes that 'Liu Shao-chi's long-range contribution is that he--more than any other man at the top level--has been the individual most responsible for setting the political style of the Party and for defining the social and moral responsibilities of Party members.'

264. _____ 'Mao Tse-tung at seventy: an American dilemma.' *Virginia Quarterly Review*, 40 (Spring 1964): 182- 200. Brief biographical study of Mao in the context of Chinese history since the 1920's. Comments that 'The man who has now reached seventy is still both peasant and intellectual, both Chinese and Communist, both hardened revolutionary and imaginative romantic.'

265. Dittmer, L. 'Mao Tse-tung: the man and the symbol: review article.' *China Quarterly*, no. 68 (December 1976): 822-28. Reviews two books published coincidentally with Mao's death: Lucian Pye, *Mao Tse-tung: The Man in the Leader*, and C. P. Fitzgerald, *Mao Tse-tung and China*.

266. Hiniker, P. J. and J. J. Peristein. 'Alternation of charismatic and bureaucratic styles of leadership in post revolutionary China.' *Comparative Political Studies*, 10 (January 1978): 529-54.

267. Eggers, Gotz. 'Mao Tse-tung.' *Schweizer Monatshafte*, 44 (June 1964): 195-210.

268. MacDonald, James. 'Mao Tse-tung.' *New Society*, 11 (January 1968): 123-125.

269. MacFarquhar, Roderick. 'On photographs.' *China Quarterly*, no. 46 (April-June 1971): 289-307. Shows the importance of the hierarchical ordering of photographs, and gives examples of Mao's own interest in this matter. Discusses the significance of the Party 'line-up' on a number of occasions.

270. Payne, Robert. 'A man called Mao.' U.S. *News and World Report*, (May 1950): 19-23.

271. Pfeffer, Richard, M. 'Revolting: An Essay on "Mao's Revolution" by Richard Solomon.' *Bulletin of Concerned Asian Scholars*, 5, 4 (December

1973): 46-55. Critical commentary on R. Solomon, *Mao's Revolution and the Chinese Political Culture* (see no. 248).

272. 'Reminiscences of Chairman Mao.' *Peking Review*, 20, 42 (14 October 1977): 17-21. Excerpts from newspaper articles on the anniversary of Mao's death. Includes some information on Mao's later contacts with his mother-in-law, Mrs. Yang; the recollections of Chen Yu-ying, a nursemaid who worked for the Mao family in the 1920's; and an account of Mao's return to his home village of Shaoshan in 1959.

273. Schram, Stuart R. 'Mao Tse-tung and Liu Shao-ch'i, 1939- 1969.' *Asian Survey*, 12 (April 1972): 275-93.

274. _____ 'What Makes Mao a Maoist.' *The New York Times Magazine*, (8 March 1970): 36-82.

275. Teiwes, Frederick C. 'Chinese Politics 1949-1965: A Changing Mao.' Parts 1 and 2. *Current Scene*, 12, 1 (January 1974): 1-15; 12, 2 (February 1974): 1-19.

276. Woodman, Dorothy. 'Mao Tse-tung.' *New Statesman and Nation*, 37, 932 (15 January 1949): 48-9. Summary of Mao's life and political career up to 1949 and comment on role of Chinese Communist Party in the Border Regions.

Entries in Biographical Works

277. Boorman, Howard L. *Biographical Dictionary of Republican China.* 4 vols. New York: Columbia University Press, 1967- 70; 'Mao Tse-tung,' vol. III, 2-22.

278. Hsueh, Chun-tu. *Revolutionary Leaders of Modern China.* New York: Oxford University Press, 1971; 'The Early Life of Mao Tse-tung,' 395-421.

279. Klein, Donald W. *Biographic dictionary of Chinese Communism, 1921-1965.* Cambridge, Mass: Harvard University Press, 1971. Vol. 2. 676-688.

280. Lewytzkyj, Borys and Juliusz Stroynowski, eds. *Who's Who in the Socialist Countries.* New York: K G Saur Publishing Inc., 1978. Brief summary of Mao's life and political career.

281. Martin, Bernard and Shui Chien-tung. *Makers of China; Confucius to Mao.* New York: Halsted Press Division, Wiley, 1972. 238.

282. Wei-chen, pseud. *Who's Who in Communist China.* New York: Free Trade Union Committee, American Federation of Labor, 1954. 5-6.

283. *Who's Who in Communist China.* 2nd edition. Hong Kong: Union Research Institute, 1969. Vol. 2. 509-514.

V. Early Life to 1921

Books

284. Eunson, Roby. *Mao Tse-tung. The Man Who Conquered China.* New York: Franklin Watts, Inc., 1973. 152. This book begins and ends with the rapprochement between China and the U.S. in the early 1970's, but most of the book is about Mao's early career, in particular his school days and student life. An elementary introduction to Mao without any serious political analysis.

285. Feigon, Lee. *Chen Duxiu: Founder of the Chinese Communist Party.* Princeton, New Jersey: Princeton University Press, 1983. 279. Mao described Chen Duxiu as 'commander-in-chief' of the May Fourth Movement. Helps to put Mao's early revolutionary activities in context.

286. Graham, Gail. *A Cool Wind Blowing: The Early Life of Mao Tse-tung.* London: Angus and Robertson, 1979. 77. An account of Mao's life from 4 May 1919 as a library clerk to the Changsha uprising, September 1927, which led to the execution of Mao's first wife. This is a simple account, written like a novel, with a personal rather than a political emphasis.

287. Li Jui. *The Early Revolutionary Activities of Comrade Mao Tse-tung.* White Plains, New York: M.E. Sharpe, 1977. 354. Translated by Anthony W. Sariti. Edited by James C. Hsiung. Introduction by Stuart Schram notes that this was the only book-length biography to be published in China, and discusses why this biography published in Chinese in 1957 has not been translated into English before. During the 1960's the book and its author were denounced in Beijing and it was repudiated as an official biography because it was not adulatory enough and gave too much prominence to Liu Shaoqi. Schram notes that although Li's biography at first seemed too 'crudely hagiographic' to be treated as a serious source, compared with the eulogies of Mao in the Cultural Revolution it now appears 'honest and sober.' Li provides a political biography of the period from Mao's student days to his experience in the early labour movement in Hunan from 1920 to 1926. There is an appendix on the Peasant Movement in Hunan.

The author had access to manuscripts of Mao, including detailed notes from his student days, and his account is based on detailed historical research. Schram's introduction takes issue with Li on the development of Mao's thought on a number of points, claiming Li is responsible for some deliberate distortions and omissions. Schram is sceptical about Li's interpretation of many events, but does not attempt to challenge the basic 'story line.'

288. Meisner, Maurice. *Li Ta-chao and the Origins of Chinese Marxism.* Cambridge, Mass: Harvard University Press, 1967. 326. See pp. 262-266 for influences of Li on Mao. States 'the earliest political writings of the young Mao Zedong, published in 1919, faithfully echoed the Nationalist, Populist and Bolshevik ideas of his teacher.'

289. Scalapino, Robert A. and George T. Yu. *Modern China and Its Revolutionary Process: Recurrent Challenges to the Traditional Order.* Berkeley: University of California Press, 1985. 814. The authors devote a chapter to the early careers of Mao Zedong and Jiang Jieshi.

290. Siao, Emi. *Mao Tse-tung: his childhood and youth.* Bombay: People's Publishing House, 1953. 76. First published in Peking, 1949.

291. Siao-yu. *Mao Tse-tung and I were Beggars. A Personal Memoir of the Early Years of Chairman Mao.* London: Souvenir Press, 1944. 266. (First published in the U.S. by Syracuse University Press, 1959). This is the only personal memoir of Mao's early years apart from his own recollections in Snow's *Red Star* and a book by Siao-yu's communist brother, Emi Siao (see no. 290). Siao-yu met Mao at school. In 1914, they organised the Xinmin Study Association. In the summer of 1917, they went on a walking holiday through Hunan, living the life of tramps. This edition has a useful historical commentary and notes by Robert L. North.

Articles

292. Anonymous. 'The Flame Over the Hsiang River.' *Selections from China Mainland Magazines,* no. 621 (29 July, 1968): 23- 26. Originally published in 1967. Article on Mao's early life.

293. Anonymous. 'The Great Voyage.' *Selections from China Mainland Magazines,* no. 614 (12 February, 1968): 23-26. Originally published in 1967. On Mao's early life.

294. Anonymous. 'The Hsiang River is Roaring.' *Selections from China Mainland Magazines*, no. 614 (12 February, 1968): 14- 17. Originally published in 1967. On Mao's early life.

295. Bailey, Paul. 'The Chinese Work-Study Movement in France.' *China Quarterly*, no. 115 (September 1988): 441-461. More than 1500 Chinese students went to France on a work-study scheme between 1919-1921. They included many future leaders: Zhou Enlai, Deng Xiaoping, Chen Yi, Li Fuchun, Nie Rongzhen, Li Lisan, Cai Chang, Xu Teli and Li Weihan. Mao helped to organise support for these students, and had some correspondence with Cai Hesen who wrote urging Mao to prepare for an 'October 1917 style' revolution in China.

296. Chen, Pan-tsu (Ch'en T'an-ch'iu). 'Reminiscences of the First Congress of the Communist Party in China.' *The Communist International*, American edition, 14.10 (October 1936): 1361-66.

297. Hu Shih. 'My former student, Mao Tse-tung.' *Freeman*, 1 (July 1951): 636-39.

298. Li Rui. 'Mao Zedong in his school days.' *Beijing Review* 27, 18 (30 April 1984): 22-26.

299. _____ 'Mao Zedong in his school days.' *Beijing Review*, 27, 19 (7 May 1984): 26-29.

300. McDonald, Angus, W. Jr. 'Mao Tse-tung and the Hunan Peasant Movement, 1920. An Introduction and Five Translations.' *China Quarterly*, no. 68 (December 1976): 751-77.

301. Scalapino, R. 'The Education of a young revolutionary: Mao Zedong in 1919-1921.' *Journal of Asian Studies*, XLII, no. 1 (November 1982): 29-61. Describes Mao as a 'liberal' at that time.

302. Schwartz, Benjamin. 'Themes in Intellectual History: May Fourth and after.' *The Cambridge History of China*, vol. 12: 406-451. Republican China 1912-1949 Part 1, ed. John K. Fairbank. Cambridge: Cambridge University Press, 1983. Covers the May 4th movement--the 'Five-four' movement, 5th month, 4th day--through to the ascendency of Marxism.

303. Witke, Roxane. 'Mao Tse-tung, Women and Society in the May Fourth Era.' *China Quarterly*, no. 31 (July-September, 1967): 128-47. Miss Chao's

suicide was the subject of at least nine impassioned articles by Mao Tse-tung (see no. 48) which set the style of the 'case study' a new genre of May Fourth polemical literature. In the traditional prototypes the famous woman might commit suicide on the death of her husband or fiance, thus being set up as the ideal of female self-abnegation. 'In Mao's studies the bride commits suicide not for love or respect of the groom, but because she hates him.' Other writings by Mao on the woman problem appeared in at least four periodicals published in Hunan in 1919-20: *Xiang jiang ping-lun* (Hsiang River Review), *Xin Hunan* (New Hunan), *Nujie zhung (Women's Bell)*, and *Da Gung Bao*. Mao found women were particularly oppressed by old ways of thinking. He called upon them to unite to abolish 'man-eating feudal morality . . . and to sweep away the goblins (that destroy) physical and spiritual freedom.' Mao attacked unequal demands for chastity. 'Where are the shrines for chaste boys?' he asked.

VI. 1921 to 1935

Books

304. Beauvoir, Simone de. *The Long March*. London: Andre Deutsch and Weidenfeld and Nicholson, 1958. 513. One of de Beauvoir's main informants for this book was Ding Ling, the veteran woman writer.

305. Borkenau, Franz. *World Communism: A History of the Communist International*. Introduction by Raymond Aron. Ann Arbor, Michigan: University of Michigan Press, Ann Arbor Paperbacks, 1962. This is a reprint of Borkenau's classic work *The Communist International* first published in 1938 (London: Faber and Faber). Chapters 18 and 19 (pp. 296-331) examine the background to the Chinese Revolution and the history of the Communist Party up to 1935. This is primarily a political survey and does not have much material on Mao. Borkenau does however raise questions about the suppression of Li Lisan in 1931 and Mao's subsequent 'police regime' in the Soviet areas, and criticises Edgar Snow for not looking into this aspect of Mao's past.

306. Braunthal, Julius. *The History of the International*. Vol. 3. London: Victor Gollancz, 1980. 600. Chapter 15 (pp. 342-48) provides a very brief summary of the history of the Chinese Communist Party from 1921 to 1949, and incorporates a short survey of Mao's theories of revolution.

307. Chassin, Lionel Max. *L'ascension de Mao Tse-tung, 1921- 1945*. Paris: Payot, 1953. 216. An important work on Mao's role in the revolutionary movement.

308. Chen Chang-feng. *On the Long March with Chairman Mao*. Peking: Foreign Languages Press, 1972. 2nd edition. 124. The reminiscences of Colonel Chen Chang-feng. A rather romantic account from 1930 to 1936. The author appears to have been close to his hero as batman and bodyguard throughout most of the Long March and afterwards in Yanan. Appended to the main text is an article first published in the *People's Daily* describing later meetings with Mao; a reproduction of Mao's autograph in Chen's notebook, and an official summary of the history of the Long March.

309. Chen, Po-ta. *Notes on Mao Tse-tung's 'Report of an investigation into the peasant movement in Hunan.'* Peking: Foreign Languages Press, 1954. 62.

310. _____ *Notes on ten years of civil war, 1927-36.* Peking: Foreign Languages Press, 1954. 108. (Translated from 2nd Chinese edition, published in 1953. First edition was published in 1944). Purports to show how Mao used the theory of Marxism-Leninism to solve the key problems of the Chinese revolution during the Second Revolutionary Civil War, 1927-1936. The author mentions (pp. 105-108) more than a dozen other distinguished propagandists of Marxism-Leninism. They have all died. In any case, 'It is only Comrade Mao Tse-tung who has been able correctly to apply Marxism-Leninism . . . concretely analyse the Chinese Society and . . . the development of the Chinese Revolution.'

311. Cole, G.D.H. *A History of Socialist Thought.* Vol. 4, Part 2. *Communism and Social Democracy 1914-1931.* London: Macmillan, 1961. 940. Chapter 25 provides a summary history of the rise of the Communist party in the 1920's and up to the Long March. Mao's role is discussed in the context of changing Party policies and the leadership struggles. Cole also explains the role played by the Comintern.

312. Elegant, Robert S. *Mao vs. Chiang: the fight for mainland China, 1925-1949.* New York: Grosset, 1969.

313. Fairbank, J. K., ed. *The Cambridge History of China.* Vol. 12. *Republican China 1912-1949, Part 1.* Cambridge: Cambridge University Press, 1983. 1002. Authoritative history with essays covering political, social, economic, intellectual and cultural trends in the period from 1912. The essays with most relevance for a study of Mao are: Jerome Chen 'The Chinese Communist Movement to 1927' (pp. 505-526) and C. Martin Wilbur 'The Nationalist Revolution: from Canton to Nanking, 1923-28' (pp. 527-720). In addition, Benjamin Schwartz's essay 'Themes in Intellectual History: May Fourth and After' (pp. 406-450) ends with a discussion on the ascendancy of Marxism. (See nos. 335, 353, 302).

314. Isaacs, Harold. *The Tragedy of the Chinese Revolution.* London: Secker and Warburg, 1938. 502. An excellent pioneering account of the failures of the Chinese revolutionary movement in its early years.

315. Ishida, Tyoko. *The political leadership of Mao Tse-tung in the Kiangsi Soviet.* Tokyo: University of Tokyo, 1965.

316. Martynov, A. (ed.) *Velikii Pokhod*, (The Great March). Moscow, 1959. A valuable collection of first-hand accounts of the Long March translated into Russian.

317. Peng Shuzhi. *L'Envol du Communisme en Chine*. Paris: Gallimard, 1983. 480. The first volume of Peng Shuzhi's memoires. Valuable as an unofficial history written by a survivor of the first generation of Chinese Communist leaders. The book includes meticulous descriptions of the birth of the communist movement in Changsha, the shaping of the communist nucleus in Shanghai around Chen Duxiu, and portraits of the founders of the C.C.P.

318. Rue, John E. *Mao Tse-tung in Opposition 1927-1935*. Stanford, California: Stanford University Press, 1966. 387. A scholarly and detailed account of the power struggle in the Chinese Communist Party during a period when the Party leadership adhered as closely as possible to the Comintern line. They attacked Mao for his strategy of creating a revolutionary base among the peasantry and for his land reform policies, his guerrilla tactics and his ideology. The title refers to Mao's opposition to Moscow's line on how the Chinese Party should evolve.

319. Salisbury, Harrison. *The Long March: The Untold Story*. London: Macmillan, 1985. 419. Salisbury seeks to tell the full story of the Long March with the support of the Chinese authorities, and uses interviews with survivors of the March, plus archive material. Final chapter on Cultural Revolution asks why Mao turned on his comrades of the Long March.

320. Shaffer, Lynda. *Mao and the Workers. The Hunan Labor Movement, 1920-1923*. Armonk, New York: M.E. Sharpe, 1982. 251. Examines Mao's achievements from late 1920 until the Spring of 1923 as the leader of a successful effort to unionise the workers of Hunan, his own province. In the conclusion the author discusses Mao's response to the 'dilemma of pursuing a labor movement during the national bourgeois stage of the revolution.' She concludes that Mao's experience disillusioned him not with the workers but with the national bourgeoisie. On Mao's affirmation in July 1923 that 'because of historical necessity and current tendencies, the work for which the merchants should be responsible in the national revolution is both more urgent and more important than the work that the rest of the people should take upon themselves,' she draws a different conclusion from that of S. Schram, *Mao Tse-tung*, pp. 73-74.

321. Smedley, Agnes. *China's Red Army Marches.* New York: Vanguard Press, 1934. 315. Stories based on events in which the Red Army took part.

322. Strong, Anna Louise. *China Fights for Freedom*, London: Lindsay Drummond, 1939. 231. An historical overview of the revolutionary movements in China covering Chiang Kai-shek's Nationalists as well as the Communists. Chapter 6 examines the Jiangxi Soviet. Chapters 12 and 13 describe the author's visits to the Eighth Route army and her meetings with Zhu De (Chu Teh) and others.

323. _____ *China's Millions.* New York: Coward-McCann, 1928. 413. A sympathetic view of the problems of China in the 1920's.

324. Tang Leang-Li. *The Inner History of the Chinese Revolution.* London: Routledge, 1930. 365.

325. Trotsky, Leon. *Problems of the Chinese Revolution.* London: New Park Publications, 1969. 354. (Original English language edition published in New York in 1932.) This edition has an Introduction by Tom Kemp in which he considers *inter alia* Mao's policy in relation to Stalinism. Kemp believes that in the controversy over the Chinese Revolution, Trotsky has been 'vindicated all along the line.' He cites 'the theory of the Permanent Revolution which Trotsky defends so ably and exhaustively.'

326. Tuter, Frederic. *The Adventure of Mao on the Long March.* New York: Citadel, 1971. 121.

327. Waller, Derek J. *The Kiangsi Soviet Republic: Mao and the National Congresses of 1931 and 1934.* Berkeley: Center for Chinese Studies, University of California. 114. (China Research Monographs, 10). This monograph begins with an introductory note on the experience of creating a 'soviet area' in Jingangshan, which failed early in 1929, and the establishing of a 'soviet' in Jiangxi (Kiangsi) during 1929. The monograph explores the political processes of establishing the Jiangxi Soviet and the power struggle at the top of the Party, including the switch in 1931 after the downfall of Li Lisan from Party activity in the city to the countryside. Waller argues that by the Second Congress Mao had lost control over the soviet government and that the two Soviet Congresses 'far from being stepping stones on Mao's road to power, were in reality evidence of his temporary decline.' (p. 114).

328. Wang Ming and Kang Hsing. *Das Revolutionare China von Heute.* Moscow-Leningrad: Verlagsgenossenschaft Auslandischer Arbeiter in der USSR, 1934. 94. The current situation in China is expounded from the point of view of the Comintern by two Chinese writers. At a later stage of the revolution Wang Ming was an adversary of Mao in Yanan.

329. Wilbur, C. M. and L. Y. Hsia (eds). *Documents on Communism, Nationalism and Soviet Advisers in China, 1918-1927.* New York: Columbia University Press, 1956. 617. Selection from documents taken from Soviet Embassy in raid by Peking police on 6 April, 1927.

330. Wilson, Dick. *The Long March, 1935. The Epic of Chinese Communist's Survival.* London: Hamish Hamilton, 1971. 331. The author 'has combined an engrossing narrative of battle and suffering and eventual triumph with a succinct critique of a political and ideological era.' The first full-length work on the Long March. Well written but the author did not have access to material which has since become available. See H. Salisbury (no. 319).

331. Womack, Brantly. *The foundations of Mao Zedong's political thought, 1917-1935.* Honolulu: The University Press of Hawaii, 1982. Stops in 1935 and fails to use some key sources on years 1917-1921.

Articles

332. 'Autumn Harvest Uprising.' *Peking Review*, 20, 32 (5 August 1977): 20-27. One of a series of articles on PLA history, this article provides a detailed account of Mao's role in the uprising in September 1927. Photographs of a building, a flag and weapons used.

333. Berkley, Gerald W. 'The Canton Peasant Movement Training Institute.' *Modern China*, 1 (1975): 161-79.

334. Bisson, T. A. 'Communist Movement in China.' *Foreign Policy Reports* (26 April 1933): 38-44. Article including bibliography and map.

335. Chen, Jerome. 'The Chinese Communist Movement to 1927.' *The Cambridge History of China*, vol. 12: 505-526. Republic China 1912-1949, Part 1, ed. John K. Fairbank. Cambridge: Cambridge University Press, 1983. Covers the early Chinese converts to Marxism, the foundation of the Party and the growing tensions inthe united front.

336. _____ 'The Communist Movement 1927-1937.' *The Cambridge History of China*, vol. 13: 168-229. 'Republican China 1912-1949,' Part 2, ed. John K. Fairbank and Albert Feuerwerker. Cambridge: Cambridge University Press, 1986.

337. _____ 'Reflections on the Long March.' *China Quarterly*, no. 111 (September 1987): 450-465. A detailed critique of the article by B. Yang *China Quarterly*, no. 106, 'The Zunyi Conference as one step in Mao's rise to power.'

338. 'Communists in China.' *Far Eastern Review*, 24 (September 1928): 388.

339. Dorrill, William F. 'Transfer of Legitimacy in the Chinese Communist Party: Origins of the Maoist Myth.' *China Quarterly*, no. 36 (October-December 1968): 45-60. Examines the official interpretation of Party history which, claiming that Mao's leadership was established at Zunyi in 1935, attributed previous setbacks to the 'errors' and ideological deviations of other CCP leaders. The author reexamines the Maoist claim to legitimacy at selected key points, notably at the Fourth Plenum and the rise of the Returned Student leadership. He concludes that there must be serious doubts as to the general reliability of the official account of Mao's role in Jiangxi. He adds '. . . we may ponder whether this tampering with the historical record revealed, at a comparatively early stage, significant weaknesses as well as strengths in Mao's character as a leader.'

340. Gurley, J. G. 'Formation of Mao's economic strategy, 1927-1949.' *Monthly Review*, 27 (July 1975): 58-132.

341. Heinzig, Dieter. 'The Otto Braun Memoirs and Mao's Rise to Power.' *China Quarterly*, no. 46 (April-June 1971): 274-288. Examines the value of the new light thrown on the Zunyi Conference by Otto Braun's memoirs.

342. Hu, Chi-hsi. 'Mao, Lin Biao and the Fifth encirclement campaign.' (With translation of 'On the short, swift thrusts' by Lin Biao), *China Quarterly*, no. 82 (June 1980): 250-80. The author examines the true extent of Mao's influence in the Red Army during this crucial campaign, against the claims made in Mao's 'Problems of strategy in guerilla war against Japan' (*Selected Works*, Chinese edition, Beijing 1966, p. 396) and in the light of Lin Biao's article from *War and Revolution*, which (originally published in July 1934) was read to Edgar Snow in 1936 (see: E. Snow *Random Notes on Red China, 1936-1945*, Cambridge, Mass: Harvard University Press, 2nd edition, p. 30). Who really developed the concept of

'when the enemy advances we retreat . . .? Why was Lin Biao apparently arguing for the development of a 'blockhouse' strategy at that time? What was the role of Otto Braun? Was Lin Biao in his article 'waving the red flag to oppose the red flag'? Hu considers these and other questions.

343. Kampen, Thomas. 'The Zunyi Conference and Further Steps in Mao's Rise to Power.' *China Quarterly*, no. 117 (March 1989): 118-134. Following the article by Benjamin Yang *China Quarterly*, no. 106 (see no. 354), the author gives additional details, provides a new interpretation and gives some explanation for the difficulties in studying this period of Communist Party history. *Inter alia*, he shows that Mao's rise was never as dramatic and final as he and his supporters would have liked.

344. Li Ang. 'Mao Tse-tung and Chu Te.' *Prospect*, no. 190 (1 January 1970): Hong Kong. Li Ang first met Mao in 1921 in Shanghai. He later withdrew from the Party. Includes some intriguing anecdotes about the young Mao.

345. 'Long March of Mao Tse-tung' (with map). *Far Eastern Economic Review*, 93 (17 September 1976): 1-8.

346. McDonald, Angus W., Jr. 'The Hunan Peasant Movement: its urban origins.' *Modern China*, 1.2 (April 1975): 180-203.

347. 'Moscow, Wang Ching-wei and the Chinese Communists.' *China Weekly Review*, 53 (16 August 1930): 399-401. In the 1920's, Wang Jingwei was a member of the Executive Bureau of the Guomindang. Mao worked with him for a time in coordinating the measures of the Communist Party and the Guomindang. In 1940, Wang defected to the Japanese.

348. Roy, Manabendra Nath. 'Lessons of the Chinese Revolution.' *Labour Monthly*, 9 (November 1927): 660-68.

349. _____ 'Mao Tse-tung: a reminiscence.' *New Republic*, 125 (September 1951): 14-15.

350. Schram, Stuart R. 'Mao Zedong and the Role of the Various Classes in the Chinese Revolution, 1923-1927' in *Chugoku no seiji to keizai/The Polity and Economy of China* (The Late Professor Yuji Muramatsu Commemoration Volume). Tokyo: Toyo Keizai Shinposha, 1975. 227-239.

351. _____ 'On the Nature of Mao Tse-tung's "Deviation" in 1927.' *China Quarterly*, no. 18 (April-June, 1964): 55-66. Discusses Mao's role in the autumn of 1927 in relation to Chinese Communist Party Central Committee resolution of November 1927 censoring Mao for his 'purely military viewpoint,' and Mao's policy towards the organisation of rural Soviets. Schram argues that Mao's memoirs as dictated to Edgar Snow are correct in their interpretation of his role in 1927 and that Mao was to the 'left' of the Comintern in this period not to the 'right' as claimed by Wittfogel (see no. 891). Schram also reflects on wider questions of Mao's originality as a Marxist strategist.

352. Steiner, Leo. (Translator). 'The Declaration of the Chinese Communist Party on the Political Situation.' *Novyi Vostok* (The New East) (1922), no. 2. 600-612.

353. Wilbur, C. Martin. 'The Nationalist Revolution: from Canton to Nanking, 1923-28.' *The Cambridge History of China*, vol. 12: 527-721. Republican China Part 1, ed. John K. Fairbank. Cambridge: Cambridge University Press, 1987. A detailed account of the revolutionary movement and the respective efforts of the nationalists and the communists through the years of the united front to the split. Puts Mao's work in context.

354. Yang, B. 'The Zunyi Conference as one step in Mao's rise to power: a survey of historical studies of the Chinese Communist Party.' *China Quarterly*, no. 106 (June 1986): 235-71. 'This article is based on a critical study of publications in the West and, particularly, in China, in an effort to give a factual account of the Zunyi Conference and an analysis of the concomitant rise to power of Mao Zedong.' The author concludes that 'Mao was not so powerless before the Conference, nor did he become so dominant after it.' In appendices there are translations of conference documents based on the official 'Materials on C.C.P. history' published in Beijing in 1983, and the 'Documental Materials of the Zunyi Conference,' 1985.

355. Yang, B. and Jerome Chen. 'Resolutions of the Tsunyi Conference.' *China Quarterly*, no. 40 (1969): 1-38. Based on Taiwanese and Western accounts, subsequently shown to be inaccurate. See Benjamin Yang's article in *China Quarterly*, no. 106 (see no. 354) and T. Kampen's article in *China Quarterly*, no. 117 (see no. 343).

VII. 1935 to 1949

Books

356. Alley, Rewi. *Six Americans in China*. Beijing: International Culture Publishing Corporation, 1985. 234. The author who has been in China for 57 years knew his six subjects personally: Ma Haide (George Hatem), Edgar Snow, Anne Louise Strong, Agnes Smedley, Joseph Warren Stillwell and Evans Fordyce Carlson. Very readable account with personal remniscencies set in the story of China's revolutionary struggles.

357. Band, Claire and William. *Dragon Fangs: Two Years with Chinese Guerrillas*. London: Allen and Unwin, 1947. 347. Experiences with guerilla forces fighting the Japanese. Chapter XVI 'Yenan Diary' has comments on Mao by 'Elder Hsu'--one of his former teachers.

358. Barber, Noel. *The Fall of Shanghai. The Communist Take-Over in 1949*. London: Macmillan, 1979. 251. A lively account of how the city fell into the hands of the Communists. Some insights into morale in the cities as the revolutionary forces advanced.

359. Belden, Jack. *China Shakes the World*. Harmondsworth, Middlesex: Penguin, 1970. 686. This is a classic account of the Civil War 1946-1949 from inside the Chinese Communist lines. Belden was an experienced American war reporter who had spent several years in China in the 1930's. Beldon looks at the growth of Communist influence primarily from the viewpoint of the peasants or the Red Army rank and file.

360. Bertram, James. *North China Front*. London: Macmillan, 1939. 514. Based on the author's travels in Japan and North China in the first year of the Sino-Japanese war. Describes interviews with Mao, Zhou Enlai and Zhu De. Photographs.

361. Bisson, T. A. *Yenan in June 1937: Talks with the Communist Leaders*. Berkeley: University of California Press, 1973. 72. Bisson was an American intellectual who interviewed Mao in Yanan a year after Edgar Snow. This monograph reprints Bisson's notebooks. Introduction by Owen Lattimore.

362. Braun, Otto. *A Comintern Agent in China, 1932-1939*. London: C. Hurst, 1982. 278. Translated by Jeanne Moore. (Published in German as *Chinesische Aufzeichnungen*, Berlin, GDR: Dietz Berlag, 1973. Introduction by Dick Wilson. Braun was Comintern military adviser to the Chinese Communists from 1932, and was the only Westerner to take part in the Long March. He played an active role as military adviser up to 1936, when he was blamed by Mao for the forced evacuation of Jiangxi in 1934; but was not recalled by Moscow for another three years. Braun used the Chinese name Li De and is mentioned by that name in Edgar Snow's *Red Star Over China*. Braun was ordered by Moscow to remain silent about his activities in China, and did so until 1964, when he wrote an article in *Neues Deutschland* attacking Mao. Braun broke his silence to promote the campaign against Maoism being waged by the Soviet bloc in the mid-1960's. But Braun's book is believed by experts to tell a genuine story and is an interesting commentary on the Chinese Communist leadership and on the events of that period. Braun and Mao developed a strong dislike of each other. Mao claimed Braun was too authoritarian and dominated military decision-making, and excluded him from meetings in Yanan. According to Braun, Mao tried to have him liquidated on his return to Moscow.

363. Carlson, Evans Fordyce. *Twin Stars of China*. New York: Dodd, Mead and Co., 1940. Book by U.S. Brigadier who observed Chinese guerilla resistance to Japan in 1938 and was impressed by the confidence of the Communist officers and troops.

364. Chassin, L. M. *The Communist Conquest of China: a history of the civil war, 1945-9*. London: Donald Moore Books, 1965. 264. First published in France in 1952 as *La Conquete de la Chine par Mao Tse-toung*. The author did most of the research for this book as Vice-Chief of Staff for National Defence, 1946-49, and thus, had the best French information, notably the reports of the Deuxieme Bureau. 'General Chassin traces the rise of Mao's forces from their beginnings in the Ching Kang (Jinggang) Mountains to their emergence as one of the most formidable armies in the world.' Includes detailed descriptions of key battles.

365. Chen, Yung fa. *Making revolution: the Communist movement in eastern and central China, 1937-1945*. London: University of California Press, 1986. Shows how middle- and lower-level CCP cadres operated in the field, using previously under-researched collections of inner-Party documents held in Taiwan. In commenting on the writings of Mark Selden and Chalmers Johnson, Chen shows that their conclusions have been too generalized. After

1941 new leaders, Liu Shaoqi and Chen Yi, applied the Maoist strategy, developed around Yanan, to central and eastern China.

366. Cole, G.D.H. *A History of Socialist Thought*. Vol. 5. *Socialism and Fascism 1931-1939*. London: Macmillan, 1961. 350. Chapter 12 covers 'Communism in China in the 1930s.' Mao is at the centre of this analysis. Cole examines Mao's role in establishing regional Soviets and his theoretical justifications of his strategy, in particular Mao's work *On New Democracy* published in 1941.

367. Fairbank, John K. and Albert Feuerwerker, eds. The Cambridge History of China. Vol. 13. *Republican China* 1912-1949, Part 2. Much of this volume has a bearing on Mao's thought and his revolutionary strategy. The most relevant chapters are: Jerome Chen 'The Communist Movement 1927-1937' (pp. 168-229); Lyman Van Slyke 'The Chinese Communist movement during the Sino-Japanese War 1937-1945' (pp. 609-722); Suzanne Pepper 'The KMT-CCP conflict 1945-1949' (pp. 723-788); and Stuart Schram 'Mao Tse-tung's Thought to 1949' (pp. 789-870). (See nos. 336, 428, 416, 868).

368. Gibbons, David Sprague. *Dominant political leadership and political integration in a transitional society: China, Chiang Kai-shek and Mao Tse-tung, 1935-1949*. Princeton, N.J.: Princeton University, 1968. 459. This PhD thesis explores the role of political leadership in imposing order on a divided society and promoting modernisation. Chapter 4 covers Mao's political socialization and rise to power and examines his personaltiy and leadership style as displayed in 1935. Chapter 5 compares the leadership role of Mao and Jiang (Chiang) between 1935 and 1949.

369. Han, Suyin. *Birdless Summer*. London: Cape, 1968. 347. The third volume of autobiography covers the period 1938 to 1948. Her life is interwoven with the great events of those years in China.

370. Johnson, Chalmers. *Peasant Nationalism and Communist Power. The Emergence of Revolutionary China, 1937-1945*. Stanford, California: Stanford University Press, 1962. 256. Stresses the importance of nationalism and resistance to the Japanese.

371. Lattimore, Owen. *The Situation in Asia*. Boston: Little, Brown, 1949. 238. A perceptive assessment of political prospects. Lattimore points out that the coalition government to be established in China in 1949 will be much more communist dominated than would have been the case in a coalition in

1946 if the United States had not continued to give military aid to Chiang Kai-shek. In the 1949 coalition the non-Communists 'can expect to wield no more than moderate influence.'

372. Payne, Robert. *Journey to Red China*. London: William Heinemann, 1947. 196. Based on a visit to Yanan in 1946 during the short-lived truce between Communists and Nationalists. Includes interviews with Zhu De in which he says 'Chinese communism is democracy plus capital' with Peng Teh-huei, and with Hsiao San, who reminisced about Mao who he remembered as a young man. A readable atmospheric account. Payne writes 'the agrarian revolution is being carried out by men who call themselves Communists but whose agrarian practices seem to approach nothing more radical than old-fashioned liberalism.'

373. Schaller, Michael. *The U.S. Crusade in China*, 1938-1945. New York: Columbia University Press, 1979. 364. Includes a detailed account of American covert actions.

374. Selden, Mark. *The Yenan Way in Revolutionary China*. Cambridge, Mass: Harvard University Press, 1971. 310. Analyses the philosophical basis of Mao's government in North-West China in the late 30's and 40's. Sees Maoism as offering a new form of revolution.

375. Service, John S. *Lost Chance in China. The World War II Despatches of John S. Service*. New York: Random House, 1974. 409. Includes detailed accounts of conditions in the Communist held areas of China and some insights on the leadership including Mao.

376. Smedley, Agnes. *Battle Hymn of China*. London: Victor Gollancz, 1944. 365. Based on the author's experiences in China, in Yanan and with the Eighth Route Army.

377. _____ *China Fights Back: An American Woman with the Eighth Route Army*. London: Victor Gollancz, 1938. 286. Shows the Eighth Route Army in the detailed problems of its combats in north Shaanxi. Her lively reporting includes close-ups of Lin Biao and Zhu De.

378. Snow, Edgar. *Journey to the Beginning*. London: Victor Gollancz Ltd, 1959. 434. Edgar Snow's reminiscences on his years in China include an account of his meetings with Mao in Shaanxi.

379. Snow, Helen Foster. *Inside Red China*. New York: Da Capo Press, 1979. 356. A reprint of the 1939 edition published by Doubleday, Doran, New York, this is an unabridged republication of the enlarged edition published in New York in 1977 supplemented with a new introduction by Harrison Salisbury. Helen Snow, then wife of Edgar Snow, published this, her first book, under the pen name *Nym Wales*. (Nym means name; Wales because she was part Welsh). It is, like Snow's *Red Star*, a classic first-hand account of a revolutionary era. Reporting from Yanan after the Long March, she gives painstaking attention to biographic detail, and seems to have met every Communist leader of consequence of the 1930's.

380. _____ *My China Years*. London: Harrap, 1984. 349. This book is about her life in China with Edgar Snow. Part III, 'Yenan,' describes her trips to the Communist area in 1937. Chapter 35 describes meetings with Mao, Zhu De and Zhou Enlai.

381. _____ *Red Dust*: autobiographies of Chinese Communists as told to Nym Wales (pseudonym). Stanford, California: Stanford University Press, 1952. 238.

382. Stein, Gunther. *The Challenge of Red China*. New York: McGraw Hill, 1945. 490. The author was correspondent for the *Manchester Guardian* and the *Christian Science Monitor*. He visited Yanan and had extensive interviews with Mao. Some excellent photographs and some wood-cuts produced by the Art College of Yanan University.

383. Thaxton, Ralph. *China Turned Rightside Up: Revolutionary Legitimacy in the Peasant World*. New Haven: Yale University Press, 1983. 266. The author believes that modern writers have tended to 'minimize the impact of peasant initiatives on the course of revolutionary events in the countryside.' On the contrary, he tries to show that the 'peasants were preparing the ground in which the Communist Party would grow.'

384. Van Slyke, Lyman P. *The Chinese Communist Movement. A Report of the United States War Department, July 1945*. Stanford, California: Stanford University Press, 1968. 274. Originally published in 1952, in slightly different form, as an appendix to the official transcript of the 1951 Senate hearings on the Institute of Pacific Relations. This report, commissioned by the Military Intelligence Division of the War Department, was completed in June 1945, classified Secret and submitted to the Chief of the Military Intelligence Service, Brigadier General Paul E. Peabody. Peabody drew up his own covering statement (see appendix). The report went virtually

unnoticed until 1949 when the publication of Dean Acheson's White paper in China created a furore. Representative Walter Judd, long-time admirer of Chiang Kai-shek, attacked the White Paper, charging that the State Department had deliberately omitted the Peabody Summary.

385. Van der Sprenkel, Otto, ed. *New China: Three Views*. London: Turnstile Press, 1950. 241. Essays covering the Maoist victory and founding of a new regime in 1949. Prints Mao's well known speech of June 1949, 'On people's Democratic Dictatorship.'

386. Wales, Nym (Helen Foster Snow). *My Yenan notebooks*. Madison, Conn: 1961.

387. Wang, Anna. *J'ai combattu pour Mao*. Paris: Gallimard, 1967. 306. Translated from German by Magda Michel. The author was a young German woman who married the Chinese Communist Wang Pingnan and lived in China from 1936 to 1955. Her memoirs relate her own experiences to historical developments in the period 1936-1945 and includes a visit to Yanan, where she met Mao.

388. White, Theodore H. and Annalee Jacoby. *Thunder Out of China*. First published, New York: 1946. Reprinted with foreword by Harrison Salisbury, New York: Da Capo, 1980. 345. This is a report by White on his time in China, 1939-1945. Shows how Communists won popular support.

389. Wylie, Raymond F. *The emergence of Maoism: Mao Tse-tung, Ch'en Po-ta and the search for Chinese theory 1935-1945*. Stanford, California: Stanford University Press, 1980. 351. The author's analysis of politics with CCP falls into two periods: 1935-40, when basic ideas of Chinese Marxism were developed; and, 1940-45 when Mao and Chen Boda worked to establish Mao's thought as the official party line.

390. Yen Chang-lin. *In His Mind a Million Bold Warriors: Reminiscences of the Life of Chairman Mao Tse-tung during the Northern Shensi Campaign*. Peking: Foreign Languages Press, 1972. See also *Chinese Literature* (Peking) 1, 2, 1961: 3-43-3-39.

Articles

391. Barnett, R. W. 'Interview with Chou En-Lai on the Prospects of Civil War in China.' *Amerasia*, 5 (7 May 1941): 123-27.

392. Chen, Po-ta. 'Commemorating the 25th anniversary of Chairman Mao's "Talks at the Yenan Forum on Literature and Art".' *Peking Review*, 10 (May 1967), no. 22, 20-24.

393. Chiang Shan. 'Edgar Snow and his "Red Star Over China".' *Peking Review*, 21, 16 (21 April 1978): 20-22. Describes Edgar Snow's visits to northern Shaanxi.

394. 'Chinese Communists and their Programme.' *World Today*, 5 (February 1949): 71-80. Article based on author's own experience in some Communist-controlled areas in 1944, and supplemented by broadcasts from the Communist area and other sources. Notes the favourable reports on Communist role from foreign correspondents and U.S. Army observers allowed into Communist areas by National Government in 1944. Article assesses 'democratic governments' at different levels within 'liberated Areas,' land reform and economic conditions. Article on communist system, not on Mao or individual personalities.

395. Chou En-lai. 'Learn from Mao Tse-tung--Excerpts from the third part of a report at the First All-China Youth Congress on May 7, 1949.' Peking Review, 21, 43 (2 October 1978): 7-15. Chou explains how the youth of China can learn from Mao's style of study and style of work to 'be honest, seek truth from facts, work in a down-to-earth way and advance steadily and valiantly.' In an overview of Mao's career he shows how 'Mao has persisted in giving the universal truth of Marxism-Leninism concrete expression on Chinese soil.'

396. 'Development on China's United Front: Chou En-lai's statement on the Activities of the Eighth Route Army; with Editorial Reply in the Ta Kung Pao and subsequent article by Chou En-lai.' Excerpts. *Amerasia*, 5 (June 1941): 167-72.

397. Garver, John W. 'The Origins of the Second United Front. The Comintern and the Chinese Communist Party.' *China Quarterly*, no. 113 (March 1988): 29-59. Reexamines Mao's attitude to Moscow's pressure for the Chinese Communists to join the United Front in the light of newly available C.C.P. documents and periodical literature in China. It is now clear that talks began as early as the Autumn of 1935 and that the Soviet Union played a pivotal role. Why did Mao give way? (1) Because his own position was still weak relative to the C.C.P. Internationalists who were not eliminated until the Zheng Feng movement, 1942-44. (2) He still hoped to get material assistance from the Russians at some point. (3) Mounting

nationalist pressure in China was probably the most important factor. Mao's standing as a genuine Chinese patriot is confirmed.

398. Green, O. M. 'Communism and China War.' *Great Britain and the East*, 53 (28 September 1939): 292.

399. Hanson, H. 'People Behind the Chinese Guerillas.' *Pacific Affairs*, 11. (September 1938): 285-98.

400. Hsia, T. A. 'Twenty Years After the Yenan Forum.' *China Quarterly*, no. 13 (January-March 1963): 226-253. 'The Yenan Forum was a major event in the determination of the nature of future Chinese Communist literature. For the first time in history, the Chinese Communist Party could boast of a "policy for literature and art". All writers under the control of that policy were henceforth obliged to conform.'

401. Hsu, M. H. (translator). 'Chinese red explains communism: interview.' *China Weekly Review* (Shanghai) 86 (10 September 1938): 54-5.

402. Hsu, Y. 'Government of Yenan; a study of a Chinese Communist Area.' *Science and Society*, 9, 4 (1945): 289-317.

403. Isaacs, H. R. 'Perspectives of the Chinese Revolution: a Marxist view.' *Pacific Affairs*, 8 (September 1935): 269-83. See also reply by H. Chan, *Pacific Affairs*, 8 (December 1935): 477-81.

404. 'Kuomintang versus Soviets.' *Labour Monthly*, 14 (July-August 1932): 450-58 and 514-20.

405. Kyoko, Tanaka. 'Mao and Liu in the 1947 land reform: allies or disputants?' *China Quarterly*, no. 75 (September 1978): 566-93. Examines three major questions: (1) to what extent the CCP leadership was split over agrarian policy; (2) whether or not Mao represented a moderate policy and Liu a radical one, as alledged in the 1960's; (3) why 'left deviations' took place? The author concludes that both men came eventually (by mid-1948) to realise that poor peasant expectations could not be reconciled with the protection of middle peasant interests. He concludes 'Their alleged split over the 1947 land reform and rectification seems to be more an *ex post facto* explanation than a fact.'

406. Lattimore, Owen. 'Unpublished Report from Yenan, 1937.' In *Studies in the Social History of China and South-east Asia: Essays in Memory of*

Victor Purcell, edited by Jerome Chen and Nicholas Tarling. Cambridge: Cambridge University Press, 1970. 153-164.

407. Leaf, E. H. "Rustling silks and padded cotton.' *China Weekly Review* 83 (25 December 1937): supplement. On Mao Zechen (Ho), Mao Zedong's wife.

408. Lee, Leo Ou-Fan. 'Literary Trends: The Road to Revolution 1927-1949.' *The Cambridge History of China*, vol. 13: 421-91. 'Republican China 1912-1949,' Part 2, ed. John K. Fairbank and Albert Feuerwerker. Cambridge: Cambridge University Press, 1986. Covers the Yanan Forum on Literature and Art convened by Mao in May 1942.

409. Lieberthal, Kenneth. 'Mao versus Liu? Policy towards Industry and Commerce: 1946-49.' *China Quarterly*, no. 47 (July/September 1971): 494-520. Article evaluates charges made during the Cultural Revolution that Mao Zedong and Liu Shaoqi differed in their views of urban revolution in China after liberation, in particular the differences that emerged during Liu's visit to Tientsin in April-May 1949. Suggests these differences almost certainly trumped up in Cultural Revolution by selective quotes.

410. Liden, David Leroy. 'Party Factionalism and Revolutionary Vision: Cadre Training and Mao Tse-tung's Effort to consolidate His Control of the Chinese Communist Party, 1936-1944.' Ph.D. dissertation, University of Michigan, 1978.

411. Lindsay, M. 'Post-war Government and Politics of Communist China.' *Journal of Politics*, 9 (November 1947): 543-64.

412. 'New situation in China.' *Labour Monthly*, 21 (September- October 1939): 437-44; 553-60; 629-36.

413. North, R. C. and J. H. Paasche. 'China in the world revolution.' *Far Eastern Survey*, 18 (27 July 1949): 172-3. About the rise of Mao Zedong.

414. Okazaki, S. 'Moscow, Yenan, Chungking.' Translated by A. J. Grajdanzeu. *Pacific Affairs*, 14 (March 1941): 107-12.

415. Palmer, Norman D. 'Mao Tse-tung: Red star.' *Current History*, N.S. 16 (1949): 86-92.

416. Pepper, Suzanne. 'The KMT-CCP Conflict 1945-1949.' *The Cambridge History of China*, Vol. 13, 723-88. 'Republican China 1912-1949.' Part 2, ed. John K. Fairbank and Albert Feuerwerker. Cambridge: Cambridge University Press, 1986.

417. Schwartz, Benjamin. 'On the "originality" of Mao Tse-tung.' *Foreign Affairs*, 34, no 1 (October 1955): 67-76. Article on 3 volumes of Mao's *Selected Works* available in English through New York International Publishers 1954 and 1955. Notes some tampering with Mao's texts and editorial slant of foot notes. Suggests *Works* may shed further light on role of '. . . shadowy group known as "the returned student faction" or "28 Bolsheviks"' (see 'Strategic Problems of China's Revolutionary War' 1936 and 'Resolutions on Some Problems of the History of our Party' 1945 in Mao's *Works*. Notes circumstantial evidence Stalin supported '28 Bolsheviks' 1931-35. *Works* also throws light on Mao's attitudes to United Front policy in period of 1931-37. Schwartz says *Works* was designed to give Mao the role of 'philosopher-king' in Marxist tradition like Lenin and Stalin.

418. 'Spread of Communism in China and Leaders of Communist China; Some Aspects of the Civil War; Photographs and Maps.' *Illustrated London News*, 212 (17 January 1948): 74-75.

419. Snow, E. 'Chinese Communists and wars on two continents: interviews.' *China Weekly Review*, 91 (13-20 January 1940): 244-46, 277-80.

420. Snow, E. 'Interview with Mao Tse-tung, Communist leader.' *China Weekly Review*, 78 (14-21 November 1936): 377-79.

421. Stevens, C. R. 'Content analysis of the wartime writings of Chiang Kai-shek and Mao Tse-tung.' *Asian Survey*, 4 (June 1964): 890-903.

422. Strong, A. L. 'Eighth Route Regions in North China.' *Pacific Affairs*, 14 (June 1941): 154-65.

423. _____ 'Kuomintang--Communist Crisis in China.' *Amerasia*, 5 (March 1941): 11-23.

424. _____'Thought of Mao Tse-tung.' *Amerasia*, 11 (June 1947): 161-74.

425. _____'World's eye view from a Yenan cave: interview with chairman of the Chinese Communist Party.' *Amerasia*, 11 (April 1947): 122-26.

426. Tang, Peter S. H. 'Stalin's role in the communist victory in China.' *American Slavic and East European Review*, 13 (1954), no. 3. 375-388.

427. Thompson, D. W. 'Chinese Rural Construction.' *London Quarterly Review*, 161 (April 1936): 175-85.

428. Van Slyke, Lyman. 'The Chinese Communist Movement during the Sino-Japanese War 1937-1948.' 609-722. *The Cambridge History of China*, Vol. 13. 'Republican China 1912-1949; Part 2, ed. John K. Fairbank and Albert Feuerwerker. Cambridge: Cambridge University Press, 1986.

429. Wales, Nym (Helen Foster Snow). 'Why the Chinese Communists Support the United Front; Interview with Lo Fu.' *Pacific Affairs*, 11 (September 1938): 311-22.

430. Yutang, Lin. 'Conflict in China: role of Mao Tse-tung.' *Far Eastern Survey*, 14 (18 July 1945): 194-95.

VIII. 1949 to 1959

Books

431. Asian Peoples' Anti-Communist League, Republic of China. *Mao Tse-tung and 'let a hundred flowers bloom and a hundred schools of thought contend' campaign.* Taipei, 1958. 52.

432. Asian Peoples' Anti-Communist League, Republic of China. *Mao Tse-tung can never be a Tito.* Taipei, 1957. 61.

433. Asian Peoples' Anti-Communist League, Republic of China. *Mao's regime as I see it.* Taipei, 1958.

434. Asian Peoples' Anti-Communist League, Republic of China. *A perspective review of the Maoist regime's rearmament and war preparations.* Taipei, 1970. 82.

435. Barnett, A. Doak. *Communist China: The Early Years 1949-1955.* New York: Praeger, 1964. 336. A detailed history of the period from Liberation to the eve of the Great Leap Forward.

436. Cameron, James. *Mandarin Red. A Journey behind the 'Bamboo Curtain.'* New York: Rinehart, 1955. 334.

437. Chao, Kuo-chun. *Agrarian Policy of the Chinese Communist Party.* London: Asia Publishing House, 1960. 399. A detailed study of the stages in the evolution of the agrarian policies of the Chinese Communist Party. Appendices include: 'Model Regulations for Advanced Agricultural Producers Co-operatives, 30 June 1956.' 'Revised Draft Programs on Agricultrual Development in the Nation, 1957-1967, 25 October 1957.' 'Resolution on Some Questions Concerning the People's Communes 10 December 1958.' 'Press Communique on the Progress of China's National Economy in 1959, 22 January 1960' which concludes 'The great achievements of 1959 powerfully testify to the absolute correctness of the general line for building socialism, the big leap forward rate of development and the people's commune form of organization, all of which were proposed

by the Chinese Communist Party and Comrade Mao Tse-tung.' 'On the basis of the great triumph of 1959, the workers, peasants and revolutionary intellectuals are confidently striving for a continued leap forward in the national economy in 1960, for catching up with the level of Britain within ten years . . ..'

438. Domes, Jurgen. *Peng Te-huai: The Man and the Image*. London: C. Hurst and Co. 1985. 164. An important biography of the man who challenged Mao over the Great Leap Forward and thus destroyed his own career. Shows how, as China's first minister of defence, Peng introduced professionalisation of the officer corps and regularisation of the ranks, which were at variance with the policies of Mao and Lin Biao.

439. Doolin, Dennis J. (Translator). *Communist China: the Politics of Student Opposition*. Stanford: The Hoover Institution, 1964. Translated texts of student speeches and wall posters during the Hundred Flowers period.

440. *Duplicity of Mao's 'bloom-contend' policy*. Taipei: Free China Review, 1957. 112.

441. Eskelund, Karl. *The Red Mandarins. Travels in Red China*. London: Alvin Redman, 1959. 175. Based on a three month visit in 1956-1957. Chapter 18, 'The Will of the People' refers to the beginning of the Hundred Flowers movement. Relates on pp. 150-151, Mao's anecdote, 'How to make a cat eat pepper.'

442. Floyd, David. *Mao against Khrushchev: A Short History of the Sino-Soviet Conflict*. London: Pall Mall Press, 1964. 456. Brief background on relations between CPSU and Chinese Communists and relations between Stalin and Mao. The bulk of the book traces the evolution of Soviet-Chinese relations from 1953 to 1963, when the Sino-Soviet rift was complete. Part 2 provides a Chronology of Documents and Significant Events, including the texts of or extracts from key documents. This is a book focussing on foreign policy. There is little on Mao himself. Part 2 prints extracts from Mao's article on Stalin in *Pravda* 10 March, 1953: 'The Greatest Friendship,' pp. 217-18.

443. Hinton, Harold C. *Communist China in World Politics*. London: Macmillan, 1966. 527. A good overview of the foreign policy of the People's Republic. Part Two 'Communist China on the World Stage' has a chapter on 'Maoism.'

444. Hinton, William. *Fanshen: A Documentary of Revolution in a Chinese Village*. New York: Random, 1968. 656. Having worked in China for UNRRA Hinton stayed on in the Liberated Area of North China as a tractor technician and teacher until 1953. Living in Long Bow he gathered the material for this classic work.

445. Khrushchev, Nikita, *Khrushchev Remembers*. 2. vols. Translated by Strobe Talbott. London: Deutsch, 1971 and 1974. Vol. 1, 639. Vol. 2, 603. In vol. 1, chapter 18 Khrushchev gives his personal version of the relations between Mao and the Soviet leadership and the causes of the Sino-Soviet split. Khrushchev claims: 'Ever since I met Mao I've known . . . that Mao would never be able to reconcile himself to any other Communist Party being in any way superior to his own . . ..' Khrushchev recalls various meetings with Mao and comments on Mao's domestic and foreign policies. In vol. 2, chapter 11, Khrushchev reverts to the origins of the Sino-Soviet split and his meetings with Mao and gives more detail about Stalin's treatment of Mao and the Chinese Party after 1949. Khrushchev also comments on developments since his own fall from power, for example, the conflict over the Sino-Soviet border and the Cultural Revolution. Although covering a wide period, both volumes of Khruschev's memoires concentrate particularly on the 1950's.

446. MacFarquhar, Roderick, ed. *China Under Mao: Politics Takes Command*. Cambridge, Mass.: The M.I.T. Press, 1966. 525. Comprises twenty-four articles previously published in *China Quarterly* covering all aspects of Chinese life since 1949.

447. MacFarquhar, Roderick. *The Hundred Flowers Campaign and the Chinese Intellectuals*. New York: Praeger, 1960. 324. A detailed account of the aborted liberalisation of the intellectuals in 1957. Includes many translated extracts.

448. _____ *The Origins of the Cultural Revolution, 1: Contradictions Among the People 1956-1957*. London: Oxford University Press, 1974. 439. Excellent scholarly account.

449. _____ *The Origins of the Cultural Revolution, 2: The Great Leap Forward 1958-1960*. London: Oxford University Press, 1983. 470. Excellent pioneering work based on the latest available materials.

450. MacFarquhar, Roderick and John K. Fairbank (eds.) *The Cambridge History of China*, vol. 14. The People's Republic, Part 1: The Emergence of

Revolutionary China 1949-1965. Cambridge: Cambridge University Press, 1987. 722. Includes chapters by Merle Goldman (2), Mineo Nakajima, Kenneth Lieberthal, Nicholas Lardy, Suzanne Pepper. (See nos. 471, 472, 485, 480, 479, 489.)

451. Moraes, Frank. *Report on Mao's China.* New York: MacMillan Co., 1953. 212. The author reports on a tour of China, April to June 1952 as a member of the Government of India's cultural delegation. His personal impressions are quite wide-ranging and informative. Includes a brief account of a meeting with Mao, and, later, compares Mao to Gandhi and Nehru.

452. Schwartz, Benjamin I. *Communism and China.* Cambridge, Mass.: Harvard University Press, 1968. 254. A study of politics and polemics in the 1950's and 60's, including the Hundred Flowers Movement, the 'Maoist Vision,' and the 'Maoist Image of World Order.'

453. Snow, Edgar. *Red China Today: The Other Side of the River.* Harmondsworth, Middlesex: Penguin Books, 1970. 749. This is a revised edition, with a new preface 'China in the 1970s,' of a book first published by Random House in 1962 in which Edgar Snow went back to China and described the changes taking place. A wide-ranging book, with flashbacks to the 1930's, but concerned especially with the 1950's.

454. Teines, Frederick C. *Leadership, Legitimacy and Conflict in China.* London: Macmillan, 1984. 167. Three essays analysing 'leadership politics at the apex of the Chinese system.' The first says that the concept of the 'two-line struggle' is inadequate for understanding the politics of the People's Republic between 1949 and 1976, because it 'seriously underestimates Mao and overestimates the cohesion of other political leaders.' The second essay looks at the problem of legitimacy, and in particular the perceptions of the party elite. The third essay examines the guidelines for political behaviour, both 'normative' and 'prudential.'

455. _____ *Politics and Purges in China: Rectification and the Decline of Party Norms 1950-1965.* White Plains, New York: M.E. Sharpe, 1979. 730. The author shows that from 1949 to the Cultural Revolution elite behaviour was guided by a defined set of organisational norms. 'Mao . . . who made these understandings an integral part of his leadership in the early 1940's, reaffirmed them on numerous occasions in the 1950-65 period. Nevertheless, it was Mao's actions in the years preceding the Cultural Revolution which gravely weakened the norms, and his decision which shattered them in 1966.'

456. Wei, Wen-ch'i. *Mao Tse-tung's 'lean-to-one-side' policy*. Lackland Air Force Base, Texas, Air Force Personnel & Training Research Center, Air Research & Development Command. 1955. 52.

457. Warner, Denis Ashton. *Hurricane from China*. New York: Macmillan, 1961. 210. The author analyses the 'threat' that China under Mao poses to the rest of the world. He examines China's relations with the Soviet Union, and the prospects for revolution in the Third World. He estimates that by 1981 'China will rank third amongst the great military powers of the world *and an easy first in militancy.*' (Author's italics). He believes that to Mao 'the world is a great guerrilla battlefield.' The title is taken from the first line of a poem, written by Guo Xiaoquan in 1960 to celebrate Hate America Week. 'The hurricane against U.S. imperialism sweeps across heaven and earth.'

458. Winnington, Alan. *Breakfast with Mao. Memoirs of a Foreign Correspondent*. London: Lawrence and Wishart, 1986. 255. Very little on Mao but shows the views of a disillusioned reporter on the Hundred Flowers movement and the Great Leap Forward. Argues that Mao was 'not a major theorist, social philosopher or economist.' His concern was always with pressing issues and political in-fighting. He was 'eclectic.'

459. Wittfogel, Karl August. *Mao Tse-tung, liberator or destroyer of the Chinese peasants?* New York: Free Trade Union Committee, American Federation of Labor, 1955. 22.

460. Ying, Esther Cheo. *Black Country Girl in Red China*. London: Hutchinson, 1980. 190. The author, daughter of an English working-class mother and Chinese father, spent the war years in England and returned to China in February 1949 at the age of 17. Describes her life in China in the 1950's including her relationship with Alan Winnington.

Articles

461. Bernal, Martin Gardiner. 'Mao and the Writers.' *New York Review of Books*, 13, 7 (23 October 1969): 32-36. A review article which discusses: M. D. Goldman, *Literary Dissent in Communist China*; T. A. Hsia, *The Gate of Darkness: Studies on the Leftist Literary Movement in China*; D. W. Fokkema, *Literary Doctrine in China and Soviet Influence*; O. Lang, *Pa Chin and his writings: Chinese youth between two revolutions*; and R. L. MacFarquhar, *The Hundred Flowers*.

462. Blumier, Jay. 'On the correct handling of contradictions within Mao Tse-tung.' *Socialist Commentory* (July 1957): 5-7.

463. Bonwit, R. 'Communist China's Leap Forward.' *Pacific Affairs*, 31 (June 1958): 164-72.

464. Borkenau, F. 'Chances of a Mao-Stalin rift: will China's Communists take the Tito road?' Translated by M. J. Goldbloom. *Commentary*, 14 (August 1952): 117-23.

465. Bridgham, Philip, Arthur Cohen and Leonard Jaffe. 'Mao's Road and Sino-Soviet Relations: A View from Washington, 1953.' *China Quarterly*, no. 52 (October-December 1972): 670-98. This article was originally produced under the title 'Chinese and Soviet Views on Mao as a Marxist Theorist and on the Significance of the Chinese Revolution for the Asian Revolutionary Movement' by the C.I.A. in September 1953. Covers period 1949-52. Of interest partly for Soviet assessments of Mao's thought in this period.

466. Charles, David A. 'The Dismissal of Marshal Peng Teh-huai.' *China Quarterly*, no. 8 (October-December 1961): 63-76. Discusses the significance of the dismissal of Marshal Peng in September 1959 from his post as Minister of Defence as part of the campaign against right-wing opportunism launched in August that year. Peng had questioned relevance of Mao's theories on military organisation and strategy and had allegedly been in treasonable contact with the Soviet Party leadership. So Peng's dismissal was also important in promoting the growing bitterness of the Sino-Soviet dispute.

467. Davidoff, G. 'Les dirigeants de la Chine d'aujourd'hui.' *France Illustration*, 6 (21 January 1950): 53-4.

468. Feng Lin. 'Use of Tongue and Use of Fists.' *Peking Review*, 20, 30 (22 July 1977): 19-20. Refers to Mao's speech at the Second Plenary Session of the 8th Central Committee of the CCP in 1956, criticising Khrushchev's ideas on 'peaceful transition.' Mao defended the example of the October Revolution without which 'by and large Leninism is thrown away.' The proletariat said Mao should be prepared for . . . 'two possibilities: one, a gentleman uses his tongue, not his fists, but two, if a bastard uses his fists, I'll use mine.' Thus, Mao 'expounded the dialectical relationship between peaceful struggle and armed struggle and the law of the development of revolution.'

469. Foster, William Z. 'A letter to Mao Tse-Tung.' *Political Affairs*, 39 (March 1959): 22-31.

470. 'From Land Reform to Communes in China.' *World Today*, 15 (March 1959): 124-30.

471. Goldman, Merle. 'The Party and the intellectuals.' *The Cambridge History of China*. Vol. 14: 218-258. The People's Republic, Part 1: The Emergence of Revolutionary China 1949- 1965, eds. R. MacFarquhar and J. K. Fairbank. Cambridge: Cambridge University Press, 1987. Describes how Mao at Yanan attacked those writers who demanded that art be independent of politics, for example, Wang Shiwei. Shows the establishment of party controls over intellectuals between 1949 and 1955. Examines the Hundred Flowers campaign 1956-57 and concludes with some analysis of the Anti-Rightist campaign which widened the gap between the Party and the intellectuals still further.

472. Goldman, Merle. 'The Party and the Intellectuals: Phase Two.' *The Cambridge History of China*. Volume 14: 432-77. 'People's Republic, Part 1: the Emergence of Revolutionary China 1949-1965. Edited by Roderick MacFarquhar and John K. Fairbank. Cambridge: Cambridge University Press, 1987. Goldman examines the impact of the 1958 Great Leap Forwrd on the intellectuals, the resistance to Mao's ideological class struggle and the role of young radicals supporting Mao, and Mao's attack on the cultural bureaucracy in the 1964-1965 Rectification Campaign.

473. Green, O. M. 'Whither Mao Tse-tung?' *Fortnightly Review*, 179, 173 (May 1953): 308-12.

474. el Hashimi, S. 'Chinese communism abroad.' *Contemporary Review*, 185 (March 1954): 149-53.

475. Haven, A. 'Peking Takes Stock.' *Contemporary Review*, 191 (January 1957): 12-15. Article on the Eighth Party Congress.

476. Herber, Robert C. 'Mao and Polycentric Communism.' *Orbis*, 2 (Summer 1958): 175-193.

477. Hinton, H. C. 'Eighth Congress of the Chinese Communist Party.' *Far Eastern Survey*, 26 (January 1957): 1-8.

478. Houn, F. W. 'Eighth Central Committee of the Chinese Communist Party: A Study of an Elite.' *American Political Science Review*, 51 (June 1957): 392-404.

479. Lardy, Nicholas R. 'The Chinese Economy under Stress, 1958- 1965.' *The Cambridge History of China*, vol. 14: 360-397. The People's Republic Part 1: The Emergence of Revolutionary China 1949-1965, eds. Roderick MaFarquhar and John K. Fairbank. Cambridge: Cambridge University Press, 1987. Covers the economic strategy of the Great Leap and the Party's response to the famine crisis.

480. Lieberthal, Kenneth. 'The Great Leap Forward and the split in the Yenan leadership.' *The Cambridge History of China*, vol. 14: 293-359. The People's Republic Part 1, 1949-1965, eds. Roderick MacFarquhar and John K. Fairbank. Cambridge: Cambridge University Press, 1987. Covers the origins of the Great Leap, the Lushan conference, 1959, the Tenth Plenum, and Rectification.

481. Ling, N. J. 'Three Years of Communist Rule in China.' *Review of Politics*, 15 (January 1953): 3-33.

482. MacFarquhar, R. 'Communist China's Intra-party Dispute.' *Pacific Affairs*, 31 (December 1958): 323-35.

483. 'Mao Tse-tung and the Chinese Communists' Rectification Movement.' *World Today*, 13 (August 1957): 330-41.

484. Mark, M. 'Chinese Communism.' *Journal of Politics*, 13 (May 1951): 232-52.

485. Nakajima, Mineo. 'Foreign Relations: from the Korean War to the Bandung Line.' *The Cambridge History of China*, vol. 14: 259-292. The People's Republic Part 1, 1949-1965, eds. Roderick MacFarquhar and John K. Fairbank. Cambridge: Cambridge University Press, 1987. Covers relations between Mao and Stalin, the Korean War and the Bandung Line.

486. North, R. C. 'Rise of Mao Tse-tung.' *Far Eastern Quarterly*, 11 (February 1952): 137-45.

487. Oksenberg, Michael C. 'Policy Making Under Mao, 1949-68: An Overview.' In *Management of a Revolutionary Society*. Edited by John Lindbeck. Seattle: University of Washington Press, 1971. 79-115.

488. _____ 'Policy making under Mao Tse-tung, 1949-1968.' *Comparative Political Studies*, 3 (April 1971): 323-60.

489. Pepper, Suzanne. 'New directions in Education.' *The Cambridge History of China*, vol. 14: 398-431. The People's Republic Part 1: The Emergence of Revolutionary China 1949-1965, eds. Roderick MacFarquhar and John K. Fairbank. Cambridge: Cambridge University Press, 1987. Covers the 'Great Leap in Education' in 1958 and the 'Walking on Two Legs' slogan of the 1960's.

490. Pollack, Jonathan. 'Perception and Process in Chinese Foreign Policy: The Quemoy Decision.' University of Michigan: Ph.D. dissertation, 1976. Thanks to the Freedom of Information Act the author was able to use materials which would otherwise not have been available. He shows that M. S. Kapitsa disagrees with Mao on what was the specific position of each side at the Khrushchev-Mao meeting of August 1958 concerning Sino-Soviet military cooperation.

491. Strong, T. B. and H. Keyssar. 'Anna Louise Strong: three interviews with Chairman Mao Zedong.' *China Quarterly*, no. 103 (September 1985): 489-509. The text of three interviews which Anna Louise Strong, veteran American reporter on the Chinese Revolution, held with Mao in March 1959, January 1964 and November 1965. Strong described the context and content of the interviews in a manuscript discovered by her two biographers, printed here. She was not given permission to print the interviews when they were held, and failed to get authorisation to publish them when she approached the authorities in 1967. Includes a section on Mao's views on Khrushchev.

492. Schwartz, Benjamin. 'New trends in Maoism?' *Problems of Communism*, July/August 1957: 1-8.

493. 'September 1956 Congress of the Chinese Communist Party.' *World Today*, 12 (November 1956): 469-78.

494. Steiner, H. Arthur. 'Ideology and politics in communist China.' *Annals of the American Academy of Political and Social Science*, 321 (January 1959): 29-39.

495. _____ 'Maoism or Stalinism for Asia?' *Far Eastern Survey*, 22 (14 January 1953): 1-5.

496. _____ 'On the Record with Mao and His Regime.' *Journal of Asian Studies* 17, 2 (February 1958): 215-22.

497. Waler, Richard L. 'Chairman Mao and the cult of Personality.' *Encounter* (June 1960): 31-42.

IX. 1960 to 1969

Books

498. Asian Peoples' Anti-Communist League, Republic of China. *Why does Mao Tse-tung want to follow the leftist line of adventure?* Taipei, 1962. 32.

499. Barcata, Louis. *China in the Throes of the Cultural Revolution: An Eye Witness Report.* New York: Hart Publishing Company, 1967. 299. This report on the Great Proletarian Cultural Revolution is based on a visit made in the Spring of 1967.

500. Barnett, A. Doak. *Cadres, Bureaucracy, and Political Power in Communist China.* New York: Columbia University Press, 1967. 563. The author describes the working of the 'mass line' in China. He shows how the Party uses ideology, propaganda and persuasion in its political campaign.

501. _____ *China after Mao, with selected documents.* Princeton, N.J.: Princeton University Press, 1967. 287. The author analyses some of the basic unsolved problems facing China's leaders in the mid-60's and considers Mao's prescription for revolution at home and abroad. He discusses possible future changes.

502. Baum, R. *Prelude to Revolution. Mao the party and the peasant question 1962-66.* New York: Columbia University Press, 1975. 222. Developed from a doctoral dissertation began in 1967-68 this book examines in depth some of the underlying causes and consequences of Mao's oft expressed anxiety over the future of Chinese socialism and examines specifically Mao's seemingly obsessive preoccupation in the early 1960's with the possible threat of 'capitalist restoration in China, and the mass campaign--the Socialist Education Movement--he initiated in an attempt to raise the class consciousness of the Chinese people.

503. Bennett, Gordon and R Montaperto. *Red Guard: The Political Biography of Dai Hsiao-ai.* New York: Doubleday, 1971. 267. This is an account of the Cultural Revolution as it was experienced by Dai Xiao'ai (Dai Hsiao-ai) a student Red Guard from Guangzhou Dai describes his initial

enthusiasm for the revolution, his visits to Beijing as a fervent follower of the Great Leader, Chairman Mao, and his work as a faction leader. He relates the growing disillusionment which led to his decision to leave his family and friends and seek asylum in Hong Kong.

504. *The brilliance of Mao Tse-tung's thought illuminates the whole world.* Peking: Foreign Languages Press, 1966. 68.

505. Brugger, Bill. China: *Radicalism to Revisionism 1962-1979*. London: Croom helm, 1981. 275. 'Examining the way in which Mao governed and the fluctuations in his attitude, this volume questions whether he in fact violated the accepted rules of procedure as party leader. Modern recapitulation tends to separate Mao from the advisers surrounding him, but this book assesses whether such a point of view is justifiable.'

506. Brule, Jean Pierre. *La Nouvelle revolution de Mao*. Paris: Editions du Centurion, 1967. 224.

507. Chan, Anita. Children of Mao. *Personality Development and Political Activism in the Red Guard Generation*. Seattle: University of Washington Press, 1985. 254. Based on interviews in Hong Kong, this book sets out to examine 'how and why some of China's urban young people became fervent political activists, why so many became zealous Red Guards in the Cultural Revolution, and why they divided into rural factions that battled each other in defence of Chairman Mao.' The author shows that those young people who strove hardest to live up to the Maoist credo tended to develop more highly authoritarian personality traits than their less devoted or less politically successful school mates. Such personality traits were not necessarily permanent. In the aftermath of the Cultural Revolution their conformity to the authoritarian social character tended to fade.

508. *CCP Documents of the Great Proletarian Cultural Revolution, 1966-1967*. Hong Kong: Union Research Institute, 1968. 692. A collection of 122 documents issued by the CCP central authorities and 10 documents issued by the Peking municipal authorities. Twenty-five of the documents are published here in English for the first time. Ten of the documents were published officially. When available the official English edition is used.

509. Chen, Jack. *Inside the Cultural Revolution*. London: Sheldon, 1976. 483. The author worked in China from 1950 to 1970 as a journalist, editor and artist, contributing to *People's China, Peking Review, Cartoons* and *People's Daily*. This book covers the phases of the Cultural Revolution from

its earliest manifestations to the January Storm of 1967 in Shanghai, and to the Five-One-Six Movement which climaxed in the Lin Biao affair and the attempt to assassinate Mao. The author believes that 'The enemies of progress have been sorted and are in retreat, but they have not been eliminated . . .. When conditions are favourable they will attack again.'

510. Ching, Shui-hsien. *Rifle Rectifies Rifle in Mao's Cultural Revolution.* Taipei: Asian Peoples' Anti-Communist League, 1969. 75. An analysis of the process of rectification in the People's Liberation Army, both before and during the Cultural Revolution. It begins with a review of movements within the army from 1953 onwards and proceeds to examine the role of the army as an instrument of rectification in the Cultural Revolution. An appendix lists the names of senior military cadres purged during the Cultural Revolution.

511. Chuang, H. C. *The Little Red Book and Current Chinese Language.* Berkeley: Center for Chinese Studies, University of California, 1968. 58. Monograph no. 13 of the series 'Studies in Chinese Communist Terminology.' Examines Mao's linguistic style as exemplified in *Quotations from Chairman Mao Tse-tung* and traces the historical origin of certain expressions.

512. Chung, Hua-min and Arthur C. Miller. *Madame Mao--A Profile of Chiang Ch'ing.* Hong Kong: Union Research Institute, 1968. 320. An English edition of *Chiang Ch'ing chen chuan* (A Biography of Jiang Qing) published in 1967.

513. *Collected Works of Liu Shao-ch'i Before 1944.* Hong Kong: Union Research Institute, 1969. 471. *Collected Works of Liu Shao-ch'i 1945-1957.* Hong Kong: Union Research Institute, 1969. 484. *Collected Works of Liu Shao-ch'i, 1958-1967.* Hong Kong: Union Research Institute, 1968. 405. These three titles comprise a total of 143 documents by Liu Shao-qi including 'self-examinations.' The introduction is by Zhang Guodao (Chang Kuo-tao), one of the founders of the CCP.

514. Dittmer, Lowell. *Liu Shao-ch'i and the Chinese cultural revolution: The politics of mass criticism.* Berkeley: University of California Press, 1974. 386. Shows Liu Shaoqi's policies as the anti-thesis of Mao's in the epoch-making 'struggle between two lines.' The author predicts that Liu's 'road not taken will endure as a meaningful point of reference in the political development of China.'

515. Deliusin, Lev Petrovich. *The 'Cultural Revolution' in China.* Moscow: Novosti Press Agency Publishing House, 1967. 103. A Soviet analysis of the Cultural Revolution.

516. Dutt, Gargi and V. P. Dutt. *China's Cultural Revolution.* New York: Asia Publishing House, 1970. 260. Beginning in the period of the Great Leap Forward, the authors trace the origins and development of the Cultural Revolution.

517. Elegant, Robert S. *Mao's Great Revolution.* New York: World Publishing Company, 1971. 478. Describes the origins and development of the Cultural Revolution from 1959 with particular attention to Mao's position and his role in the political machinations of the CCP. Includes (pp. 347-367) excerpts from the Three Trials of Wang Guangmei (Wang Kwang-mei), the wife of Liu Shaoqi, during the day and night of 10 April 1967. A good example of the style of 'struggle' sessions, and the methods used.

518. Fan, K. H. (ed). *The Chinese Cultural Revolution: Selected Documents.* New York: Grove Press, 1968. 320. A collection of documents from Chinese Communist sources from 1939 to 1967. Each section has an introductory note by the editor.

519. *Forward along the high road of Mao Tse-tung's thought.* Peking: Foreign Languages Press, 1967. 36.

520. Gao Yuan. *Born Red : A Chronicle of the Cultural Revolution.* Stanford: Stanford University Press, 1987. 380. A personal account of the years 1966-1969 by one who was a teenager at the time. Gao shows how everyone he knew became victims of a mass movement.

521. Gel'bras, V. G. *Mao's pseudo socialism.* Moscow: Novosti Press Agency Publishing House, 1968. 156.

522. Gittings, John. *Survey of the Sino-Soviet Dispute: A Commentary and Extracts from the Recent Polemics 1963-1967.* London: Oxford University Press, 1968. 410. A masterly analysis of the attacks and counterattacks. Includes major historical documents.

523. Granqvist, Hans. *The Red Guard: a Report on Mao's Revolution.* New York: Praeger, 1967. 159. The author looks at current pronouncements and events in China under the momentum of the Cultural Revolution. He comments on the changing political scene.

524. Gray, Jack and Patrick Cavendish. *Chinese Communism in Crisis: Maoism and the Cultural Revolution.* New York: Frederick A. Praeger, 1968. 279. Follows the historical development of the Cultural Revolution, and examines the political role of the intelligentsia in the context of intellectual movements in China in the twentieth century. The authors see the origins of the Cultural Revolution in the rectification of errors in popular culture and in the educational structure. The appendix, approximately half the book, contains twelve documentary sources.

525. *The Great Cultural Revolution in China.* Compiled and edited by the Asia Research Center. Melbourne & Sydney: Paul Flesch and Co., 1968. 507. A collection of documents covering the origins and development of the Cultural Revolution from 1963 to the end of 1966. The documents come from Chinese communist newspapers, Party publications, speeches of leaders, etc. Part II includes an annotated personnel directory of key officials involved in the early stages of the Cultural Revolution. There is also a chronology of events covering the period November 1965 to November 1966 and a list of Chinese Communist newspapers and periodicals.

526. *The Great Power Struggle in China.* Hong Kong: Asia Research Center, 1969. 503. This is a companion volume to *The Great Cultural Revolution in China* (see no. 525). It is a collection of documents covering the later stages of the Cultural Revolution and arranged under nine headings: The Red Guard Movement; Spread of the Revolution to the Countryside and to Industrial and Mining Enterprises; January Revolution; Nationwide Struggle to Seize Power; Reverse in the Power Struggle; the Impact of the Power Struggle; the Army's New Role in Cultural Revolution; the Cultural Revolution in the Army; and Problems Involving the Army.

527. *The Great Socialist Cultural Revolution.* Peking: Foreign Languages Press, 1966.

528. *Great Victory for Chairman Mao's Revolutionary Line.* Peking: Foreign Languages Press, 1967. 88. This is a collection of speeches by Zhou Enlai, Jiang Qing and others, together with editorials from *Renmin Ribao* and *Jiefang Zhunbao* on the birth of the Peking Municipal Revolutionary Committee, 20 April 1967.

529. Grey, Anthony. *Hostage in Peking.* London: Michael Joseph, 1970. 343. The experiences of a British journalist held in solitary confinement for two years during the Cultural Revolution.

530. Harman, Richard Synder. *The Maoist Case against Liu Shao-ch'i.* Charlottsville: University of Virginia, 1969. 300. The case against 'China's Khrushchev,' the 'top-party person taking the capitalist road' who was at last openly identified as a 'revisionist scab.'

531. Hinton, William. *Turning Point in China. An Essay on the Cultural Revolution.* New York: Monthly Review Press, 1972. 112. The author disagrees with popular western interpretations of the Cultural Revolution of 1966 to 1969 which see it as a military takeover, a personal power struggle or an effort to guarantee the succession to Mao Zedong. He postulates a real struggle for power between contending social interests, and describes, in detail, the forces polarised in the two camps.

532. Hsiung, V. T. *Red China's Cultural Revolution.* New York: Vantage Press, 1968. 188. Begins with an overview of the early years of the Communist struggle in China. The book focusses on the complexities of Mao's thought and examines the role of individuals and factions in China and the split in the international communist movement.

533. Huck, A. *The Security of China.* London: Chatto & Windus, 1970.93. While the Maoist picture of the world in revolutionary fermant is the antithesis of the traditional Chinese view of a stable world order with China at its centre, the two views are not difficult to reconcile. 'Both have a determined interest in removing alien (distant, foreign, "imperialist") influence from the periphery of China.'

534. Hunter, Neale. *Shanghai Journal: An Eyewitness Account of the Cultural Revolution.* New York: Frederick A. Praeger, 1969. 311. The author taught English at the Foreign Languages Institute in Shanghai from 1965 to 1967. He views the Cultural Revolution as a successful movement to reestablish the dominance of Mao's works.

535. Hwang, Tien-chien. *Moscow-Peiping relations and Khrushchev-Mao struggle.* Taipei, Asian Peoples' Anti-Communist League, Republic of China, 1963. 78.

536. _____ *Transformation of Mao-Lin faction's tactical line for power seizure.* Taipei: Asian Peoples' Anti-Communist League, Republic of China, 1968. 94.

537. Kadathaskottiya, Ashok. *Man, god or sphinx? A Political spotlight on Mao Tse-tung.* Colombo: Tribune Publications, 1968. 218.

538. Karnow, Stanley. *Mao and China: From Revolution to Revolution*. New York: Viking Press, 1972. 592. Account of Mao's struggles within the Party apparatus in the 1960's. Relates personality of Mao as indicated by his thought and actions, to the events of the Cultural Revolution. An objective study of Mao's role.

539. Karol, K. S. *The Second Chinese Revolution*. London: Jonathan Cape, 1975. 472. The author visited China in 1965 and 1971. A critical account of the Cultural Revolution through to the fall of Lin Biao.

540. Knight, Sophia. *Window on Shanghai. Letters from China Today*. London: Andre Deutsch, 1967. 256. In the foreword, Dr. Joseph Needham says 'Here is a stop-press account of what it was like for one young westerner to live through it' (the Cultural Revolution). The author who went to China immediately after graduation to teach English had been in Shanghai long enough by the time the Cultural Revolution began to feel at home. In a series of letters to her mother she describes what she saw in the streets, at meetings, on her travelling holidays and in the foreign languages institute where she was working. On the whole a sympathetic account of the activities of the Red Guards and of Mao's leadership.

541. Kwong, Julia. *Cultural Revolution in China's Schools, May 1966-April 1969*. Stanford: Hoover Institution Press, 1988. 200.

542. Lewis, John Wilson. *Communist China: crisis and change*. New York: Foreign Policy Association, 1966. 63.

543. Lewis, John W. (ed). *Party Leadership and Revolutionary Power in China*. New York: Cambridge University Press, 1970. 422. Papers presented at a conference on the Chinese Communist Party held in England, July 1968. Includes an account of Mao's rise to power; and analysis of Communist ideology, party motivation and elitism; and a study of the power struggle between the central authorities and local leaders. Concludes with an examination of the role of the army in the Cultural Revolution.

544. Leys, Simon. *The Chairman's New Clothes: Mao and the Cultural Revolution*. New York: St. Martin's Press, 1978. 261. A translation of the 1971 French publication, *Les habits neufs du President Mao*. Part 1: gives a useful historical perspective which describes and analyses the origins of the Cultural Revolution, particularly in relation to the power struggles of the 1950's. Part 2: 'A Diary of the Cultural Revolution through 1967, 1968 and

1969.' Appendices include several key documents, e.g. 'Hai Jui reprimands the emperor' and short biographical sketches.

545. Li, Tien-min. *Chou En-lai*. Taipei: Institute of International Relations, 1970. 426. Uses original materials to trace Zhou Enlai's role during the Cultural Revolution. The final chapter gives an analysis of the interrelations between Zhou, Mao Zedong, Liu Shaogi and Lin Biao.

546. Li, Ting-sheng. *The CCP's Persecution of Chinese Intellectuals in 1949-69*. Taipei: Asian Peoples' Anti-Communist League, 1969. 67. Examines the incidents, before the Cultural Revolution, in which intellectuals were repressed. The author then discusses the reeducation campaign of the Cultural Revolution and concludes that Mao will never succeed in moulding the intelligentsia into a pliable force in his hands.

547. Liang, Kuo-hsin. *Mao's regime--as I see it*. Taipei: Asian Peoples' Anti-Communist League, Republic of China, 1966. 104.

548. Lifton, Robert Jay. *Revolutionary Immortality: Mao Tse-tung and the Chinese Cultural Revolution*. New York: Random House, 1968. 178. The author is a psychiatrist with a leaning towards psychoanalysis. He combines psychological and historical analysis to reveal the Cultural Revolution as a reaction to the anticipated death of Mao Zedong and the dictator's fear that his revolution may lose its impetus.

549. Lin, Mo-han. *Raise higher the banner of Mao Tse-tung's thought on art and literature*. Peking: Foreign Languages Press, 1961. 40.

550. Lin, Piao. *The international significance of Comrade Mao Tse-tung's theory of people's war*. Peking: Foreign Languages Press, 1965.

551. Lindquist, Sven. *China in Crisis*. London: Faber and Faber, 1963. 125. Based on two years in China in 1961-62. Gives some insights into the economic situation and changing political attitudes.

552. Loescher, Gil with Ann Dull Loescher. *The Chinese Way. Life in the People's Republic of China*. New York: Harcourt Brace Jovanovich, 1974. 206. Based on visits to China in 1971 and 1973. The authors are sympathetic to what they see and hear in Mao's China.

553. *Long Live Victory of the Great Cultural Revolution Under the Dictatorship of the Proletariat*. Peking: Foreign Languages Press, 1968. 49.

Comprises: Lin Biao's speech at the Rally Celebrating the Eighteenth Anniversary of the Founding of the People's Republic of China on 1 October 1967; Zhou Enlai's speech at the National Day Reception on 30 September 1967; 'Long Live Victory of the Great Cultural Revolution Under the Dictatorship of the Proletariat,' by the Editorial Departments of *Renmin Ribao, Hong Qi and Jiefang Zhunbao* on 1 October 1967; 'A Great Revolution to Achieve the Ascendancy of Mao Tse-tung's Thought,' editorial of *Hong Qi*, no. 15, 1967; '"Fight Self, Repudiate Revisionism" Is the Fundamental Principle of the Great Proletarian Cultural Revolution,' editorial of *Renmin Ribao*, 6 October 1967; and 'To Repudiate Revisionism, it is Essential to Fight Self,' editorial of *Jiefang Zhunbao*, 8 October 1967.

554. MacFarquhar, Emily. *China: Mao's last leap*. London: Economist Newspapers, 1968, 26.

555. Malraux, Andre. *Anti-memoires*. Translated by Terence Kilmartin. New York: Holt, Rhinehart and Winston, 1968. Interview with Mao in August 1965 recorded, pp. 356-77.

556. Mehnert, Klaus. *Peking and the New Left: At Home and Abroad*. Berkeley: Center for Chinese Studies, University of California, 1969. 156. This is a study of the new youth organisation--the 'Hunan Provincial Proletarian Revolution Great Alliance Committee,'--formed shortly after Mao Zedong visited the province in the autumn of 1967.

557. Myrdal, Jan and Gun Kessle. *China: The Revolution Continued*. Translated from the revised Swedish edition by Paul Britten Austin. New York: Pantheon Books, 1970. 201. Presents an account of the Cultural Revolution at village level, based on interviews with the people of Liu Ling in northern Shaanxi.

558. Myers, James Townsend. *The Apotheosis of Chairman Mao*. Washington, D.C.: George Washington University, 1969. 174.

559. Nee, Victor and Don Layman. *The Cultural Revolution at Peking University*. New York: Monthly Review Press, 1969. 91. This book began as a Master's thesis written by Victor Nee at Harvard. It analyses the political controversy at Beijing University beginning with the Hundred Flowers movement and continuing through the Great Leap Forward and the growth of elitism in the first half of the 1960's. There is a detailed chronological account of the upheaval in the university, 1965-66. The appendix includes several articles from Red Guard newspapers.

560. Peng, She-tse, Pierre Frank, Joseph Hansen, and George Novack. *Behind China's 'Great Cultural Revolution*. New York: Merit Publishers, 1967. 63. Contains four articles published previously between August 1966 and February 1967: 'Peng Shu-tse on Background of Chinese Events'; 'Second Interview with Peng Shu-tse: Mao's "Cultural Revolution";' 'Meaning of the Shanghai Events,' by Pierre Frank; 'The Upheaval in China, an Analysis of the Contending Forces,' by George Novack and Joseph Hansen.

561. Robinson, Joan. *The Cultural Revolution in China*. Baltimore, Maryland: Penguin Books, 1969. 151. Comprises: Introduction; The Cultural Revolution Seen From Shanghai; Documents; Reports and Conversations; and Postscript. Part 2, 'The Cultural Revolution Seen From Shanghai' is an account of the Cultural Revolution given to Joan Robinson in November 1967, by a member of the committee temporarily in control of Shanghai.

562. Robinson, Thomas W., ed. *The Cultural Revolution in China*. Berkeley, California: University of California Press, 1971. 509. Five case studies on the early period of the Cultural Revolution (1966-1967) from the Rand Corporation. The studies cover ideology, policy-making, leadership, foreign policy and the revolution in the countryside.

563. *Roots of Chinese developments*. Moscow: Novosti Press Agency Publishing House, 1968. 78.

564. Strong, A. L. *Letters from China 1962-1964*. 2 vols. Peking: New World Press, 1963 and 1964. Sympathetic commentary on current developments in China.

565. _____ *Letters from China, Nos. 21-30*. Peking: New World Press, 1965. 217 Sympathetic view of China's policies at home and abroad, including comments on the war in Indochina.

566. *Summary of the Forum on the Work in Literature and Art in the Armed Forces With Which Comrade Lin Piao Entrusted Comrade Chiang Ching*. Peking: Foreign Languages Press, 1968. 48. Includes: Lin Biao's Letter to members of the Standing Committee of the Military Commission of the Party Central Committee (22 March 1966); Summary of the Forum on the Work in Literature and Art in the Armed Forces With Which Comrade Lin Biao Entrusted Comrade Jiang Qing; Two Diametrically Opposed Documents (editorial of *Hong Qi*, no. 9, 1967); An Important Document for the Proletarian Cultural Revolution (editorial of *Renmin Ribao*, 29 May 1967);

Pick Up Your Pens and Hold on to Your Guns, Fight to Defend Proletarian State Power (editorial of *Jiefang Zhunbao*, 29 May 1967).

567. *Take the road of integrating with the workers, peasants, and soldiers.* Peking: Foreign Languages Press, 1970. 94

568. Tang Tsou. *The Cultural Revolution and Post-Mao Reforms: A Historical Perspective*. Chicago: University of Chicago Press, 1986. 351. A collection of the author's essays written over a period of twenty years. Includes some thought provoking analysis of Mao's motives.

569. Taylor, Jay. *China and Southeast Asia: Peking's Relations with Revolutionary Movements*. New York: Praeger, 1974. 376. Focusses on 'Under what circumstances is Peking likely to give what kind of support to which revolutionaries abroad?' The author examines China's internal 'debate' and its effect on foreign policy between 1965 and 1972. He concludes 'differences within the leadership in interpreting external threats and opportunities in Southeast Asia were primarily along the lines of great-power versus more limited interests, of boldness versus caution, and of long-term goals versus short-term gains.'

570. Tai, Sung An. *Mao Tse-tung's Cultural Revolution*. Indianoplis: Pegasus, Bobbs-Merrill, 1972. 211. Intended as a brief interim version of a larger work in progress. It describes and makes some evaluation of the progress of the Cultural Revolution to 1970. It is based on Chinese sources in the People's Republic and in Hong Kong. The author says '. . . it is apparent that Chairman Mao has lost his Utopian crusade to remake China in his militant revolutionary image.' There is some comment on the position, at the time, of the group later known as the Gang of Four and on Lin Biao. Useful appendices list members of the Ninth Central Committee of the CCP and leading members of the Revolutionary Committee in the major cities, e.g. Shanghai.

571. Urban, George. *The Miracles of Chairman Mao*. London: Tom Stacey Ltd, 1971. 182. Describes the adulation of the Great Leader and the many incredible works attributed to him during the Cultural Revolution.

572. Wang, Ssu-ch'eng. *The delicate relationship between Mao Tse-tung, Liu Shao-chi and Chou En-lai*. Taipei: Asian People's Anti-Communist League, Republic of China, 1963. 24.

573. _____ *Why Mao Tse-tung is bellicose*. Taipei: Asian Peoples' Anti-Communist League, Republic of China, 1966. 84.

574. Wint, Guy. *Communist China's crusade: Mao's road to power and the new campaign for world revolution*. New York: Praeger, 1965. 136.

575. Zagoria, David. *The Sino-Soviet Conflict, 1956-1961*. Princeton, New Jersey: Princeton University Press, 1962. 484. The author had previously worked in the Central Intelligence Agency. This study draws on authoritative and highly secret sources especially in regard to the meetings at Bucharest and Moscow.

Articles

Originally published in China, arranged by author

576. Chang, Yu-tien; Yang Yuan-huan and Liu Ko-cheng. 'Peking Television University is a Strong Fortress of the "Three-Family Village" Gangster Inn.' *Renmin Ribao* (People's Daily), (11 June 1966). Translated in *Survey of China Mainland Press*, no. 3723 (22 June 1966): 1-6. An attack on Wu Han, president of the University by three students of Beijing Television University, for misleading students concerning the nature of the Cultural Revolution.

577. Chen, Yung-Kuei, and others. 'Resolutely defend Chairman Mao's proletarian revolutionary line.' *Hung ch'i (Red Flag)*, no. 12 (1967).

578. Chen, Yung-Kuei. 'Study Chairman Mao's works for the sole purpose of applying them.' *Peking Review*, 11 (March 1968), no. 12, 21-23.

579. _____ 'Tachai marches forward under the radiance of Mao Tse-tung's thought.' *Selections of China Mainland Magazine*, no. 572 (April 1967): 6-10.

580. Feng, Fu-sheng. 'PLA. activist in studying Chairman Mao's works.' *Peking Review*, 11 (March 1968), no. 13, 14-16.

581. Hsu, Kuang-ping. 'Mao Tse-tung's thought illuminates Lu Hsun.' *Chinese Literature*, no. 1 (1967), 35-40.

582. Hsuan, Wei-tung. 'Put Mao Tse-tung's Thought in Command of Kindergarten Education.' *Kuang-ming jih-pao* (31 March 1969). Translated

in *Survey of China Mainland Press*, no. 4400 (23 April 1969): 1-6. The program for kindergarten education set out in 1960 is denounced as the 'black fruit of renegade, traitor and scab Liu Shao-chi's (Liu Shaoqi) counter-revolutionary revisionist line.'

583. Hung, Chin-ping. 'Inner-party struggle guided by Mao Tse-tung's thought is the life of the Party.' *Peking Review*, 11 (November 1968), no. 46, 17-20.

584. Hung Yin-hang. 'A Great victory for Mao Tse-tung's Thought on the Financial and Monetary Front.' *Chinese Economic Studies*, 3, 3 (Spring 1970): 179-90. A translation of an article in *People's Daily*, 6 July 1969, which claims that China's people's currency has become an exceptionally stable currency of the world thanks to 'the invincible thought of Mao Tse-tung.' In an overview of the Chinese economy since Liberation Mao is credited with the achievement of stability whereas Liu Xiaoqi, 'the renegrade, traitor and scab' is blamed for advocating 'the reactionary nonsense of "deficit spending and inflation".'

585. Keng, Chang-so. 'Always follow Chairman Mao in making revolution.' *Hung ch'i (Red Flag)*, no. 4 (October 1968).

586. Ku, Ah-tao. 'Follow Chairman Mao closely and wage revolution forever.' *China Pictorial*, no. 7 (1968): 20-23.

587. Kuo, Feng-lien. 'Arm the peasants with the thought of Mao Tse-tung.' *Selections from China Mainland Magazines*, no. 612 (January 1968): 16-24.

588. Kuo, Mo-jo. 'We must be Chairman Mao's good pupils all our lives.' *Peking Review*, 10 (June 1967), no. 24, 23-24.

589. Lin Piao. 'Long Live the Victory of the People's War.' *Peking Review*, 8, 36 (3 September 1965): 9-30.

590. Liu, Ku-chih. 'Read Chairman Mao's works, rebel against the word "ego".' *Selections of China Mainland Magazine*, no. 564 (February 1967): 22-25.

591. Liu, Shih and Chi, Szu. 'Using Mao Tse-tung's thought to open up a "forbidden zone"--curing deaf-mutes.' *Peking Review*, 11 (November 1968), no. 46. Cited as an example of a 'great victory of Mao Tse-tung's thought.' Describes the achievement of Mao Tse-tung Thought Progaganda Team of

Medical Workers from the PLA 3016 Unit's Health Section. Using acupuncture many of its mute students were enabled to speak. Of 168 students 129 can shout 'Long Live Chairman Mao' and 47 can sing 'The East is Red.'

592. Shapiro, Michael. 'Mao Tse-tung's thought lights the whole world.' *Peking Review*, 10 (July 1967), no. 31, 17-18.

593. Shen, Yu-ying. 'Ten questions raised and answered--thought on creative study and application of Chairman Mao's work in struggle.' *Selections of China Mainland Magazine*, no. 599 (October 1967): 7-19.

594. Tsui, Fu-yung. 'Cultivate new communists with the thought of Mao Tse-tung.' *Hung ch'i (Red Flag)*, no. 15 (December 1966).

595. Wang, Tse-chun. 'Creatively study and apply Chairman Mao's writings in supporting the struggle of proletarian revolutionaries to seize power.' *Hung ch'i (Red Flag)*, no. 4 (February 1967).

596. Wang, Yung-hsing. 'Making revolution and promoting production depends on the thought of Mao Tse-tung.' *Hung ch'i (Red Flag)*, no. 1 (January 1967).

597. Yang, Cheng-wu. 'Thoroughly establish the absolute authority of the Great Supreme Commander Chairman Mao and of his great thought.' *Peking Review*, 10 (November 1967), no. 46, 17-24.

598. Yang, Shih. '"Quotations from Chairman Mao Tse-tung" fly through the world.' *Chinese Literature*, no. 7 (1967): 107-109.

599. Yang, Tao-ken. 'March toward new heights in flexible study and application of the works of Mao Tse-tung.' *Hung ch'i (Red Flag)*, no. 1 (January 1967).

600. Yen, Hsieh-chung. 'I will defend Chairman's Mao's revolutionary line all my life.' *China Reconstructs*, 17 (December 1968): 48-50.

Originally published in China, arranged by title

601. Kuang-ming jih-pao. 'Advance Victoriously Along the Splended Route Indicated by Chairman Mao.' (7 March 1969). Translated in *Survey of China Mainland Press*, no. 4386 (28 March 1969): 1-5. Describes the reorgan-

isation of a Middle School in Tianjin. Children of workers and poor peasants are admitted without examination.

602. 'An Example of Primary School students in Studying the Thought of Mao Tse-tung.' (31 May 1966). Translated in *Survey of China Mainland Press*, no. 3713 (7 June 1966): 11-14. Describes a visit to a children's group for the study of Mao's works.

603. 'Arts Faculties Must be Thoroughly Revolutionized.' (1 April 1969). Translated in *Survey of China Mainland Press*, no. 4396 (16 April 1969): 6-8. It is proposed that arts faculties should be modelled on the Yanan Anti-Japanese University, with students selected for their loyalty to Mao and with leadership drawn from the working class.

604. 'Chairman Mao's "March 7" Directive is the Beacon Light Guiding Us Forward.' (12 March 1968). Translated in *Current Background*, no. 854 (24 May 1968): 27-33. Describes how the teachers and students of a middle school studied Mao's Directive of 7 March.

605. 'Chronology of the Two-Road Struggle on the Educational Front in the Past Seventeen years.' (6 May 1967). Translated in *Chinese Education*, 1 (Spring 1968): 3-58. A chronological account of the struggle between Mao's 'proletarian educational line' and the 'revisionist educational line' associated with Liu Shaoqi from 1949 to 1967.

606. 'Completely Carry Out Our Great Leader Chairman Mao's Latest Instruction, and Firmly Execute the Battle Order Issued by the Proletarian Headquarters.' (28 August 1968). Translated in *Chinese Education*, 2 (Spring-Summer 1969): 18-25.

607. 'Do We Need Foreign Language Courses?' (7 March 1969). Translated in *Survey of China Mainland Press*, no. 4383 (25 March 1969): 11. It is argued that the study of foreign languages is necessary in order to propagate Marxism-Leninism and Mao Zedong's thought throughout the world.

608. 'Hungch'i Middle School in Penhsi, Liaoning, Forms Textbook Compiling Group.' (8 May 1969). Translated in *Survey of China Mainland Press*, no. 4419 (20 May 1969): 6-7. Stresses the importance of emphasising the thought of Mao Zedong in new textbooks.

609. 'New Peking University Forges Ahead.' *China Pictorial*, 6 (June 1970): 32-35. Describes the work of the worker--PLA Mao Zedong Thought Propaganda Team in Beijing University.

610. 'New Peking University Marches Forward in Big Strides Along the Road Pointed Out by Chairman Mao.' (16 September 1968). Translated in *Survey of China Mainland Press*, no. 4267 (27 September 1968): 7-11. Describes how two rival Red Guard factions at Beijing University were reconciled to working together, thanks to the efforts of a Mao Zedong's Thought Propaganda Team.

611. 'Our Great Leader Chairman Mao and Vice-Chairman Lin Piao Receive Revolutionary Fighters.' *Peking Review*, 11 (January 1968), no. 1, 7-8. More than 26,000 party and government cadres and representatives of the masses from various areas and the PLA attended.

612. 'Peking Agricultural Labor University Studies Chairman Mao's Latest Instruction in a Big Way and Severely Repudiates China's Khrushchev's Revisionist Line for Education.' (6 September 1968). Translated in *Survey of China Mainland Press*, no. 4260 (18 September 1968): 1-2. A denunciation of the alleged 'counter-revolutionary revisionist line' of Liu Shaoqi in the field of education.

613. 'Propaganda Team in Hopei Normal University Helps University's Revolutionary Committee Further Carry Out Policy Toward Intellectuals.' (7 July 1969). Translated in *Survey of China Mainland Press*, no. 4461 (24 July 1969): 1-3. Describes how the worker-PLA Mao Tse-tung's Thought Propaganda Team reeducated the intellectuals of the University.

614. 'Proposals to the Party Central Committee and Chairman Mao Concerning the Introduction of a Completely New Academic System of Arts Faculties in Universities.' (21 July 1966). Translated in *Survey of China Mainland Press*, no. 3742 (20 July 1966): 1-5. A letter from students of China People's University demanding the 'resolute, thorough and early smashing of the old education system.'

615. 'Protest Against Anti-China Provocation in Britain.' *Peking Review*, 10, 29 (14 July 1967): 40. Describes the incidents outside the Chinese embassy in Portland Place when 'with the connivance of the British Government . . . a handful of anti-China elements, in the name of the "Campaign for nuclear disarmament" created disorders and provocations.' On 4 July 1967 'Some of them went so far as to burn a copy of *Quotations from Chairman Mao*

Tse-tung which is most treasured by the revolutionary people of the world
. . . Staff members . . . who have enormous love for the great leader
Chairman Mao, immediately rushed out to stop the ruffians' shameless
crime.'

616. 'The Red Sun Rises in the Hearts of the Red Young Fighters.' (11
March 1968). Translated in *Current Background*, no. 845 (24 May 1968):
25-26. Primary school children organise Mao Zedong's Thought study classes.

617. 'Revolutionization of Teachers' Thinking is a Question of Primary
Importance.' (6 January 1969). Translated in *Survey of China Mainland
Press*, no. 4346 (27 January 1969): 4-5. Suggests that teachers should
'heighten their awareness of the struggle between the two lines, break with
the counter-revolutionary revisionist line for education . . . and stand on the
side of Chairman Mao's proletarian revolutionary line.'

618. 'Sailing the Seas Depends on the Helmsman.' *Peking Review*, vol. 11,
no. 1 (January 1968): 25-27. A literal translation of one of the best loved
Chinese revolutionary songs in praise of Chairman Mao, with music.

619. 'Tear Aside the Bourgeois Mask of "Liberty, Equality and Fraternity".'
(4 June 1966). Reprinted in *Survey of China Mainland Press*, no. 3714 (8
June 1966): 1-8. This is an article from *Renmin Ribao* (*People's Daily*)
attacking the 'bourgeois' outlook, which is opposed to Mao Zedong's
thought.

620. 'Tsinghua University Undergoes Great Changes Under Chairman Mao's
Brilliant Idea, "The Working Class Must Exercise Leadership Over
Everything".' (9 May 1969). Translated in *Survey of China Mainland Press*
no. 4423 (26 May 1969): 1-6. Describes the work of the Worker-PLA Mao
Zedong's Thought Propaganda Team in Tsinghua University.

621. 'What Chairman Mao Says We Do.' (13 July 1966). Translated in
Survey of China Mainland Press, no. 3748 (28 July 1966): 12-14. Letters
written by students of the Department of Law at Hupeh University and the
Department of Chinese, Beijing Normal College proposing reforms in line
with Mao Zedong's Thought.

Published in the West

622. Achminor, Herman F. 'Crisis in Mao's realm and Moscow's China policy.' *Orbis*, 40 (Winter 1968), no. 4, 1179-1192.

623. Alexandrov, K. 'Mao Tse-tung and Liu Shao-chi.' *Bulletin of Institute for the Study of USSR*, 6 (July 1959): 36-41.

624. Baum, Richard D. 'Ideology Redivivus.' *Problems of Communism*, 16 (May-June 1967). Presents the Cultural Revolution as Maoist attempt to revive revolutionary ideology beginning to decline under impact of modernisation. Part of a symposium 'The New Revolution' III.

625. Behr, E. 'Mao meets the press.' Translated by A. Farbstein. *Atlas*, 9 (February 1965): 104-5.

626. Bjelajac, Slavko N. 'Communism's discordant leadership: Mao and Khrushchev.' *Orbis*, 7 (July 1963): 386-99.

627. Bennett, Gordon. 'Madam Mao's Polemicist Laureate: Mrs Mao's Literary Ghost.' *Far Eastern Economic Review*, 62 (24 October 1968): 197-199. Analyses the writings and career of Yao Wenyuan, later designated a member of the Gang of Four, during the Cultural Revolution.

628. Bridgham, Philip. 'Mao's "Cultural Revolution": Origin and Development.' *China Quarterly*, 29 (January-March 1967): 1-35. Follows Mao's political line from the Lushan conference in 1959 through to the outburst of the Cultural Revolution.

629. Bridgham, Philip. 'Mao's Cultural Revolution: The Struggle to Consolidate Power.' *China Quarterly*, 41 (January-March, 1970): 1-25. The author shows that in spite of a 'flurry of activity at the Centre' the Party has yet to assume its assigned role of leadership within the provincial Revolutionary Committee system. 'The primary cause for this snail's pace in Party building appears to be Mao Tse-tung's insistence that the same three-way alliance principle underlying the new government (Revolutionary Committee) structure also govern the process of Party reconstruction. Until such time as sufficient 'new blood' ('new cadres') is brought into the leadership, it appears that the party will continue to lead a shadowy, ghost-like existence at provincial and local levels of the new structure of power.' The author concludes that reforms 'to the extent that they embody visionary aims can never be completed.' But it would be misreading Mao to

think that he will 'abandon the pursuit of these chimerical goals . . . The Cultural Revolution will continue, although perhaps under a new name in Communist China.'

630. 'But has he tried walking on it?' *Economist*, 220 (30 July 1966): 439. Facetious poem on Mao's swim with 5000 others plus extracts from New China News Agency on same event.

631. Chang, Parris H. 'Leadership Purges in China: The Fallen Idols.' *Far Eastern Economic Review*, 61 (22 August 1968): 351-353. Suggests that the purges within the Chinese leadership have been more extensive than originally anticipated, both at central and provincial levels.

632. _____ 'Mao's great purge: a political balance sheet.' *Problems of Communism*, 18 (March-April 1969): 1-10.

633. _____ 'The Second Decade of Maoist Rule.' *Problems of Communism*, 18 (November-December 1969): 1-14. Examines new leadership selected at Ninth Party Congress in April 1969, considers the recent past and looks to the future. Part of a symposium 'China in Flux.'

634. _____ 'Struggle Between the Two Roads in China's Countryside.' *Current Scene*, 6 (15 February 1968): 1-14. Considers 'the major issues of contention within the Party about rural policies, identifying major participants and their different perspectives, and offers some observations on the problems encountered by the Party.'

635. Chen, Chien-chung. 'An analysis of the "power-seizure" struggle within the Chinese Communist regime.' *Asian Outlook*, 2 (March 1967): 15-21.

636. _____ 'New situation of the Maoist power seizure struggle.' *Asian Outlook*, 3 (September 1968): 13-22.

637. Chen, Theodore Hsi-en. 'A Nation in Agony.' *Problems of Communism*, 15 (November-December 1966). Looks at wider significance of Cultural Revolution in the Communist attempt to create 'socialist man.' Part of a symposium 'The New Revolution.'

638. _____ 'The New Socialist Man.' *Comparative Education Review*, 13 (February 1969): 88-95. In this article the author sets out 'to delineate the image of the New Socialist Man--the modern version of the Confucian chun-tzu or Superior Man--as conceived by Mao and his followers, through

a searching inquiry into the ideological inner source as well as an examination of the specific educational means by which the New Socialist Man is molded.'

639. Cheng, Chu-yuan. 'The roots of China's cultural revolution.' *Orbis*, 11 (Winter 1968): 1160-78.

640. Chi, Wen-shun. 'The Great Proletarian Cultural Revolution in Ideological Perspective.' *Asian Survey*, 9 (August 1969): 563-579. Examines the ideological issues at the heart of the Cultural Revolution debates in China.

641. Chin, Ssu-k'ai. 'The Mao-Liu struggle from another angle.' *Chinese Law & Government*, 3 (Summer-Fall 1970): 189-205.

642. Chou, Yi-min. 'The Mao-Lin factions deadlocked power seizure struggle.' *Asian Outlook*, 2 (July 1967): 11-16.

643. Chu, Hung-ti. 'Education in Mainland China.' *Current History*, 59 (September 1970): 165-169. An analysis of changes in education during the Cultural Revolution. The author concludes that Mao's reforms 'may be no more successful than the Great Leap Forward.'

644. Cohen, Arthur A. 'The Man and his Politics.' *Problems of Communism*, 15 (September-October 1966). Considers aspects of Mao in symposium on 'What is Maoism?'

645. Dai, Shen-yu. 'Peking's "Cultural Revolution".' *Current History*, 51 (September 1966): 134-139.

646. Dellinger, Dave. 'Report from Revolutionary China.' *Liberation*, 11 (January 1967): 4-10.

647. Doolin, Dennis. 'The Revival of the "Hundred Flowers" Campaign : 1961.' *China Quarterly*, no. 8 (October-December 1961): 34-41. Shows that recent revived campaign has been more restrained than in 1959. Revival may reflect China's need for 'specialists and technicians and that it is not necessary for them to be completely "Red".'

648. Elegant, Robert S. 'Mao vs. China: seeking the "perfect proletarian government".' *New Leader*, 50 (January 1967): 3-7.

649. Ernst, Wolfgang. 'The Foreign Trade Policy of the Mao Tse-tung clique.' *Chinese Economic Studies*, 3 (Fall 1969): 33-47.

650. Field, Robert Michael. 'The Performance of Industry during the Cultural Revolution: Second Thoughts.' *China Quarterly*, no. 108 (December 1986): 625-642. Includes statistics for the 'Ten Years of Disorder,' 1966-1976.

651. Field, Robert Michael, Kathleen M. McGlynn and William B. Abnett. 'Political Conflict and Industrial Growth in China: 1965-1977.' In Congress of the United States, Joint Economic Committee, *Chinese Economy Post Mao*, Washington, D.C.: U.S. Government Printing Office, 1978. 239-83. Shortages of raw materials, work stoppages, the breakdown of transport were caused by political disruption.

652. Fincher, John. 'Mao's China: Old Images and New Reflections-- Thirteen Books on China, Her Policies and Politics, in Review.' *Current Scene*, 5 (31 March 1967): 1-12.

653. Franke, Wolfgang. 'The revolutionary theory and practice of Mao Tse-tung: a contribution to the discussion of the history of communism.' *Modern World*, 1960-1961, 48-53.

654. Fraser, Blair. 'China: chaos, purges and a billion marching feet.' *Maclean's*, 80 (March 1967): 11-18.

655. Freeberne, M. 'Great splash forward.' *Problems of Communism*, 15 (November 1966): 21-27. Examines Mao's swim in the Yangtse in July 1965 and how it has been used to promote cult of Mao. Part of a symposium 'The New Revolution.'

656. Gayn, Mark. 'China Convulsed.' *Foreign Affairs*, (January 1967): 246-59. Discusses Mao's 'Yenan complex' as factor in the Cultural Revolution.

657. _____ 'Mao's Last Revolution.' *The 1968 World Book Year Book*. Chicago: Field Enterprises Educational Corporation, 1968.

658. Gelman, Harry. 'Mao and the Permanent Purge.' *Problems of Communism*, 15 (November-December 1966). Considers origins of Cultural Revolution and nature of 1966 purge, and the roles of Mao, Liu Shaoqi and Lin Biao. Part of a symposium 'The New Revolution.'

659. Gerber, William. 'China under Mao.' *Editorial Research Reports*, (August 1968): 565-82.

660. Gittings, John. 'The Anti-Liu Shao-chi Campaign: the Crimes of China's K.' *Far Eastern Economic Review*, 60 (18 April 1968): 176-179. An analysis of the accusations made against Liu Shaogi in the field of foreign policy.

661. _____ 'New Light on Mao: His View of the World.' *China Quarterly*, no. 60 (December 1974): 750-66. Article examining light thrown on Mao by two volumes of Mao's speeches and writings published in China during Cultural Revolution: *Long Live Mao Tse-tung's Thought* 1967 and 1969. Gittings focusses on Mao's views of international relations.

662. _____ 'The Party is Always Right.' *Far Eastern Economic Review*, 64 (5 June 1969).

663. Goodman, David S. G. 'The Provincial Revolutionary Committee in the People's Republic of China, 1967-1979: An Obituary.' *China Quarterly*, no. 85 (March 1987): 49-71.

664. Griffith, Samuel B. 'Mao Tse-tung--"Sun in the East".' *United States Naval Institute Proceedings*, 1951.

665. Gurley, John G. 'Maoist Economic Development: The New Man in the New China.' *The Center Magazine*, 3, 3 (May 1970): 25-33.

666. Harding, Harry Jr. 'Maoist Theories of Policy-Making and Organization.' In *The Cultural Revolution* edited by Thomas W. Robinson. 113-164. Berkeley, California: University of California Press, 1971.

667. Hook, Brian. 'China's cultural revolution: the pre-conditions in historical perspective.' *World Today*, 23 (November 1967): 454-64.

668. Hsiao, Gene T. 'The Background and Development of "The Proletarian Cultural Revolution".' *Asian Survey*, 7 (June 1967): 389-404. Examines the origins and development of the Cultural Revolution. Concludes 'Mao is in control of the situation and may eventually win the struggle with the continued support of the majority of the PLA.'

669. Hwang, Shao-tzu. 'Anatomy of Mao Tse-tung's thought.' *Asian Outlook*, 3 (December 1968): 9-12.

670. Israel, John. 'The Red Guards in Historical Perspective: Continuity and Change in the Chinese Youth Movement.' *China Quarterly*, no. 30 (April-June 1967): 1-32. Examines the origin of the Red Guards; their role in the struggles of the Cultural Revolution and suggests some historical precedent.

671. Kitts, Charles. 'The Great Proletarian Cultural Revolution.' *Issues & Studies*, 6 (August 1970): 29-35. A brief study focussing on the domestic issues in the Cultural Revolution.

672. Ladany L. 'Mao's China: the decline of a dynasty.' *Foreign Affairs*, 45 (July 1967): 610-23. Examines the period just before the Cultural Revolution, arguing that Mao's power was in decline and that the prominent role of the army indicated weakness at the top of Mao's 'dynasty.' The article also includes a brief outline of the outbreak of the Cultural Revolution in 1966 in Beijing.

673. Lee, H. Y. 'Mao's strategy for revolutionary change: a case study of the cultural revolution.' *China Quarterly*, no. 77 (March 1979): 50-75. The author considers: (1) what was Mao's role in the Cultural Revolution; (2) what faults did he attribute to the pre-Cultural Revolution political system; (3) what were his objectives in the Cultural Revolution; (4) how did he actually lead the movement; (5) was there any discernible pattern in his leadership?

674. Lisann, Maury. 'Moscow and the Chinese Power Struggle.' *Problems of Communism*, 18 (November-December 1969). Discusses Soviet attempts to influence internal Chinese power struggle in favour of Mao's opponents. Part of a symposium on 'China in Flux.'

675. Lowenthal, R. 'Mao's revolution.' *Encounter*, 28 (April 1967): 3-9.

676. MacFarquhar, Roderick. 'Mao's last revolution.' *Foreign Affairs*, 45 (October 1966): 112-124.

677. Machnel, Klaus. 'The Economic Policy of the Mao Tse-tung clique.' *Chinese Economic Studies*, 3 (Fall 1969): 48-69.

678. Malayavin, P. 'The foreign policy of Mao.' *Military Review*, 50 (October 1970): 56-60.

679. Meisner, Maurice. 'Utopian Goals and Ascetic Values in Chinese Communist Ideology.' *Journal of Asian Studies*, 28, 1 (November 1968): 101-110.

680. Michael, Franz. 'The Struggle for Power.' *Problems of Communism*, 16 (May-June 1967). Considers Mao's dual struggle to secure utopian revolutionary communism in China and promote his role as leader of world communism abroad. Part of a symposium 'The New Revolution' III.

681. Murphy, Charles J. V. 'Red China's Sinkiang revolution: beset by failures, an aging Mao Tse-tung lashes out.' *Fortune*, 74 (November 1966): 134-139.

682. Myers, James T. 'De-Stalinization and the new cult of Mao Tse-tung.' *Orbis*, 9 (Summer 1965): 472-93.

683. _____ 'The Fall of Chairman Mao.' *Current Scene*, 6 (15 June 1968): 1-18. 'This article seeks to explore the background of civil strife and disorder and to determine what role may be assigned to . . . Mao Tse-tung in the break-down of civilian authority and the threatened disintegration of the Chinese revolution.'

684. Noumoff, S. J. 'China's Cultural Revolution as a Rectification Movement.' *Pacific Affairs*, 40 (Fall-Winter, 1967/68): 221-234.

685. Oldham, C.H.G. 'Technology in China: Science for the Masses?' *Far Eastern Economic Review*, 60 (16 May 1968): 353-355. Examines the struggle between the 'two-lines' in technology and its significance for the future of Chinese science.

686. 'Philosophy under Mao Tse-tung.' *Hibbert Journal*, 62 (August 1964): 131-33.

687. Pfeffer, Richard M. 'The Pursuit of Purity.' *Problems of Communism*, 18 (November-December 1969): 12-25. Interpretation of Cultural Revolution as Mao's attempt to ensure his vision of the Chinese Revolution prevails. Part of a symposium 'China in Flux.'

688. Possony, Stefan R. 'Mao's strategic initiative of 1965 and the U.S. response.' *Orbis*, 11 (September 1967), no. 1, 149-181.

689. Powell, David E. 'Mao and Stalin's Mantle.' *Problems of Communism*, 17 (March-April 1968). Compares Mao's justification of Cultural Revolution with Stalin's for the 1930's Great Purge and the 1940's 'vigilance campaign.' Part of a symposium 'The New Revolution' IV.

690. Prybyla, Jan S. 'The Soviet View of Mao's Cultural Revolution.' *Virginia Quarterly Review*, 44 (Summer 1968): 385-398.

691. Pye, Lucien W. 'Reassessing the Cultural Revolution.' *China Quarterly*, no. 108 (December 1986): 597-612. Re-examines the Cultural Revolution under the broad questions: (1) What have we learned that is new about how it all began? (2) What can we now say in trying to explain how Chinese society could possibly have produced such a convulsion? (3) How did individuals experience the Cultural Revolution? (4) What has been the impact of the Cultural Revolution on the major institutions of Chinese society? The author concludes that the 'pledge of "never again" has opened an escape valve for dramatic systmatic change,' and yet 'paradoxically, the haunting memories . . . may also intimidate the current Chinese leaders and prevent them from allowing the degree of liberalization and decentralization essential for the success of the reforms in the economic realm.'

692. Ra'anan, Uri. 'Rooting for Mao: the virtues of "anti-revisionism".' *New Leader*, 50 (March 1967): 6-10.

693. Robinson, Thomas W. 'The Wuhan Incident : Local Strife and Provincial Rebellion during the Cultural Revolution.' *China Quarterly*, no. 47 (July/September 1971): 413-438. Examines the Wuhan incident as the turning point in Mao's Cultural Revolution policies.

694. Scalapino, Robert A. 'Mao Tse-tung and the "new left".' *AFL-CIO Free Trade Union News*, 26 (March 1971): 4-5.

695. Schapiro, Leonard and John W. Lewis. 'The Roles of the Monolithic Party under the Totalitarian Leader.' *China Quarterly*, no. 40 (October-December 1969): 39-64. Examines the usefulness of terms, *Bolshevism*, *fuhrerism*, *monolithic* and *movement-regime* in the light of the experience of Lenin, Mussolini, Stalin, Hitler and Mao. Gives particular attention to Mao's role in relation to the CCP in the Cultural Revolution. Concludes that 'Mao seeks to establish a new order that will displace the bureaucratic order built up in the past two decades,' and that 'Mao, like Stalin, is intent on by-passing the Party as the supreme, monopolistic instrument of power.'

696. Schram, Stuart R. 'The Limits of Cataclysmic Change: Reflections on the Place of the "Great Proletarian Cultural Revolution" in the Political Development of the People's Republic of China.' *China Quarterly*, no. 108 (December 1986): 613-624. Reexamines old questions in the light of the latest information and explores new issues, in particular 'whether cultural change is more effectively fostered by debate, and the gradual dissemination of new ideas, or by mass mobilization.'

697. _____ 'The Man and His Doctrines.' *Problems of Communism*, 15 (September-October 1966). Discusses different aspects of Mao's thought, in symposium on 'What is Maoism?'

698. Schulman, Irwin J. 'Mao as Prophet.' *Current Scene*, 8 (7 July 1970): 1-6. Examines 'the charismatic leadership and the role of myth as ways of viewing Mao's relationship to the Chinese Communist Party, and to the people of China.'

699. Schurmann, Franz. 'What is Happening in China?' *New York Review*, (20 October 1966): 18-25 and (12 January 1967): 32-35. Discusses Mao's expectation of American confrontation with China in the light of U.S. escalation in the Vietnam War.

700. Schwartz, Benjamin. 'Some Broad Perspectives on Leader, and Party in the Cultural Revolution.' In *Party Leadership and Revolutionary Power in China*, edited by John W. Lewis. London: Cambridge University Press, 1970. Examines ideas behind Mao's attack on the Party and influences on dominant themes in the Cultural Revolution.

701. _____ 'Upheaval in China.' *Commentary*, (February 1967): 55-62. Article which stresses Mao's 'nostalgic idealization' of the Yanan days.

702. Simon, Sheldon W. 'Maoism and inter-party relations.' *China Quarterly*, no. 35 (July-September 1968): 40-57. Examines the effect of the Cultural Revolution on the Chinese Communist Party's relations with the hitherto pro-Beijing Japan Communist Party. Shows that Chinese foreign policy makers in the Cultural Revolution developed a paranoic world view which led to 'a self-fulfilling prophesy' pursuing 'a policy of subversion against that party which, in fact, forced it into an anti-CCP posture.'

703. Sims, Stephen A. 'The New Role of the Military.' *Problems of Communism*, 18 (November-December 1969). Looks at the greater role of the

military in Chinese politics as a result of the Cultural Revolution. Part of a symposium on 'China in Flux.'

704. Snow, Edgar. 'Interview with Mao.' *The New Republic*, (27 February 1965). Also in Franz Schurmann and Orville Schell *The China Reader*, vol. 3 *Communist China*. New York: Random House, 1966. 359-75.

705. _____ 'The man alongside Mao.' *New Republic*, 155 (3 December 1966): 15-18. On Lin Biao.

706. _____ 'Mao and the new mandate.' *World Today*, 25 (July 1969): 289-305.

707. Solomon, Richard H. 'On Activism and Activists: Maoist Conceptions of Motivation and Political Role Linking State to Society.' *China Quarterly*, no. 39 (July-September 1969): 76-114. Discusses Chinese Communists' attempts to replace Confucian values by revolutionary values through mass agitation and self-criticism. This 'politics of activism' was developed well before the Cultural Revolution but in Solomon's view was an underlying cause. He argues the Cultural Revolution was Mao's attempt to revitalize a bureaucratic Party and government.

708. _____ 'The Pattern of the Chinese Revolution.' *Current History*, 55 (September 1968): 129-134, 173-183. Examines the Cultural Revolution and discusses how Mao has sought to liberate 'the boundless energy of the masses.'

709. Spitz, Allen. 'Maoism and the People's Courts.' *Asian Survey*, 9 (April 1969), no. 4, 255-263.

710. _____ 'Mao's Permanent Revolution.' *Review of Politics*, 30, 4 (October 1968): 440-454.

711. Stolte, Stefan C. 'The four gospels accoridng to Mao Tse-tung.' *Institute for the Study of the USSR Bulletin*, 15 (February 1968): 14-22.

712. Tang Tsou. 'Mao Tse-tung and peaceful coexistence.' *Orbis*, 8 (Spring 1964): 36-51.

713. Tang Tsou and Morton H. Halperin. 'Maoism at home and abroad.' *Problems of Communism*, 14 (July-August 1965): 1-13.

714. Tao, J. 'Mao's world outlook: Vietnam and the revolution in China.' *Asian Survey*, 8 (May 1968): 416-32.

715. Taylor, Charles. 'The death of Maoism.' *Progressive*, 31 (March 1967): 12-16.

716. Terrill, Ross. 'The new revolution: the siege mentality.' *Problems of Communism*, 16 (March-April 1967): 1-10. Interprets the Cultural Revolution as arising out of growing fear of U.S. aggression, which promotes a siege mentality.

717. Ting Wang. 'Power Struggle in Peking: Plots and Counterplots.' *Far Eastern Economic Review*, 59 (25 January 1968): 147-152. Examines, in particular, the career of Kang Sheng, and his talent for survival.

718. Walker, Richard L. 'China's new regime.' *The New Leader*, (October 1962): 19-21.

719. _____ 'Peking's Approach to the Outside World.' In F.N. Trager and W. Henderson (eds.) *Communist China, 1949-1969. A Twenty Year Appraisal*. New York: New York University Press, 1970. Considers the foreign policy implications of the Maoist cult.

720. Wang, Hsueh-wen. 'On Mao Tse-tung's "Educational Revolution".' *Chinese Communist Affairs*, 5 (December 1968): 25-34.

721. _____ 'The Problem of the Schooling System in the Maoist Education Reform.' *Issues & Studies*, 6 (March 1970): 42-55. Examines the impact of Mao's concepts of education on institutes of higher learning, and rural and urban schools.

722. Wang, Yun. 'An analysis of Maoist criticism of the "theory of many centers".' *Issues & Studies*, 5 (October 1968), no. 1, 10-18.

723. Wilson, Dick. 'The Cultural Revolution: The China After Next.' *Far Eastern Economic Review*, 59 (1 February 1968): 189-195. Examines the standpoint of Mao's opponents and the policies of Liu Shaoqi in opposition to Maoism.

724. Yahuda, Michael B. 'Chinese foreign policy after 1963: the Maoist phases.' *China Quarterly*, (October-December 1968): 93-113. After the USSR signed the Nuclear Test Ban Treaty in July 1963, China claimed to

be independent of the Soviet Union in all fields. With the Cultural Revolution 'Maoist foreign policy fulfills the function of reinforcing Maoist formal political authority in China.' It is suggested that the 'myth of global popular adoration of Chairman Mao and the "Thought of Mao Tse-tung" seems to have become a function of the legistimisation of Mao.' However, 'the introversion of Maoist foreign policy . . . coupled with its inconsistencies and many failures . . . may mean that the possibility of its surviving the passing of Mao has been diminished.'

725. 'Yao Wen-yuan: Newcomer in China's Politburo.' *Current Scene*, 7 (15 July 1969): 1-24. An analysis of Yao's career which gives particular attention to his role during rectification campaigns and his rise during the Cultural Revolution. An appendix presents selections from Yao's articles published in the period 1965 to 1968.

Published in the Soviet Union

726. Andronov, I. 'Genesis of Maoism.' *New Times* (Moscow), April 1969: 5-8.

727. Apalin, G. 'Ideological bases of Maoist foreign policy.' *International Affairs* (Moscow), June 1968: 47-55.

728. Delyusin L. and L. Kyuzadzhyan. 'A threat to socialism in China.' *Current Digest Soviet Press*, 19 (July 1967): 7-9.

729. Kapchenko, N. 'The heart of Maoism and its policies.' *International Affairs* (Moscow), May 1969: 10-17.

730. Luvov, O. 'Concerning the events in China: the political manoeuvers of Mao Tse-tung's group.' *Current Digest of the Soviet Press*, 21 (January 1969): 3-6.

731. Pasenchuk, V. and V. Viktokov. 'On the events in China: the anti-pupular policy of the Peking rulers.' *Current Digest of the Soviet Press*, 20 (May 1968): 3-7.

732. Rumyantsev, A. 'In international themes: Maoism and the anti-Marxist essence of its philosophy.' *Current Digest of the Soviet Press*, 21 (March 1969): 10-15.

733. Zanegin, B., Mironov, A. and Mikhaylov, Ya. 'China and its Cultural Revolution: A Soviet Analysis.' (Originally published under the title: *K Sobytiyam v Kitaye* [On Events in China], by the Publishing House of Political Literature, USSR, 1967). Translated in Joint Publications Research Service, no. 48239 (16 June 1969). A wide-ranging analysis of the causes and processes of the Cultural Revolution. Includes consideration of Mao's current policy and his goals.

734. Zanegin, B. 'The failure of Peking's foreign policy.' *Current Digest of the Soviet Press*, 20 (June 1968): 5-7.

X. 1970 to 1976

Books

735. Barnett, A. Doak. *Uncertain Passage*. Washington: Brookings, 1974. 387. An authoritative and comprehensive work. Chapter 1 looks at the conflicts of values and the problem of institutional stability. Chapter 2 analyses the political roles of the military. Chapter 3 focusses on the regime's developmental problems. Chapter 4 examines problems of leadership and the succession question. Chapter 5 is concerned with foreign policy and Chapter 6 summarizes the implications for U.S. policy towards China.

736. Bonavia, David. *Verdict in Peking. The Trial of the Gang of Four*. London: Burnett Books, Hutchinson, 1984. 225. Includes transcripts from the Chinese TV broadcasts of excerpts from the trial. This is a useful commentary which helps to balance the official publication *A Great Trial in Chinese History*, Beijing: New World Press, 1981 (see no. 745). NB Chapter 12 'The plot to kill Mao.'

737. Chan, Anita, Stanley Rosen and Jonathan Unger. *On Soviet Democracy and the Chinese Legal System: The Li Yizhe Debates*. Armonk, New York: M.E. Sharpe, 1985. 310. A study of the activities of three dissidents, Li Zhengtian, Chen Yiyang and Wang Xizhe, from the 1970's to the early 1980's. Examines the origins of the group who were responsible for the famous wall-poster 'On Socialist Democracy and the Legal System' November 1974, which attacked the policies of Mao's wife, Jiang Qing and the Shanghai faction. Includes translated essays, statements and interviews.

738. Chi, Hsin. *The Case of the Gang of Four*. Hong Kong: Cosmos Books Ltd., 1977. 295. A collection of articles originally appearing in *The Seventies*, a Chinese magazine published in Hong Kong, which attempts to explain the downfall of the Gang of Four. This is related to their relationship with Mao in the last years of his life, see, for example 'II. Theory and the Gang of Four' and 'V. The Political Ups and Downs of Teng Hsiaoping.' The Appendix has the first translation of the three documents allegedly written by Deng (Teng) and labelled 'the three poisonous weeds by the Gang of Four' 'On the General Program of Work for the Whole Party and the

Whole Nation.' 'Some Problems in Accelerating Industrial Development.' 'On Some Problems in the Fields of Science and Technology.' Also Deng's comments on 26 September 1975 on the Presentation of Hu Yaobang's report.

739. Derbyshire, Ian. *Politics in China from Mao to Deng*. Edinburgh: W. & R. Chambers, 1987. 134. A summary of political history since 1949 with particular attention to the changes during the years between 1972 and 1987. It is designed for students of politics, journalists and political commentators.

740. Domes, Jurgen. *China after the Cultural Revolution. Politics between Two Party Congresses*. London: Hurst, 1976. 283. (First published in German in Munich by Wilhelm Fink Verlag, 1975). This work concentrates on 'the field of political decision-making and the resulting activities in domestic and foreign policy . . . from the Spring of 1969 to the Autumn of 1973.' The focus is on practical politics beginning with the 'Last Phase of the Cultural Revolution.' In the conclusion 'Revolutionary Leadership and Crises,' Domes says that China's development since the Cultural Revolution seems to indicate that 'Communist rule is subject to the same laws as have been confirmed in the course of other revolutionary movements.' Stage 1, charismatic leadership is followed by Stage 2, transitional leadership. He believes that the prospect for a change in China towards (stage three) institutionalized leadership seem very likely.'

741. Gardner, John. *Chinese Politics and the Succession to Mao*. London: Macmillan, 1982. 217. A well-written account of the political history of the People's Republic since the late 1960's, and a useful introduction to the study of Chinese politics.

742. Ginneken, Jaap van. *The Rise and Fall of Lin Piao*. Harmondsworth, Middlesex: Pengiun Books, 1976. 348. First published as *De linkse stroming in China*, in Amsterdam, 1974. Translated by Danielle Adkinson. This book begins with the confusion surrounding the disappearance of Lin Biao, Minister of Defence and Vice-Chairman of the Communist Party, in September 1971. It subsequently emerged that Lin Biao had been aiming to seize power, and it was believed he was forced to escape in a plane which crashed in the People's Republic of Mongolia. The author tracks Lin Biao's growing prominence after 1959 and his role in the Cultural Revolution. He suggests Lin Biao was opposed to rapprochement with the U.S. and also in conflict with Zhou Enlai (Chou En-lai) over appointment of leading Party cadres.

743. Goldwasser, Janet and Stuart Dowty. *Huan-Ying: Workers' China*. New York: Monthly Review Press, 1975. 404. Describes a seven week visit to China. An uncritical report on China under Mao.

744. Goodstadt, Leo. *China's Watergate. Political and Economic Conflicts, 1969-1977*. New Delhi: Vikas Publishing House, 1979. 219. This account begins with the downfall of the Gang of Four, which included Mao's widow Jiang Qing (Chiang Ching) at the end of 1976. Goodstadt traces the struggle between Zhou Enlai (Chou En-lai) and Lin Biao (Lin Piao) in the late 1960's and the death of Lin after the failure of his conspiracy against Mao. He goes on to examine Mao's isolation in the years before his death as Chou and Deng Xiaoping (Teng Hsiao-ping) promoted anti-leftist policies.

745. *A Great Trial in Chinese History*. Beijing: New World Press, 1981. 246. This official report of the trial of the Gang of Four throws light on the period from the Cultural Revolution to Mao's death with particular attention to Mao's wife and by implication the late Chairman himself. Photographs of leading personalities as defendants in the dock.

746. Hinton, William. *Shenfan. The Continuing Revolution in a Chinese Village*. London: Secker and Warburg, 1983. 789. Based on a return visit in 1971 to Long Bow, the village which was documented in *Fanshen*. *Shenfan*, which means 'deep-digging,' presents a new aspect of the Great Leap Forward, with insight into Mao's methods, and his errors in unleasing the Cultural Revolution. Good descriptive material brings the village to life.

747. Kim, Ilpyong J. and Vic Falkenheim. *Chinese Politics from Mao to Deng*. New York: Paragon, 1989. 256. This collection of essays shows how the reforms of the CCP under Deng 'were a reaction to the Maoist era of cultural revolution and mass oppression.'

748. Kissinger, Henry. *The White House Years*. London: Weidenfeld, 1979. 1521. These memoirs cover Kissinger's years as President Nixon's National Security Adviser in the first Nixon Administration (1969-1972). This was the period in which the U.S. reversed its previous hostility to China, and increasingly close diplomatic relations developed between the two governments. Kissinger describes the initial 'ping pong diplomacy' (Chapter 18), Kissinger's first secret journey to Beijing (Chapter 19), and Nixon's visit to China in 1972 (Chapter 24). Kissinger describes in Chapter 24 his (and Nixon's) first meeting with Mao and comments on Mao's manner and personality. He also gives his assessment of the implications of the visit.

749. _____ *Years of Upheaval*. London: Weidenfeld and Nicolson, 1982. 1283. This is the second volume of Kissinger's memoirs of his period as architect of U.S. foreign policy under President Nixon (sequel to *White House Years*), and covers the period 1973 to the end of the Nixon Administration in 1974. The most dramatic phase of U.S. diplomacy with China was over by 1973, but Chapter 15 (pp. 678-699) describes Kissinger's visit to China in November 1973, when he met Zhou Enlai and also talked with Mao. Kissinger describes Mao's comments on foreign policy which involved a general survey of world developments, and included Mao's advice on how the U.S. should hold its alliances together. Kissinger comments: 'Starting from opposite ends of the ideological spectrum, we had become tacit partners in maintaining the global equilibrium.'(p.693)

750. Leys, Simon. *Chinese Shadows*. New York: Viking Press, 1977. 220. Based on a six month stay in China in 1972. The author is negatively impressed.

751. Lotta, Raymond (ed). *And Mao makes 5: Mao Tse-tung's last great battle*. Chicago: Banner Press, 1978. 522. Lotta begins by examining the power struggle at the top of the Party in the period 1973-1976 between Mao and the Gang of Four on the one side and Zhou Enlai (Chou En-lai) and Deng Xiaoping (Teng Hsiao-ping) on the other. The issue was whether to pursue the goals of the Cultural Revolution or to reverse them. Lotta's account covers the overthrow of the Gang of Four shortly after Mao's death and the triumph of the new moderate leadership.

752. Menon, M.S.N. *Dragon Changes Its Skin*. New Delhi: Perspective Publications, 1974. 224. The author is particularly concerned with relations between China and India.

753. Nixon, Richard. *The Memoirs of Richard Nixon*. London: Sidgwick and Jackson, 1978. 1120. Nixon's extensive memoirs cover his life from 1913 to the end of his Presidency in 1974. In his account of his first Administration Nixon includes a description of his historic visit to China in 1972 (pp. 557-80) and records conversations with Mao and Zhou Enlai.

754. Snow, Edgar. *The Long Revolution*. London: Hutchinson, 1973. 269. This book is based on Snow's last trip to China in 1970-71, and was unfinished when he died in 1972. It includes background information on the Cultural Revolution, but is primarily about Snow's travels and interviews on his last visit, including an interview with Mao himself. The book ends with a discussion of China's reasons for rapprochement with the U.S. The

appendices include Snow's accounts of interviews with Mao and Zhou Enlai in 1965.

755. Worsley, Peter. *Inside China*. East Ardsley, Wakefield: EP Publishing Limited, 1978. 270. (First published by Penguin Books in 1975). The author, a professor of sociology, has based this book largely on what he was told and what he observed during a three week visit to China in 1972. On the whole a sympathetic account of the regime at that time. In light of what we now know it appears an unnecessarily kind interpretation.

756. Wu Tien-wei. *Lin Biao and the Gang of Four*. Carbondale and Edwardsville: Southern Illinois University Press, 1983. 283. Examines two campaigns of the 1970's, the campaign to criticise Lin Biao and Confucius, and the campaign against the Gang of Four.

757. Yao, Ming-le. *The Conspiracy and Murder of Mao's Heir*. London: Collins, 1983. 231. This is a dramatic account of the abortive attempts to assassinate Mao. It claims to be based on top secret documents, and shows that Lin Biao was not shot down over Mongolia but was blown up with the connivance of Mao himself after a last supper together.

Articles

758. Ascherson, Neal. 'The Great Leap Backwards.' *Observer*, London, 5 March 1972. Extracted in A. Lawrance, *China's Foreign Relations Since 1949*, Routledge and Kegan Paul, 1975. Suggests that in the current detente with the United States, China is 'actually retreating from active involvement in world politics, and tying up dangerously loose ends in order to concentrate on her own affairs.' No longer is the Maoist model of world revolution to be exported.

759. Bonavia, D. 'Stability at Stake as Mao retires.' *Far Eastern Economic Review*, 92 (25 June 1976): 10-11.

760. Chao, Ching-chuan. 'Using Chairman Mao's philosophical thinking to guide work of delivering letters.' *Peking Review*, 13 (March 1970), no. 11, 7-11.

761. Forster, Keith. 'The Politics of Destabilization and Confrontation: the Campaign against Lin Biao and Confucius in Zhejiang Province, 1974.' *China Quarterly*, no. 107 (September 1986): 433-462. A detailed account of the campaign in one province, based on articles published between 1976-79

in the *Hangzhou Daily*, and compared where possible with evidence published in 1974. The author concludes that local followers of the radical leaders in the Politburo in that province were more successful in penetrating the power structure than has been previously assumed.

762. Gayn, M. 'Who After Mao?' *Foreign Affairs*, vol. LI, no. 2 (January 1973): 300-309.

763. Goodstadt, L. 'Back to the four cleans.' *Far Eastern Economic Review*, 83 (14 January 1974): 144.

764. Gray, Jack. 'The Economics of Maoism.' In *China After the Cultural Revolution: A Selection from the Bulletin of the Atomic Scientists*. New York: Vintage Books, 1970. 115-142.

765. 'First clues.' *Economist*, 260, 6943 (25 September 1976): 66. On Hua Kuo-feng's speech at Mao's memorial meeting on 18 September, on who seems to be supporting Mao's widow and names members of family on family wreath. (Son, 2 daughters and 2 other relatives.) A very brief story.

766. 'Impossible dream.' *Far Eastern Economic Review*, 86 (7 October 1974): 86.

767. 'Mao and the Mystery Mailer?' *Economist*, 260, 6937 (14 August 1976): 55. Brief commentary on mysterious document purporting to be published by Peking's People's Publishing House called 'Criticise and overthrow the Greatest Revisionist in the Party' attacking Mao, especially for rightist foreign policy. *Economist* suggests this may be a Soviet fabrication.

768. Moody, P. R., Jr . 'Helmsman and the swindlers: notes on the passing of the era of Mao Tse-tung.' *Review of Politics*, 35 (April 1973): 219-41.

769. Nixon, Richard. 'Report to Congress' 9 February 1972. *Department of State Bulletin* (13 March 1972): 313-418.

770. 'Peking in Mourning.' *Far Eastern Economic Review*, 93 (24 September 1976): 13.

771. 'Power and personality in China: Mao Tse-tung, Liu Shao-chi and the politics of charismatic succession (with discussion).' *Studies in Comparative Communism*, 7 (Spring-Summer 1974): 21-73.

772. Robinson, T. W. 'Political succession in China.' *World Politics*, 27 (October 1974): 1-38.

773. Ross, A. 'Chairman Mao, the exorcist.' *Far Eastern Economic Review*, 91 (19 March 1976): 10-13.

774. Schwartz, B. 'Modernization and Maoist vision: some reflections on Chinese communist goals.' *Dissent*, 21 (Spring 1974): 237-48.

775. Snow, Edgar. 'A conversation with Mao Tse-tung.' *Life*, 70, no. 16 (30 April 1971): 46-48. Report of interview with Mao.

776. Van Ness, P. 'Mao Tse-tung and revolutionary self reliance.' *Problems of Communism*, 20 (January-April 1971): 68-74.

777. Walker, R. 'Mao as superman.' *Journal of International Affairs*, 26, 2 (1972): 160-6.

778. Wang, H. J. 'Conversations with Mao: Interview.' *Atlas*, 21 (January 1972): 42-4.

779. Wang Hsueh-wen. 'The "Gang of Four" incident: Official expose by a CCPCC document.' *Issues and Studies*, 13, 9 (September 1977): 46-58. Documentation produced by the Party Central Committee to condemn the Gang of Four.

780. Witke, Roxane. 'More Deluge in Mao's Way.' *Journal of Asian Studies*, 33, 1 (November 1973): 99-103.

XI. Analyses of the Thought of Mao Zedong

Books

781. Adie, W.A.C. *Chinese Strategic Thinking under Mao Tse-tung.* Canberra: Australian National University Press, 1972. 26. This pamphlet, no. 13 of Canberra Papers on Strategy and Defence, shows how the C.C.P.'s strategies are applied to the conduct of foreign relations. The author argues that 'regardless of changes in the hierarchy the Peking government's actions abroad will continue to reflect the politico-military approach ascribed to Mao although much of its past policy had now been repudiated as due to distortion of Maoism by deviationist subordinate leaders.'

782. Aikman, David B. T. *Thought of Mao Tse-tung and Marxism-Leninism.* Seattle: University of Washington, 1972.

783. Albee, Edward. *Box and Quotations from Chairman Mao Tse-tung.* New York: Atheneum, 1969. 74. Two experimental one act plays for the Arts Festival in Buffalo in 1968. *Box* is a monologue by an unseen speaker about the decline of civilisation. In *Quotations* Mao reads, from his *Little Red Book* maxims that comment on the decline of the West.

784. Bouc, Alain. *Mao Tse-tung: a guide to his thought.* Translated from the French by Paul Auster, Lydia Davis. New York: St. Martin's Press, 1977. 230. This study seeks to examine, through a description of the man himself, the depth and influence of his political thought. Begins by discussing Mao's reflections about his own country. Has several pages on the search for a balanced society and the definition of individual and social morality.

785. Briggs, Horace W. *Mao Tse-tung's Concept of Peace and New Order.* Fletcher School of Law and Diplomacy, 1971?

786. Chambre, Henri. *From Karl Marx to Mao Tse-tung; a systematic survey of Marxism-Leninism.* New York: Kennedy, 1963. 308.

787. Chen, David Hsiao-hsin. *The Thought of Mao in the Light of Chinese Tradition and Revolutionary Development.* Salt Lake City: University of Utah, 1970. 206.

788. Chen, Vincent. *Mao Tse-tung's Communist Ideology on Revolution and War.* New Haven: Yale University, 1957.

789. Chen, Yung Ping. *Chinese Political Thought Mao Tse-tung and Liu Shao-chi.* (Revised edition.) The Hague: Martinus Nijhoff, 1971. 129. A lucid exposition of the fundamentals of Chinese Communist ideology. In this revised edition the author made use of source material on the Cultural Revolution which had recently become available. A useful survey of the Mao-Liu disagreements over many years.

790. Chu, Don Chean. *Chairman Mao: Education of the Proletariat.* New York: Philosophical Library, 1980. 478. The author examines Mao's ideas on education. The revolutionary and innovative methods are explained as a pragmatic response to the social changes in China, with particularly sinitic approaches to problems of mass education in towns and countryside.

791. Cohen, Arthur A. *The Communism of Mao Tse-tung.* Chicago: University of Chicago Press, 1964. 210. The author 'attempts to distinguish' between those of his (Mao's) ideas and actions which justifiably may be described as unique in the history of the world Communist movement and those which may not.' He concludes that Mao's highest distinction is as a Communist revolutionary leader. The thought of Mao Zedong 'draws its uniqueness from revisions, improvements and even complete abandonment of various aspects of the foundation tenets and Soviet practices. The view of Mao as an intellectual, whose erudition in philosophy surpasses that of any living Communist is more picturesque than true.' In comparing Stalin and Mao, Cohen points out that whereas Stalin preferred to appear as 'merciless' Mao wished to be seen as 'compassionate.' Nevertheless Mao killed 800,000 opponents in the period 1949-1954 on the grounds that they were enemies of the people.

792. Creel, Herrlee G. *Chinese Thought: From Confucius to Mao Tse-tung.* Chicago: University of Chicago Press, 1953. 293. Mao's ideas are considered briefly in Chapter XII. The author, examining *New Democracy* and *On People's Democratic Dictatorship*, sees 'little to indicate that they were written by a Chinese.' The framework of thought is Marxist; the very rare illustrations relating to Chinese culture seem almost self-consciously added to keep the writings from seeming too 'foreign.'

793. Dai, Shen-yu. *Mao Tse-tung and Confucianism*. Philadelphia: University of Pennsylvania, 1953.

794. Devillers, Philippe. *Mao* (What They *Really* Said series). (First published in German in 1967). English Edition. London: Macdonald, 1969. 317. Written at the time of the Cultural Revolution to put Mao's 'thoughts' into the context of his life, and to highlight their significance for the contemporary world. Shows that Mao's contribution is both Marxist and Chinese-- but 'primarily, principally and deeply Chinese.' The author believes that Mao's works are 'required reading for anyone who wants to understand the "contradictions" of our age.'

795. Garvey, J. E. Marxist-Leninist China: Military and Social Doctrine. New York: Exposition Press, 1960. The author concludes that the Chinese communists are orthodox Leninists with an ingrained xenophobia.

796. Gittings, John. *The World and China, 1922-1972*. London: Eyre Methuen, 1974. 303. Despite the title this book contains a good deal of material on Mao, examining his views on world developments and their impact on China, and the continuities in Mao's thought on China's internal revolution and China's foreign policy interests.

797. Goodstadt, Leo. *Mao Tse-tung. The Search for Plenty*. London: Longman, 1972. 266. An examination of Mao's economic strategy in the context of his wider political goals and an assessment of the various phases and setbacks in China's economic development after 1949. Concludes with a discussion of the implications of Lin Biao's death for economic policy.

798. Hawkins, John N. *Mao Tse-tung and Education: His Thought and Teachings*. Hamden, Connecticut: Linnet Books, 1974. 260. The author believes that 'Mao's . . . educational thought has been a major factor in the attempt to unify, develop and strengthen the People's Republic of China . . . Mao's approach to education is crucial to the eventual emergence of the "new socialist man".' The book is based on Mao's writings over fifty-five years. It examines Mao's analysis of the basic aims, goals and priniciples of education as well as problems related to the structure of both formal and informal education. Includes an extensive and useful partially annotated bibliography, 213-250.

799. Hsiung, J. C. (ed). *The Logic of Maoism; antiques and explication*. New York: Praeger, 1974. 230. The eight contributers are all concerned with the logic of what is labelled '*Maoism*.' They examine 'the domestic and

international application of Mao's thought and programme' and also 'offer substantive critiques, and . . . methodological suggestions on how to make our studies more scientific.' Hsiung himself suggests that there is an element of self-fulfilling prophesy in regard to Mao's premise about the perfectibility of man in a 'correct' social environment. Four of the articles are based on papers delivered in 1973 at the Association of Asian studies convention. The material that has been added includes an article by Bradley Womack on the relationship between theory and practice in Mao's political philosophy.

800. Jin, Steven S. K. *The Thought of Mao Tse-tung: Form and Content.* Hong Kong: Center of Asian Studies, University of Hong Kong, 1976. 271. The author maintaining that Mao's thought is Marxist-Leninist in essence, shows that Mao eliminated some of the impurities of dialectical-materialism and added some important elements of his own.

801. Joseph, William A. *The Critique of Ultra-Leftism in China, 1958-1981.* Stanford, California: Stanford University Press, 1984. 312. This analysis focuses on three examples of 'ultra leftism' in Chinese Communist politics-- the Great Leap Forward, the Cultural Revolution as epitomised in the critiques of Liu Shaoqi and the Gang of Four's policies--and examines the nature of the critiques mounted against these forms of ultra-leftism.

802. Krivtsou, K. I. (ed). *Maoism through the eyes of Communists. The World Communist and Workers' Press on the policies of the Mao Tse-tung group.* Moscow: Progress Publishers, 1970. 326.

803. Lehmann, Johannes. *Mao, Marx und Jesus.* Wuppertal-Barmen: Judend-dienst-Verl., 1969. 117

804. Lowe, Donald M. *The function of 'China' in Marx, Lenin, and Mao.* Berkeley: University of California Press, 1966. 200. A study in the historical significance of the (1) Marxist (2) Leninist and (3) Maoist ideas of China. This is done respectively in relation to the nineteenth century West European intellectual situation; the early twentieth-century Russian intellectual situation and the twentieth century Chinese intellectual situation.

805. Schlomann, Friedrich-Wilhelm. *Die Maoisten.* Frankfurt A. M.: Soc-ietats-Verl, 1970. 300.

806. Schram, Stuart R. *La 'revolution permanente' en Chine.* Paris: Mouton, 1963. Monograph which examines theory of permanent revolution in relation to persistent elements in Mao's thinking, and compares Mao's interpretation

with the views of Marx, Lenin, Trotsky and Stalin. It also discusses how the theory reflects conditions in China in the 1950's. The term 'permanent revolution' was revived to justify the Great Leap Forward of 1958.

807. Sherman, James Charles. *Mao Tse-tung's Concept of Higher Education.* Ann Arbor: University Microfilms, 1972. 177. A dissertation written for the University of Denver, Colorado.

808. Soo, Francis Y. K. *Mao Tse-tung's Theory of Dialectic.* Dordrecht: D. Reidel, 1981. 192. This study is based on the four volumes of Mao's *Selected Works.* The author does not accept the authenticity of the 1937 text of 'On Dialectical Materialism.' (This is now recognised in China. Articles have been published on the difference between the versions of 'On Contradiction' in *Selected Works* and in the original lectures).

809. Starr, John Bryan. *Continuing the Revolution: the Political Thought of Mao.* Princeton, New Jersey: Princeton University Press, 1979. 366. Using all of Mao's writings available to date, the author concentrates on Mao's theory 'of continuing revolution under dictatorship of the proletariat.' He examines the internal logic of this theory and its evolution under various themes. Includes a lengthy bibliography of Mao's writings in chronological order with an indication of where to find English translations.

810. Summers, Gilbert Lee. *Communism in China: the myth of Maoism.* Washington, D.C.: George Washington University, 1963.

811. Thomson, George. *From Marx to Mao Tse-tung. A Study in Revolutionary Dialectics.* London: China Policy Study Group, 1971. A Marxist study of the Russian Revolution of 1917 and the Chinese Revolution of 1949 designed to show their unity and continuity as two necessary stages in the world's socialist revolution. Goes through to the Ninth Party Congress in 1969.

812. Tsai, Harry Do-ning. *The 'New Democracy' Mao Tse-tung's interpretation of Communism.* Berkeley: University of California, 1952.

813. Tsant, Yankee Pierre. *The sociological implications of Mao Tse-tung's 'New Democracy.'* Los Angeles: University of Southern California Press, 1952.

814. U.S. Department of State, Bureau of Intelligence & Research. *The Thought of Mao Tse-tung*. Washington: External Research Division, Department of State, 1962. 73.

815. Whitehead, Raymond. *Love and struggle in Mao's thought*. New York: Orbis Books, 1978. 166. The author writes 'Mao's thought is more than a philosophy; it sums up a revolutionary dynamic that has touched the lives of hundreds of millions of people in China and beyond. To study Mao or the Chinese revolution is not simply an academic exercise, it is a deeply personal encounter leading us to formulate more clearly the questions of whom we serve and where we stand.'

816. Whitehead, Raymond Leslie. *Revolutionary animosity in Mao Tse-tung's thought and a comparison of it with a Christian understanding of love*. New York: Union Theological Seminary, 1972?

817. Wakeman, Frederick, Jr. *History and Will: Philosophical Perspectives of Mao Tse-tung's Thought*. Berkeley: University of California Press, 1973. 392. Asserts (*inter alia*) that Mao's dialectic was not truly Marxian because Chinese metaphysical construction did not possess the universal ontological categories of European rationalism. Much of the book tries to show the primary qualities of Western and Chinese thought about man and nature by taking the reader through segments of each world of ideas rather than simply declaring the differences exist.

818. Wauters, Arthur. *Le communisme de Mao Tse-tung*. Bruxelles: Universite libre de Bruxelles, Institut de Sociologie Solvay, 1957. 112.

819. Ye Qing. *Inside Mao Tse-tung Thought*. (Edited by Stepan Ban, T.H. Zuan, Ralph Mortensen.) Hicksville, New York: Exposition Press, 1975. 336. Ye Qing (Yeh Ching) was a colleague of Zhou Enlai in Paris in 1921-24 and with Mao in Hunan in 1927. He was captured by the Guomindang and has been a vociferous opponent of Maoism ever since. In this book he points out the dangers and inconsistencies in Mao's teachings.

Articles

820. Bedeski, Robert E. 'Concept of the State: Sun Yat-sen and Mao Tse-tung.' *China Quarterly*, no. 70 (June 1977): 338-54. The author concludes that (1) Mao's concept of the state drew rather heavily from the ideas of Sun Yat-sen, (2) Mao adapted the Three People's Principles to conditions which Sun has foreseen--the weakening of world liberalism and

capitalism, and the eruption of Japanese aggression. 'In these respects, Mao's programme of state-building followed the broad outlines of the second united front.'

821. Bonavia, D. 'Debunking the thoughts of Mao Tse-tung.' *Far Eastern Economic Review*, 101 (22 September 1978): 8-9.

822. _____ 'Dismantling parts of Maoism--but not Mao.' *Far Eastern Economic Review*, 98 (7 October 1977): 39-41.

823. Boorman, Howard L. 'Mao Tse-tung as Historian.' *China Quarterly*, no. 28 (October-December 1966): 82-105. Discusses Mao's general view of modern history. The author comments: 'Of all the individuals, both professional and political, who write on historical subjects in the People's Republic of China, Mao Tse-tung alone may speak with freedom and with unimpeachable authority.' He concludes 'Better than any outside historian. Mao Tse-tung himself has left an account, unparalleled in Chinese historical literature, of the strategy and tactics of revolution.'

824. Brugger, Bill. 'From "Revisionism" to "Alienation", from "Great Leaps" to "Third Waves".' *China Quarterly*, no. 108 (December 1986): 643-65. Argues that the diagnosis offered by some humanist Marxists in China in the 1980's is similar to those made by radicals in the mid 1960's. 'The means offered to prevent bureaucratism . . . evoke ideas from more radical times.'

825. Chen, Vincent. 'An evaluation of Mao Tse-tung's analysis of the nature of Chinese society.' *Chinese Culture*, 9,2 (June 1968): 55-72.

826. Cohen, Arthur A. 'How original is "Maoism"?' *Problems of Communism*, 10 (November-December 1961): 34-42.

827. _____ 'What is Maoism? The Man and his Policies.' *Problems of Communism*, 15, 5 (September-October 1966), 8-16.

828. Deng Xiaoping. 'Two whatever policy does not accord with Marxism.' *Beijing Review*, 26 (15 August 1983): 14-15. The 'two whatevers' refers to the statement, attributed to Hua Guofeng and others in February-March 1977, that 'we will resolutely uphold whatever policy decisions Chairman Mao made, and unswervingly follow whatever instructions Chairman Mao made.'

829. Doolin, Dennis J. and Peter J. Golas. 'On Contradiction in the light of Mao Tse-tung's Essay on "Dialectical Materialism."' *China Quarterly*, no.19

(July-September 1964): 38-46. Article arguing that Mao's well known essay 'On Contradiction' was not written in 1937, as Chinese Party history had asserted, but much later. The authors point out that the 1945 and 1947 editions of Mao's Selected Works up to 1944 do not refer to 'On Contradiction' and cite other evidence from Party materials up to 1952. In addition, the authors argue that 'On Contradiction' is more mature than Mao's 1940 essay on 'Dialectical Materialism.' The authors suggest that 'On Contradiction' draws on Stalin's and Zhdonov's writings and that the date has been falsified to strengthen the Chinese Communist claim that Mao was a greater Marxist theoretician. Cf. Schram, 'Mao Tse-tung as Marxist Dialectician.' *China Quarterly*, no. 29 (see no. 867).

830. Fiszman, J. R. 'Appeal of Maoism in Pre-Industrial, Semi- Colonial Political Cultures.' *Political Science Quarterly*, 74 (March 1959): 71-88.

831. Forster, K. "Mao Tse-tung on the Transition Period from Capitalism to Communism (Speech).' *Journal of Contemporary Asia*, 6, 1 (1976): 101-6.

832. Frakt, P. M. 'Mao's concept of representation.' *American Journal of Political Science*, 23 (November 1979): 684-704.

833. Friedman, Edward. 'Einstein and Mao: Metaphors of Revolution.' *China Quarterly*, no. 93 (March 1983): 51-75. Considers Mao's understanding of Einsteinianism as a metaphor of continuing revolution.' After Mao's death and the arrest of the Gang of Four 'Mao's favoured Einsteinian model of infinite divisibility, the straton model, was "museumified".'

834. _____ 'Neither Mao nor Che: the practical evolution of revolutionary theory.' *Comparative Studies in Society and History*, 12 (April 1970): 134-9.

835. _____ 'On Maoist conceptualization of the capitalist world system.' *China Quarterly*, no. 80 (December 1979): 806-37. The author provides an analytical overview of the extent of Maoist committment to anti-imperialism before and after Liberation. This includes the theoretical claims that 'The theory of Mao Tse-tung is a development of Marxism-Leninism in the East . . . For the entire world struggle as a whole, it is of universal significance.' (Chen Boda). The author considers that western 'progressives' have wrongly accused the Chinese of being traitors to the cause. He concludes 'A virtue of world systems theory is its concern with core states, semi-peripheral states and peripheral states. This concern better explains why the politicised world market system continues no matter what one state does. It explains why so little is achieved at the world level despite principled and mighty efforts at

the state level . . . and why the efforts of Maoist ruling groups and others necessarily fall far short of achieving their sincerely stated goal of ending the robber's world.'

836. Glaberman, Martin. 'Mao as a Dialectician.' *International Philosophical Quarterly*, 8 (1968): 94-112. Discusses Mao's essays 'On Practice,' and 'On Contradiction' and looks briefly at 'political' text 'On the Correct Handling of Contradictions among the People.' Concludes that Mao departs strikingly from 'dialectical materialism' and that Mao's philosophy 'is the servant of his policies.'

837. Gouldner, A. W. 'Marxism and Mao.' *Partisan Review*, 40, 2 (1973): 243-54.

838. Gray, J. 'Politics in command: the Maoist theory of social change and economic growth.' *Political Quarterly*, 45 (January 1974): 26-48.

839. Gregor, A. J. and M. J. Chang. 'Maoism and Marxism in comparative perspective.' *Review of Politics*, 40 (July 1975): 307-27.

840. Hak, H. and E. von Ree. 'Was the older Mao still a Maoist?' *Journal of Contemporary Asia*, 14, 1 (1984): 82-93.

841. Ho, D.Y.F. 'Conception of Man in Mao Tse-tung thought.' (bibliog). *Psychiatry*, 41 (November 1978): 391-402.

842. Hoffman, Charles. 'The Maoist economic model.' *Journal of Economic Issues*, 5, 3 (September 1971): 12-27.

843. Holubnychy, Vsevolod. 'Mao Tse-tung's Materialist Dialectics.' *China Quarterly*, no. 19 (July-September 1964): 3-37. The thesis of this article is that mao's materialistic dialectics has a definite place of its own in the realm of the Marxist-Leninist-Stalinist philosophy. Its discernible differences are somewhat related to the dialectics of classical Chinese philosophy, and may be partly explained by the fact that Mao's reading in Marxian classics were 'possibly less extensive than his readings in Chinese classics. The rest of the differences and peculiarities come from his own thinking.'

844. Horn, R. C. 'China and Russia in 1977: Maoism without Mao.' *Asian Survey*, 17 (October 1977): 919-30.

845. 'How to define Mao Zedong thought: changes over 40 years.' *Beijing Review*, 24 (2 March 1981): 12-15.

846. Klein, Sidney. 'Capitalism, socialism and the economic theories of Mao Tse-tung.' *Political Science Quarterly*, 73 (March 1958): 28-46.

847. Knight, Nick. 'Mao Zedong's *On Contradictions* and *On Practice*: pre-liberation texts.' *China Quarterly*, no. 84 (December 1980): 641-68.

848. Kraus, R. C. 'Limits of Maoist egalitarianism.' *Asian Survey*, 16 (November 1976): 1081-96.

849. Levy, R. 'New Light on Mao: His Views on the Soviet Union's "Political Economy".' *China Quarterly*, no. 61 (March 1975): 95-117. Based on recently available *wan-sui* material.

850. Lin Chin-jan. 'A Great Creation in the History of Proletarian Revolution.' *Peking Review*, 20, 37-38 (13 September 1977): 24-28. An abridged translation of an article in *Hongqi*. The author, a supporter of Hua Guofeng emphasises the continuing validity of Mao's revolutionary line, and stresses that if any persons should try to usurp Party and state leadership 'we will, under the leadership of the Party Central Committee headed by Chairman Hua, apply the method used by Chairman Mao in launching the Great Proletarian Cultural Revolution, mobilize the people of the whole country, practice mass democracy and overthrow them.'

851. Ma Qibin et al. 'Formation and development of Mao Zedong thought.' *Beijing Review*, 25 (8 February 1982): 15-21.

852. MacInnis, Donald E. 'Maoism: the religious analogy.' *Christian Century*, 85 (January 1968): 39-42.

853. Masi, Edoarda. 'Mao's thought and the European left.' *Socialist Revolution*, 1 (July/August 1970), no. 4. 15-38.

854. Mehnert, Klaus. 'Mao and Maoism: Some Soviet Views.' *Current Scene*, 8 (1 September 1970): 1-16. The author shows how Soviet writers have presented Maoism in literary publications.

855. Meisner, Maurice. 'Leninism and Maoism: Some Populist Perspectives in Marxism-Leninism in China.' *China Quarterly*, no. 45 (January/March 1971): 2-36. This article argues Maoism cannot be understood simply

through a comparison with Leninism, and relates some 'implicit stands in Maoist thought to the general intellectual tendencies of Russian Populism.'

856. Namiotkiewicz, N. 'Chauvinist content of the three world's theory.' *World Marxist Review*, 21 (November 1970): 74-85.

857. 'National symposium on Mao Zedong's thought.' *Beijing Review*, 26 (28 November 1983): 5-6.

858. Nomura, Koichi. 'Mao Tse-tung's thought and the Chinese revolution.' *Developing Economics*, 5 (March 1967): 86-104.

859. Pfeffer, R. 'Mao and Marx in the Marxist-Leninist Tradition: A Critique of "The China Field" and a Contribution to a Preliminary Reappraisal.' *Modern China*, vol. II, no. 4 (October 1976): 421-60.

860. Ramachandran, K. N. 'Maoism.' *International Studies*, New Delhi, 8 (April 1967): 422-443.

861. Robertson, R. T. 'The Cultural Revolution (1966-1978) in Maoist and Dengist strategies of development.' *Journal of Contemporary Asia*, 14, 3 (1984): 325-42.

862. Rue, John E. 'Is Mao Tse-tung's dialectical materialism a forgery?' *Journal of Asian Studies*, 26, 3 (May 1967): 464-8.

863. Schram, Stuart R. 'Chairman Hua edits Mao's literary "On the 10 Great Relationships" heritage.' *China Quarterly*, no. 69 (March 1977): 126-35. Schram suggests that 'On the 10 Great Relationships' (25 April 1956) was an attempt by Mao to lay down a balanced line. The single overriding theme of the speech is the need to take account of all aspects of every question. Chairman Hua may feel it can serve the same purpose in 1977.

864. _____ 'From the "Great Union of the Popular Masses" to the "Great Alliance".' *China Quarterly*, no. 49 (January-March 1972): 88-105. In commenting on Mao's essay 'The Great Union of the Popular Masses' Schram develops parallels with Mao's ideas during the Cultural Revolution. He comments '. . . the Mao Tse-tung of 1919 has not yet seriously begun to assimilate Marxism, whereas the Mao Tse-tung of the Cultural Revolution had altogether moved beyond Marxism to conceptions not altogether compatible with the logic of Marxism or of Leninism.'

865. _____ 'Mao Tse-tung and the Secret Societies.' *China Quarterly*, no. 27 (July-September 1966): 1-13. Mao approached the secret societies 'not simply from the outside, as a revolutionary seeking to manipulate them, but also with a certain degree of instinctive comprehension and sympathy.' However, the explicit evidence on Mao's attitude towards and relations with the secret societies is extremely limited. Appendix has translation of 'Appeal of the Central Soviet Government of the Ko-lao-hui.' (see no. 59).

866. _____ 'Mao Tse-tung and the Theory of the Permanent Revolution, 1958-1969.' *China Quarterly*, no. 46 (April-June 1971): 221-44. The main concern of this article is not the history of Marxist doctrine, nor contrasts between Soviet and Chinese conceptions of revolution, 'but with the circumstances in which the theory emerged in China in 1958' when Mao urged the Great Leap Forward.

867. _____ 'Mao Tse-tung as Marxist Dialectician.' A Review Article. *China Quarterly*, no. 29 (January-March 1967): 155-65. Reviews A. A. Cohen, *The Communism of Mao Tse-tung* (see no. 793). Criticises *inter alia* Mr. Cohen's belief that 'On Practice' and 'On Contradiction' were not delivered in 1937, and cites Professor Wittforgel's arguments for accepting the official dating of these articles.

868. _____ 'Mao Tse-tung's Thought to 1949.' 789-870. *The Cambridge History of China*, vol. 13. 'Republican China 1912-1949.' Part 2, ed. John K. Fairbank and Albert Feuerwerker. Cambridge: Cambridge University Press, 1986.

869. _____ 'The "Military Deviation" of Mao Tse-tung.' *Problems of Communism*, 13, 1 (January/February 1964): 49-56. Article covering that aspect of Chinese nationalism that has always characterised Mao: his 'fondness for posing and solving problems in military terms.' Schram traces this tendency from Mao's first article in 1917 through to the Great Leap of 1958. Mao's 'military deviation' in internal affairs is interpreted as extreme voluntarism, his 'belief that the masses can do anything and his emphasis on political mobilization rather than technical competence.' This is an essay stressing military cost of Mao's political thought and strategy, not specifically on Mao's guerrilla tactics.

870. _____ 'The party in Chinese communist ideology.' *China Quarterly*, no. 38 (April-June 1969): 1-26. The author concentrates on those aspects of Chinese views of the party which best serve to define their originality; such decisive concepts as the nature of the Party, the locus of authority within the

Party, and the Party's relation to other organisations and social groups. The first part of the article deals with the views of Mao and Liu Shaoqi in the period from Yanan to after the Great Leap Forward.

871. Schwartz, Benjamin. 'China and the West in the "Thought of Mao Tse-tung".' *China In Crisis*, vol.1 (1968): 365-396.

872. _____ 'The Legend of the "Legend of Maoism".' *China Quarterly*, no. 2 (April-June 1960): 35-42. Reply by Schwarz to article by Wittfogel (see no. 894), contesting accuracy of Wittfogel's analysis and rejecting Wittfogel's conception of Marxism-Leninism.

873. _____ 'Mao Tse-tung and Communist Theory.' *New Leader*, 43 (April 1960): 18-21.

874. _____ 'Maoist image of world order.' *Journal of International Affairs*, 21, 1 (1967): 92-102.

875. _____ 'Modernization and Maoist Vision--Some Reflections on Chinese Communist Goals.' *China Quarterly*, no. 21 (January-March 1965): 3-10. Discusses conflict between modernisation and the Maoist vision of the 'good society' and concludes Mao will give priority to ideology so long as he is at the helm.

876. Shi, Zhongquan. 'Liu Shaoqi's contribution to Mao Zedong Thought.' *Beijing Review*, 25 (19 April 1982): 15-18.

877. Shi, Z. and Yang, Z. 'Zhou Enlai on Mao Zedong thought.' *Beijing Review*, 24 (2nd March 1981): 8-11.

878. Starr, John Bryan. 'Conceptual foundations of Mao Tse-tung's theory of continuous revolution.' *Asian Survey*, 11, 6 (June 1971): 610-28.

879. _____ 'From the 10th Party Congress to the Premiership of Hua Kuo-feng : The Significance of the Colour of the Cat.' *China Quarterly*, no. 67 (September 1976): 457-488. Examines the conflict between the Maoist and the Dengist 'lines' between August 1973 and April 1976. The title refers to Deng's famous criticism of Maoist policies; that the colour of a cat is irrelevant so long as it catches mice.

880. Sudama, T. 'Analysis of classes by Mao Tse-tung 1923-39.' *Journal of Contemporary Asia*, 8, 3 (1973): 355-73.

881. Tang, Tsou. 'Mao Tse-tung thought and the post-Mao era.' *China Quarterly*, no. 71 (September 1977): 498-527. Discusses how the 'Gang of Four' and their opponents in the succession struggle both draw on Mao's theoretical formulations.

882. Thomas, P. 'Mao-Marx Debate: a view from outside China.' *Politics and Society*, 7, 3 (1977): 331-41.

883. Townsend, J. R. 'Mao and Maoism.' (Review article). *Problems of Communism*, 15 (January 1966): 15-35.

884. Tsui, Chui-yien. 'Does Mao Tse-tung's thought originate in the Chinese tradition?' *Issues and Studies*, 4 (April 1968): 1-8.

885. Walder, A. 'Marxism, Maoism and Social Change.' *Modern China*, vol. III, no. 1 (January 1977): 101-18; vol. III, no. 2 (April 1977): 125-60.

886. Wang, Qi. 'Inheriting and developing Mao Zedong thought.' *Beijing Review*, 26 (26 December 1983): 20-26.

887. Wang, Shao-lan. 'Mao Tse-tung's thought.' *Chinese Communist Affairs*, 4 (April 1967), no. 2. 19-25.

888. Weakland, J. H. 'Family imagery in a passage by Mao Tse-tung: on essay in psycho-cultural method.' *World Politics*, 10 (April 1958): 387-407.

889. Whyte, Martin King. 'Bureaucracy and Modernization in China: The Maoist critique.' *American Sociological Review*, 38, 2 (April 1973): 149-63.

890. Wittfogel, Karl A. 'The influence of Leninism-Stalinism on China.' *Annals of the American Academy of Political and Social Science*, September 1951.

891. _____ 'The Legend of Maoism.' Part 1: *China Quarterly*, no. 1 (January-March 1960): 72-86. Part 2: *China Quarterly*, no. 2 (April-June 1960): 16-31. Article arguing that Mao was not diverging significantly from Marxism-Leninism and that he was not an original Marxist theoretician and did not, up to 1940, claim to be so. The argument is directed against western analysts, in particular John K. Fairbank and Benjamin Schwartz who in Wittfogel's view do claim Mao did abandon basic principles of Marxism-Leninism and develop an original theory--a thesis Wittfogel dubs as 'Marxist.' See reply by Schwartz (see no. 875).

892. Young, G. and Woodward, D. 'From contradictions among the people to class struggle: the theories of uninterrupted revolution and continuous revolution.' *Asian Survey*, 18 (September 1978): 912-33.

893. Zhang, B. 'Differentiations are necessary.' *Beijing Review*, 24 (21 September 1981): 16-18. The author, a staff member of *Renmin Ribao*, argues that Mao's mistakes must be excluded from Mao Zedong Thought, which he defines as 'the application and development of Marxism-Leninism in China, the proven correct theoretical principles of the Chinese revolution, the summation of experiences and the crystallization of the collective wisdom of the Communist Party of China. The most significant contributions to the development of Mao Zedong Thought were made by Comrade Mao Zedong.'

894. Zhang, Gong. 'Mao Zedong's thought on socialist economic construction.' *Beijing Review*, 26 (19 December 1983): 14-17.

XII. Mao's Military Strategy

Books

895. Asian Peoples' Anti-Communist League, Republic of China. *A research on Mao Tse-tung's thought of military insurrection*. Taipei: 1961. 94.

896. Boorman, Scott. *The Protracted Game: A Wei-ch'i Interpretation of Maoist Revolutionary Strategy*. New York: Oxford University Press, 1969. 242. 'Weiqi' (Wei-chi) has been a favourite game of strategy of Chinese generals, statesmen and literati from the Han dynasty to Mao. The structure of the game, and in particular its abstractness, makes possible a depth of analogy which has no parallel in the relatively superficial comparisons of western forms of military strategy to chess or poker. Mao in some of his writings on strategy, for example, 'On Protracted War' referred to Wei-chi. This work looks at the Jiangxi period, the Sino-Japanese War and the Civil War, showing analogies with 'Weiqi' strategy.

897. Gittings, John. *The Role of the Chinese Army*. London: Oxford University Press, 1967. 331. Examines the transformation and modernisation of the People's Liberation Army from the civil war period to the Cultural Revolution. Discusses the contradiction between 'revolutionisation' and 'professionalisation' and the changing political and social roles of the army since 1949. Includes chapters on 'The PLA and Society' and 'The People's Militia.'

898. Griffith, Samuel B. *The Chinese People's Liberation Army*. London: Weidenfeld and Nicolson, 1968. 398. This broad-ranging study 'seeks to set Communist Chinese military developments within the context of the Chinese revolution.' Chapters 1 to 6 provide a history of the Red Army to Liberation. Chapter 14 considers 'The Magnificent Military Theories of Chairman Mao Tse-tung.'

899. Hsieh, Alice. *Communist China's Military Doctrine and Strategy*. Santa Monica, California: Rand Corporation, 1963.

900. Jencks, Harlan. *From Muskets to Missiles: Politics and Professionalism in the Chinese Army, 1945-1981*. Boulder, Colorado: Westview 1982. 322. Beginning with some theoretical analysis of Party-Army relations the author has brought together a lot of information to explain the factional politics within the PLA and the Party.

901. Johnson, Chalmers. *Autopsy on People's War*. Berkeley: University of California Press, 1974. 118. Johynson sees the revolutionary struggles of the 1960's in the Third World as the consequence of Chinese efforts to create revolution and thereby provoke massive American retaliation. He concludes that the Maoist model has failed in the contemporary conditions of the Third World.

902. Laqueur, Walter. *Guerrilla: A Historical and Cultural Study*. London: Weidenfeld and Nicolson, 1977. 462. The author covers Mao's guerrilla campaigns and his strategic theory, pp. 239-62.

903. Liu, F. F. *A Military History of Modern China 1924-1949*. Port Washington, New York: Kennikat Press, 1972. 312. (Originally published by Princeton University Press, 1956.) This is primarily a history of Chiang Kai-Shek's military preparations and campaigns, and of Soviet military aid to the Guomindang. But the author includes references to Mao and to Mao's strategic ideas and the role of the Red Army.

904. Marini, Alberto. *De Clauseqitz a Mao Tse-tung*. Buenos Aires: C'irculo Militar, 1969. 236.

905. Nelson, Harvey. *The Chinese Military System: An Organizational Study of the Chinese People's Liberation Army*. Boulder, Colorado: Westview, 1982. 285. A revised edition of a work published in 1977. Useful as a study of PLA organisation.

906. Tsai, Ping-yuan. *People's war of Mao Tse-tung*. Taipei: Asian Peoples' Anti-Communist League, Republic of China, 1966. 104.

Articles

907. An, Thomas S. 'Mao Tse-tung purges military professionalism.' *Military Review*, 48 (August 1968): 88-98.

908. Boorman, Howard L. and Scott A. Boorman. 'Chinese Communist Insurgent Warfare, 1935-1949.' *Political Science Quarterly*, 81, 2 (June 1966): 171-95.

909. Davidson, Philip B. 'The strategy of Mao Tse-tung.' *Army*, 13 (April 1963), no. 9. 65-68.

910. Fuller, Francis F. 'Mao Tse-tung: military thinker. *Military Affairs*, (Fall 1958): 139-145.

911. Garthoff, Raymond L. 'Unconventional Warfare in Communist Strategy.' *Foreign Affairs*, 40 (1962): 566-75. Discusses Mao's military thought.

912. Glucksmann, Andre. 'Politics and war in the thought of Mao Tse-tung.' *New Left Review*, no. 49 (May-June 1968): 41-47.

913. Griffith, Samuel B. 'The glorious military thought of Comrade Mao Tse-tung.' *Foreign Affairs*, 42 (July 1964): 669-674.

914. Hinton, Harold C. 'Political Aspects of Military Power and Policy in Communist China,' in *Total War and Cold War* edited by Harry L. Coles. 266-92. Columbus, Ohio: Ohio State University Press, 1962.

915. Ho, Kenmin. 'Mao's 10 principles of war.' *Military Review*, 47 (July 1967): 96-98.

916. Johnson, Chalmers A. 'Civilian Loyalties and Guerrilla Warfare.' *World Politics*, 14, 4 (July 1962): 646-61. Written at a time when the U.S. administration of J. Kennedy was concerned with increasing the U.S. capability for guerrilla warfare. This is a broad article comparing Lawrence of Arabia, Mao and Guevara. Emphasises the importance of 'attitudes' which was an essential element of Mao's successes in the 1940's. Johnson considers that some analysts have overrated guerrilla tactics and understated the importance of the civilian population.

917. Katzenbach, E. L., Jr. 'Time, space and will: the political-military views of Mao Tse-tung.' *Marine Corps Gazette*, 40 (October 1956), no. 4. 36-40.

918. Katzenbach, L., Jr. and G. Z. Hanrahan. 'Revolutionary strategy of Mao Tse-tung.' *Political Science Quarterly*, 70, no. 3 (September 1955): 321-40. Discussion of Mao's military writings, from 1928 to 1938, especially *'On*

Protracted War' which authors claim probably is 'classic and timeless.' Relates Mao's writings to his actual strategy into the 1940's.

919. 'Mao's Primer on Guerrilla War.' *New York Times Magazine*, 4 June 1961. A popular presentation of Mao's ideas at a time when President Kennedy had ordered the rapid expansion of U.S. provision for guerrilla and contra-guerrilla warfare.

920. Mrazek, James L. 'The philosophy of the guerrilla fighter.' *Army Quarterly*, 96 (April 1968): 64-74.

921. Nihart, F. B. 'Mao's strategic defensive.' *Marine Corps Gazette*, (November 1952): 51-59.

922. Pak, Hyobom. 'China's militia and Mao Tse-tung's "People's War".' *Orbis*, 11 (Spring 1967), no. 1. 285-294.

923. Powell, R. L. 'Maoist military doctrines.' *Asian Survey*, 8 (April 1968): 239-62.

924. Tang, Tsou and M. H. Halperin. 'Mao Tse-tung's revolutionary strategy and Peking's international behaviour.' *American Political Science Review*, 59 (March 1963): 80-99. Article arguing that explanation for China's ability to enter the nuclear arms race and success in foreign policy, despite China's relative weakness, must be sought in Mao's revolutionary strategy at home and abroad. Examines Mao's revolutionary rise to power and his military and political theories.

XIII. Mao the Poet

Zang Kejia, a celebrated poet and Editor-in-Chief of *Shi Kan* (Poetry Magazine) who had written to Mao, received the following reply. It was dated 26 December 1961 (which happened to be Mao's birthday). The following is the full text of the letter in Mao's handwriting.

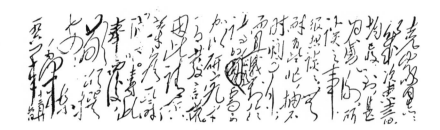

Translation

Dear Comrade Kejia,
Thank you very much for the letters you sent me. I am rather keen on the question you raise. Unfortunately, I'm busy with my work and cannot find time for it. Besides I have no right to speak on the question of poetry unless I make a study of it. So I'm afraid you will have to wait a little while.
With sincere regards
Mao Zedong

--From *Beijing Review*, vol. 26, no. 52.

**Arranged alphabetically by author, translator or
editor where known, otherwise by title**

Books

925. N. B. Jerome Chen's biography *Mao and the Chinese Revolution* OUP 1965 (see no. 191) contains thirty-seven poems translated by Michael Bullock and Jerome Chen, together with an introductory note on Mao's style. Robert Payne's biography *Portrait of a Revolutionary: Mao Tse-tung*, New York: 1961 (see no. 231) has nineteen of Mao's poems, translated with a commentary in Chapter 10.

926. Mao Zedong. *The Poems of Mao Tse-tung.* Translated by Willis Barnstone. London: Barrie and Jenkins, 1972. 144. Prints selection of thirty-five poems written by Mao between 1925 and 1963. The poems are annotated and the editor has written a brief introduction on Mao as a political leader and as a poet.

927. _____ *Poems.* Translated by Andrew Boyd and Gladys Yang. Peking: Foreign Languages Press, 1959.

928. _____ *Mao Tse-tung: Nineteen Poems.* Peking: Foreign Languages Press, 1958. Nineteen poems, 18 of which were published and widely disseminated in China early in 1957. Includes well known poem 'Snow.' Explanatory comments by Zang Kejia, editor of the monthly *Poetry*.

929. _____ *Poems.* Translated by Engle, Hua-ling Nieh and Paul Engle. New York: Dell, 1972.

930. _____ Poems. *Chinese Literature*, no. 1, 1963. Collection of six of Mao's poems composed while 'humming on horseback' between 1929-1931. Published by *People's Literature*, May 1962 in Chinese, with long commentary and annotations by Kuo Mo-jo. Published to commemorate the twentieth anniversary of Mao's talks at Yanan Forum on Art and Literature in May 1942. Describes successes of China Communist forces against Nationalists, probably published in 1962 to bolster morale in aftermath of failure of Great Leap Forward. See Ng, 'The Poetry of Mao Tse-tung' (see no. 936).

931. _____ *Poems.* Translated by Wong Man. Hong Kong: Eastern Horizon Press, 1966. Annotated selection. Includes 1925 poem 'Changsha' on exploits of Mao and his fellow students.

932. _____ 'Ten Poems' *Chinese Literature*, no. 5, 1966.

933. _____ *Ten More Poems*. Hong Kong: Eastern Horizon Press, 1967.

934. _____ *Poems*. Beijing: Foreign Languages Press, 1976. 53. Thirty-six poems with a note on the verse form by the translators.

Articles

935. Ho, Ping-ti. 'Two Major Poems by Mao Tse-tung.' *Queen's Quarterly*. Kingston, Canada: LXV no. 2, 1958. 257.

936. Ng, Yong-sang. 'The Poetry of Mao Tse-tung.' *China Quarterly*, no. 13 (January-March 1963): 60-73. Discusses in particular the six poems published in 1962. All six describe incidents in which the Communist forces were beating the Nationalists; and their publication may be an attempt to raise morale and revolutionary spirit against current difficulties in the aftermath of the Great Leap Forward.

937. Mao Zedong. 'A letter discussing poetry,' 12 January 1957. *New York Times*, 13 June 1963.

938. _____ 'An unpublished poem of Mao Tse-tung.' Translated by Jerome Ch'en. *China Quarterly*, 34 (April-June 1968): 3.

939. _____ 'Midstream' (poem) adapted by E. Birney. *New Statesman*, 60 (24 September 1960): 439. Poem written 1920, adapted by Earle Birney from literal translation by Ho Ping-ti.

940. _____ 'Trumpet of our time?' *Economist*, 210, 6289 (7 March 1964): 880. (Poems by Mao Tse-tung). On ten recently published poems by Mao written in 1961 and 1962. Quotes from three and explains political allusions to U.S. and USSR.

941. Palandri, Angela Jung. 'The Political Significance of Mao Tse-tung's Poetry. Certain Contradictions between Theory and Practice.' *East Asia occasional papers*, II. Honolulu: University of Hawaii, Asian State Program, 1970. 46-58.

942. Payne, Robert. 'Poetry of Mao Tse-tung.' *Cornhill*, 170 (Fall 1958): 177-188. Includes translation of Changsha; Pavilion of the yellow cranes; Land of the great pines; Lou pass; Sixteen word rhymes; Long March;

Liupeng mountain; Gun long mountains; Snow; Poem for Liu Yazi; Another poem for Liu Yazi, Bei Dai river; Swimming.

943. _____ 'The Poetry of Mao Tse-tung.' *The Literary Review*, 2, 1 (Autumn 1958).

944. Schram, Stuart R. 'Mao as a Poet.' *Problems of Communism*, no. 5 (1964): 38-44.

945. Tay, C. N. 'From Snow to Plum Blossoms: a commentary on some poems by Mao Tse-tung.' *Journal of Asian Studies*, 25 (February 1966): 287-308.

946. _____ 'Two poems of Mao Tse-tung in the light of Chinese literary tradition.' *Journal of Asian Studies*, 29 (May 1970) 633-55.

XIV. Historiography

Books

947. Bandyopadhyaya, Jayantanuja. *Mao Tse-tung and Gandhi: perspectives on social transformation*. Bombay, India: Allied, 1973. 156. This book begins with the historical backgrounds of Gandhi and Mao and then proceeds to examine themes such as 'People's War and satyagraha' and 'mass line and constructive program.' The author sums up the respective achievements of the two men, and offers a tentative 'third model' of social and political change.

948. Blecher, Marc. *China: politics, economics and society: iconoclasm and innovation in a revolutionary Socialist country*. Boulder, Colorado: Rienner, 1986. 232. An interpretation of developments since Liberation which appears to idealise Maoism as 'direct mass democracy in action.' On the Cultural Revolution Blecher writes that Mao 'was not given to despondency and inaction; he was an activist and an optimist' and 'students all over China spontaneously formed themselves into groups that came to be known as Red Guards.' The author maintains that the Cultural Revolution was not a reenactment of the Great Leap Forward. Includes chapters on the Chinese Communist Party's rise to power and a chapter comparing socialism in China and the Soviet Union. There is a detailed description of the Socialist Education Movement of the early 1960's and Mao's perspective of the 'Two-line struggle.'

949. Burlatsky, Fedor. *Mao Tse-tung: an ideological and psychological portrait*. Moscow: Progress, 1980. 397. The author is a distinguished social scientist. He considers Mao's psychological outlook in relation to ideology and Chinese policy options, in particular, in the relationships with the super powers. He concludes that China will find it economically beneficial to restore good relations with the USSR.

950. Deng Xiaoping. *Selected Works*. Beijing: Foreign Languages Press, 1984. 418. Contains forty-seven talks and speeches given by Deng Xiaoping from 1975 to 1982, most of which are published for the first time. The eight speeches in 1975 reflect 'the head-on struggle he waged against the Gang of

Four.' Speeches from 1977 include attacks on the 'two whatevers' doctrine of Hua Guofeng--'a doctrine aimed at perpetuating the mistakes Mao Zedong made in his later years.' The speeches after the Third Plenary Session of the Eleventh Central Committee of the C.C.P., December 1978, show Deng as the policy-maker who has been restored to power. Throughout there are repeated references to Mao's policies and to the legacy of Maoism.

951. _____ *Speeches and Writings*, 2nd expanded edition. New York: Pergamon Press, 1987. 114.

952. Harris, Peter. *Political China Observed*. London: Croom Helm, 1980. 229. 'This study of post-Maoist China is seen through the eyes of a political scientist who has spent more than ten years in Hong Kong analysing various policy shifts over the late years of Mao and his successors.' See Chapter 3 for 'The Intellectual Legacy of Mao Tse-tung' in which the author states: 'Most careful authorities, in their sober moments, would agree that Mao was never a theoretician of standing,' (p. 71) and 'The idea that Maoism was a state religion founded upon certain Marxist categories and concepts is an interpretation which appears more valid as time passes' (p. 75).

953. Kerry, Tom. *The Mao Myth and the Legacy of Stalinism in China*. New York: Pathfinder Press, 1977. 190. A collection of essays and speeches by a veteran socialist journalist and political activist. *Inter alia*, the author (1) considers whether Mao's victory in 1949 marked a break between the CCP and the Kremlin, and (2) considers the application to China of Trotsky's position as developed in his criticism of Stalin's policy of building socialism in one country.

954. Martin, Helmut. *Cult and canon: the origins and development of state Maoism*. Armonk, New York: Sharpe, 1982. 233. A detailed examination of 'state Maoism,' from its origins, through the cult of the *Little Red Book*, to the vain attempt of the Gang of Four to cite Mao's writings in order to underpin their political ambitions. A large part of the book is concerned with the way Mao's works have been used by Hua Guofeng and Deng Xiaoping in their rise to power.

955. Meisner, M. *Mao's China: A History of the People's Republic*. New York: Free Press, Collier Macmillan, 1977. 416. Looks at the successes and failures of the 'Maoist era,' to 1976, in the light of the Communists' own goals and also offers comparisons with the experience of the Soviet Union. It aims to illuminate the chief problems which were central to China's development: 'agrarian reform, industrialization, the organization of the new

state, the problem of bureaucracy, the question of permanent "revolution", and conservative reactions to radical and social change.'

956. Michael, Franz. *Mao and the Perpetual Revolution.* Woodbury, New York: Baron, 1977. 320. This book covers more than half a century of revolutionary activity in China, with close attention to the role of Mao and other Communist leaders.

957. Murphey, Rhoads. *Mao's Legacy: Lessons for the Future?* New York: Methuen, 1980. 170. The author examines the impact of Mao's ideology in China, the extent to which it has been modified, and the reasons for such modifications. China's ecomonic and social achievements are compared to those of India.

958. Onate, Andres D. *Chairman Mao and the Chinese Communist Party.* Chicago: Nelson-Hall, 1979. 289. The author presents an overview of the political history of the revolution in China. He examines *inter alia* the influences of Confucianism on Mao, and makes some critical analysis of Mao's writings.

959. Schram, Stuart R. Mao Zedong. *A Preliminary Reassessment.* Hong Kong: Chinese University Press, 1983. 104. Three lectures given at United College in April 1982 with a preface by the author. (1) *The Formative Years, 1917-1937.* Examines the emergence of trends in Mao's thinking such as an emphasis on subjective forces; the justification for the central role of the peasantry in the revolution and Mao's theory of contradictions. (2) *A Quarter Century of Achievements, 1937-1962.* Examines themes developed by Mao during the Yanan period, such as the need to adopt Marxism to Chinese conditions, and the 'mass line' and relates there to Mao's efforts after 1955 to formulate a distinctive pattern for building socialism. (3) *The Final Phase: From Apotheosis to Oblivion.* 'Considers how aspects of Mao Zedong's thought, which had hitherto coexisted in dynamic and creative tension, became dissociated, . . . (and) led to destructive excesses which turned his political and ideological legacy into something ambiguous and problematical.' Each lecture is followed by Questions and Answers. Appendix A prints a translation of 'On Questions of Party History' adopted by the Sixth Plenary Session of the 11th Central Committee of the CCP, 27 June 1981.

960. Wilson, Dick. *Mao Tse-tung in the Scales of History.* New York: Cambridge University Press, 1979. 331. First published by Cambridge University Press, Cambridge, England in 1977 in commemoration of Mao's

death. This is a valuable collection of essays by distinguished contributors showing the various aspects of the Chinese leader--as philosopher, Marxist, teacher, military strategist and economic planner.

Articles

961. Bernstein, T. P. 'How Stalinist was Mao's China?' (review article) *Problems of Communism*, 34 (March/April 1985): 118-25.

962. Bonavia, D. 'The Chairman's art.' *Far Eastern Economic Review*, 131 (27 March 1986): 58-59. On Mao Tse-tung.

963. _____ 'Rewriting Mao's Life.' *Far Eastern Economic Review*, 113 (3-9 July 1981): 10-11.

964. Chai, T. R. 'Content analysis of the obituary notices on Mao Tse-tung.' *Public Opinion Quarterly*, 41 (Winter 1977-78): 475-87.

965. Chang, P. H. 'Passing of the Maoist Era.' *Asian Survey*, 16 (November 1976): 907-1011.

966. Davies, D. 'Last of the great men.' *Far Eastern Economic Review*, 93 (17 September 1976): 5-6.

967. 'Deng Xiaoping on Mao Zedong.' *Beijing Review*, 29 (8 September 1986): 14-15.

968. Fei Xiaotong. 'His Image will not Fade.' *China Reconstructs*, no. 12 (1983): 16-17. On Mao Tse-tung.

969. Gill, G. 'Personality cult, political culture and party structure.' *Studies in Comparative Communism*, 17 (Summer 1984): 111-21.

970. Gupta, K. P. 'Mao's uncertain legacy.' (review article) *Problems of Communism*, 31 (January-February 1982): 45-50.

971. Hu Yaobang. 'The Best Way to Remember Mao Zedong.' *Beijing Review*, no 1 (1984): 16-18.

972. Hua Kuo-Feng. 'Memorial speech on Mao's death.' *Journal of Contemporary Asia*, 6, 4 (1976): 535-39.

973. Huang, K. 'How to assess Chairman Mao and Mao-Zedong thought.' *Beijing Review*, 24 (27 April 1981): 15-23.

974. Jing, Wei. 'Mao Zedong Still Fresh in Memory.' *Beijing Review*, no. 36 (1986): 15-18.

975. Jones, Mervyn. 'Two Maos.' *New Statesman*, 92, 2374 (17 September 1976): 362-64. Obituary assessment examining dominant elements in Mao's personality and the key themes and events of his political career, with particular emphasis on Mao's Chinese-centred view of the world and his commitment to 'uninterrupted revolution.'

976. King, A.Y.C. 'Voluntarist model of organization: the Maoist version and its critique.' *British Journal of Sociology*, 28 (September 1977): 363-74.

977. Leng, S. C. 'Role of Law in the People's Republic of China as reflecting Mao Tse-tung's influence.' *Journal of Criminal Law and Criminology*, 68 (September 1977): 356-73.

978. Leys, S. 'Myth of Mao: two notes and a postscript.' *Dissent*, 24 (Winter 1977): 13-21.

979. Liu, Xiuzhen. 'Personal feeling cannot replace scientific analysis.' *Beijing Review*, vol. 24, no. 38 (21 September 1981): 18-19. The author, deputy leader of a medical team of a PLA unit, now realises that his previously uncritical admiration of Mao Zedong must give way to an analysis which recognises the merits and the mistakes of the leader.

980. Melnick, A. I. 'Soviet Perceptions of the Maoist Cult of Personality.' *Studies in Comparative Communism*, 9 (Spring/Summer 1976): 129-44.

981. 'Mao is dead.' *Economist*, 260, 6941 (11 September 1976): 9- 10. Brief comment of Mao and his legacy to China.

982. 'Mao's legacy: a symposium.' *Asian Survey*, 17 (November 1977): 1001-1060.

983. 'On Questions of Party History--Resolution on Certain Questions in the History of Our Party Since the Founding of the People's Republic of China.' *Beijing Review*, vol. 24, no. 27 (6 July 1981): 10-39. This resolution was adopted by the Sixth Plenary Session of the 11th Central Committee of the CCP on June 27, 1981. In this overview of party history attention is given

to the role of Mao Zedong, before, during and after the Cultural Revolution. In an assessment of Mao's historical role it is stated 'Comrade Mao Zedong was a great Marxist and a great proletarian revolutionary, strategist and theorist. It is true that he made gross mistakes during the "cultural revolution" but, if we judge his activities as a whole, his contributions to the Chinese revolution far outweigh his mistakes. His merits are primary and his errors secondary. . . . He made major contributions to the liberation of the oppressed nations of the world and to the progress of mankind . . . Mao Zedong Thought is wide-ranging in content. It is an original theory which has enriched and developed Marxism-Leninism . . .'

984. Pye, L. 'Mao Tse-tung's Leadership Style.' *Political Science Quarterly*, 91 (Summer 1976): 219-35.

985. Raddock, D. M. 'Mao the Teacher, Society the School.' *Problems of Communism*, 25 (1976): 70-73.

986. Schram, Stuart R. 'Chinese and Leninist components in the personality of Mao Tse-tung.' *Asian Survey*, 3 (June 1963), no. 6. 259-273.

987. _____ 'Mao Tse-tung and the search for a "Chinese road" to socialism.' *Journal of Royal Central Asian Society*, 56 (February 1969): 30-41.

988. _____ 'Mao Tse-tung as a charismatic leader.' *Asian Survey*, 7 (June 1967): 383-88.

989. _____ 'Mao Zedong.' *History Today*, vol. 31 (April 1981): 22-29. An overview and assessment of Mao's career with good illustrations. 'Though Mao . . . could not transcend his own historical limitations his contribution to China's developments as a nation remains an imposing one . . . it would be a pity if, in the effort to divest Mao Zedong's political heritage of the errors and distortions of The Great Leap and the Cultural Revolution, the current leadership were to discard also the participatory and anti-bureaucratic thrust which was an integral part of mainstream Maoism.'

990. Sweezy, P. M. 'Theory and Practice in the Mao period.' *Monthly Review*, 28 (February 1977): 1-12.

Bibliographies and Reference Works

991. *Americans in China, 1971-1980: A guide to the University of Michegan National Archive on Sino-American relations.* Ann Arbor: University of Michigan Center for Chinese Studies, 1981.

992. Bartke, Wolfgang, ed. *Who's Who in the People's Republic of China.* Brighton: Harvester Press, 1981.

993. Berton, Peter and Eugene Wu. *Contemporary China: A Research Guide.* Stanford: Stanford University Press, 1967. An important guide to the Chinese periodical press which lists many of the ministerial journals of the 1950's and 1960's.

994. Berton, Peter. *Soviet Works on China: a Bibliography of Non-Periodical Literature, 1946-1955.* Los Angeles: University of Southern California Press, 1959.

995. *Bibliography for the Study of Chairman Mao's Work.* Washington, D.C.: US Department of Commerce, Joint Publications Research Service, 1961. 99. (no. 10539). A translation of a Chinese bibliography of Mao's works from 1926, arranged chronologically. Covers 210 works by Mao, plus some commentaries on his thought and biographies of Mao.

996. *Bibliography of Chinese Studies.* Selected articles on China in Chinese, English and German compiled by Nieh, Yu-hsi. A publication of the Institute of Asian Affairs, Hamburg. Published annually. First published as a separate publication 1982. Previously appendix to German Far Eastern Bibliography.

997. *Biographic Dictionary of Chinese Communism 1921-1965.* Cambridge, Massachusetts: Harvard University Press, 1971.

998. Boorman, Howard. et al. (eds). *Biographical Dictionary of Republican China.* 4 vols. New York: Columbia University Press, 1967-1968.

999. *Cambridge Encyclopedia of China.* Ed. Brian Hook. Cambridge: Cambridge University Press, 1982. 492.

1000. *Catalogue of the works of Mao Tse-tung.* Peking: Foreign Languages Press, 1970. 57.

1001. Cheng, Peter. *China*. Santa Barbara: Clio Press, 1983. 391. This is vol. 35 of World Bibliographical Series. Pp. 70-78 has forty-two annotated references to books on Mao Zedong.

1002. _____ *Chronology of the People's Republic of China, 1970-1979*. Metuchen, New Jersey: Scarecrow Press Inc., 1986. 629.

1003. Chesneaux, Jean and John Lust. *Introduction aux etudes d'histoire contemporaine de Chine*. Paris: Mouton, 1964. A general bibliography of works on contemporary China with critical notes.

1004. *China in Western Literature*. Compiled by Tung-li Yuan. New Haven, Conn: Far Eastern Publications, Yale University, 1958. 802. A continuation of Cordier's Bibliotheca Sinica.

1005. Columbia University. East Asiatic Library. *Guide to the writings of Mao Tse-tung in the East Asiatic Library*. New York: Columbia University, 1951. 16. An eight-page supplement was produced in 1952.

1006. Committee for a Free Asia. *List of Writings of Mao Tse-tung found in the Hoover Library at Stanford University*. Stanford, California: Hoover Institution Library, 1951. 25.

1007. Dilger, Bernhard and Jurgen Henze. *Das Erziehungs--und Bildungswegen der VR China seit 1969*. Eine Bibliographie. Hamburg: Bochum, 1978. P. 521 gives all Mao entries.

1008. Evans, Paul M. *John Fairbank and the American Understanding of Modern China*. Oxford: Blackwell, 1988. 366. A well-written portrait of the man who led America's China experts from the 1950's onwards. Shows *inter alia* that in his enthusiasm for Sino-American rapprochement, Fairbank played down the excesses of the Cultural Revolution.

1009. Goodman, David S. G. *China's Provincial Leaders, 1949-1985*, 3 vols. Cardiff: University College Press, 1986-87. These three volumes, each of 300 pages, provides a valuable reference work. Vol. 1: The Directory-- identifies the leaders by province or region. Vols. 2 and 3 provide detailed biographies. Uses both the Wade-Giles and Pinyin systems of transliteration throughout.

1010. _____ *Research Guide to China's Provincial and Regional Newspapers*. London: School of Oriental and African Studies, Contemporary China Institute.

1011. *Index to Selected Works of Mao Tse-tung*. Hong Kong: Union Research Institute, 1968. 180. An index to the proper nouns and terms in *Selected Works of Mao Tse-tung*, Volumes I to IV, Foreign Languages Press, Peking, 1965, and *Selected Military Writing of Mao Tse-tung*, Foreign Languages Press, Peking, 1963.

1012. Lamb, Malcolm. *Directory of Officials and Organizations in China 1968-1983*. New York and London: M.E. Sharpe, 1984. 717. A cross-referenced list of Party and state bodies and top officials, drawn from Chinese official sources.

1013. Lee, James and Gary E. Dilley. *Index to selected works of Mao Tse-tung and selected military writings of Mao Tse-tung*. Hong Kong: Union Research Institute, 1968. 180.

1014. Lieberthal, Kenneth. *A Research Guide to Central Party and Government Meetings in China, 1949-1975*. White Plains, New York: International Arts and Sciences Press, 1976. 321. Presents summaries on almost 300 meetings. These include the names of major leaders attending and those who did not and notes the major items on the agenda, speeches and reports, documents passed and other decisions and actions taken. There is a useful introduction by the author, and a foreward (by M. Oskenberg) which is, in effect, a very useful bibliographical essay on sources for research into post-1949 politics. (Reviewed in *China Quarterly*, no. 71-- September 1977).

1015. Ling, Scott K. *Bibliography of Chinese Humanities: 1941-1972*. Taipei, Taiwan: The Liberal Arts Press, 1975. Republic of China.

1016. *Mao Zedong*. A selection of photographs. Peking: People's Fine Arts Publishing House, 1978. 200. An album of color photographs of Mao.

1017. Medlin, Virgil Dewain. *Mao Tse-tung: a Bibliographical essay*. Norman, Oklahoma: Institute of Asian Affairs, University of Oklahoma, 1971. 45.

1018. O'Neill, Hugh B. *Companion to Chinese History*. New York: Facts on File Publications, 1987. 397. Nearly 1000 entries include concise biographies and entries on such diverse subjects as law, politics, philosophy, language and religion.

1019. Posner, A. and A. J. de Keijzer (eds.) *China. A Resource and Curriculum Guide*. Chicago: University of Chicago Press, 1976. 317. P. 166 ff. has biographical notes.

1020. Quested, R.K.I. *Sino-Russian Relations. A Short History*. Sydney: George Allen & Unwin, 1984. 194. An excellent concise history of Sino-Russian relations with a useful bibliographical guide.

1021. Rhoads, Edward J. M. *The Chinese Red Army, 1927-63: an Annotated Bibliography*. Cambridge, Mass.: Harvard University Press, 1964. This critical bibliography covers the origins and development of the Chinese Communist army.

1022. Shu, Austin C. W. *On Mao Tse-tung: a bibliographical guide*. East Lansing, Michigan: Asian Studies Center, Michigan State University, 1972. 78. Covers Chinese and Japanese as well as Western sources, focussing primarily on period since 1949. Not annotated.

1023. *Sino-Soviet Conflict. A Historical Bibliography*. Santa Barbara, California: ABC Clio.

1024. Starr, J. B. and N. A. Dyer. *Post-Liberation Works of Mao Zedong: a Bibliography and an Index*. Berkeley, California: Center for Chinese Studies, University of California, 1976. 222. Reviewed in *China Quarterly*, no. 75 (September 1978): 663-65. A chronologically arranged bibliography of 797 of Mao's writings and speeches since October 1949 available in English.

1025. Skinner, G. William, ed. *Modern Chinese Society: An Analytical Bibliography; Pt.1 Publications in Western Languages*. Stanford, California: Stanford University Press, 1973. A full, cross-indexed bibliography for reference.

1026. Tanis, N. E., D. L. Perkins and J. Pinto. *China in Books. A Basic Bibliography in Western Language*. Greenwich, Conn: Jai Press Inc., 1979. 328. This is volume 4 of Foundations in Library and Information Science.

1027. Tsien Tsuen-Hsuin and James K. M. Cheng. *China an annoted bibliography of bibliographies.* Boston, Mass: G.K. Hall. 604. See p. 271-273 for bibliographies on Mao.

1028. U.S. Department of State. External Research Division. *The Thought of Mao Tse-tung: a selected list of references to the published works and statements attributed to Mao Tse-tung and to the literature on the Chinese communist leader.* Washington, D.C.: 1962. 73. (External research paper 138).

1029. Wang, James C. F. *The Cultural Revolution in China: An Annotated Bibliography.* New York: Garland Publishing Inc., 1976. 246.

1030. Wu, Eugene. *Leaders of Twentieth Century China: An annotated bibliography of selected Chinese biographical works in the Hoover library.* Stanford, California: Stanford University Press, 1956. 106.

Author Index

(by item number; includes editors of texts)

Subject Index

(by item number)

Mao and Maoism are not indexed because almost all references include Mao. Topics covered in Mao's utterances are indexed where specifically mentioned; so are some of Mao's key writings. A number of names in the author index are included where they become subjects of historical comment or theoretical analysis.

About the Author

ALAN LAWRANCE is principal lecturer in modern history, Hatfield Polytechnic School of Humanities, Watford, U.K. Among his earlier publications
is *China's Foreign Relations since 1949*.

Recent Titles in Bibliographies of World Leaders

Marshal Tito: A Bibliography
April Carter

Gamal Abdel Nasser: A Bibliography
Faysal Mikdadi